The Concept of Bodhicitta in Śāntideva's *Bodhicaryāvatāra*

McGill Studies in the History of Religions,
A Series Devoted to International Scholarship

Katherine K. Young, editor

The Concept of Bodhicitta in Śāntideva's *Bodhicaryāvatāra*

Francis Brassard

STATE UNIVERSITY OF NEW YORK PRESS

Published by
State University of New York Press, Albany

Printed in the United States of America

For information, address the State University of New York Press
State University Plaza, Albany, NY 12246

Cover Illustration: *Drawing of an Ancient Urn* (watercolor), by Robert Kralj

Production by Kristin Milavec
Marketing by Patrick Durocher

Library of Congress Cataloging-in-Publication Data

Brassard, Francis, 1961–
The concept of Bodhicitta in Santideva's Bodhicaryavatara / Francis Brassard.
p. cm. — (McGill studies in the history of religions)
ISBN 0-7914-4575-5 (hc. : alk. paper). — ISBN 0-7914-4576-3 (pbk. : alk. paper)
1. Bodhicitta (Buddhism). 2. Spiritual life—Buddhism. I. Title. II. Series.
BQ4398.5.B65 2000
294.3'422—dc21 99-41324
CIP

10 9 8 7 6 5 4 3 2 1

za Rinu

asaṃprajanyacittasya śrutacintitabhāvitam,
sacchidrakumbhajalavat na smṛtāvavatiṣṭhate.
(A person who lacks alertness cannot retain what has been heard, thought about, or contemplated just as a jar with a hole that leaks water.)
Bodhicaryāvatāra

Contents

Abbreviations

A	Aṅguttara-nikāya
Abhidh-k	Abhidharmakośa
BCA	Bodhicaryāvatāra
BHS	Buddhist Hybrid Sanskrit Dictionary
D	Dīgha-nikāya
G. S	The Books of the Gradual Sayings
G. Vy	Gaṇḍavyūhasūtra
M	Majjhima-nikāya
MA	Madhyamakāvatārasūtra
M. L. S	The Collection of the Middle Length Sayings
MMK	Mūlamadhyamakakārikā
Paṭis	Paṭisaṃbhidāmagga
PED	Pali-English Dictionary
Pra.vi.si	Prajñopāyaviniścayasiddhi
S	Saṃyutta-nikāya
Śāl	Śālistaṃbasūtra
SED	The Practical Sanskrit-English Dictionary
Śs	Śikṣāsamuccaya
Sn	Sutta-nipāta
Vibh-a	Vibhaṅgaṭṭhakathā
Vism	Visuddhimagga
Vv	Vigrahavyāvartanī
Ys	Yoga sūtra

Introduction

The present study is an attempt to understand the meaning of the concept of *bodhicitta* by analyzing the features of the spiritual path suggested in the *Bodhicaryāvatāra*, a text from the Mahāyāna Buddhist tradition known to have been composed in Sanskrit by the Buddhist philosopher Śāntideva (eighth century C.E.).

The expression *bodhicitta* has usually been translated as the "thought of enlightenment" or the "desire of enlightenment." Sometimes *enlightenment* is substituted by *awakening*. When one considers the traditional Buddhist sources that discuss *bodhicitta*, it is, however, somehow difficult to get a precise picture of that concept. It appears that *bodhicitta*, although a technical term within Buddhism, has acquired various meanings due to the diversity of situations in which it is employed. In the Tantric tradition of Tibetan Buddhism, for example, this concept has obvious metaphysical connotations, whereas, in some Sanskrit texts of the Mahāyāna tradition, it has been argued that it assumes a more functional character since it involves a commitment to attain realization. In other texts, *bodhicitta* also seems to have ethical implications when it stresses the altruistic motive of the Bodhisattva (the Mahāyāna spiritual aspirant) in contrast to the "selfish" desire for emancipation of the Arhat (the saint of the "Hīnayāna" Buddhist tradition).

Scholars who attempted to define *bodhicitta* have mainly done so on the basis of a linguistic analysis of the Sanskrit term *bodhicitta*. *Bodhicitta* often occurred within expressions such as "the arising of *bodhicitta*," "the production of *bodhicitta*," or "the cultivation of *bodhicitta*." These expressions are used within the Mahāyāna literary tradition to refer to specific events in the course of the Bodhisattva's spiritual practice. Even today, they often occur in Buddhist inspirational literature to describe what the practitioner has to do in order to engage in, and to progress on, the spiritual path. Thus, given the close link that exists between *bodhicitta* and spiritual practice, to see the full significance of this concept, one should determine its spiritual function, that is, how it contributes to the spiritual development of the Bodhisattva.

There are scholars, however, who have suggested, based on more than mere linguistic analysis, such a spiritual model to evaluate the relevance of *bodhicitta*. These scholars, who were often inspired by Buddhist traditions, have, probably for the first time, given us an explicit picture of the underlying structure of, or the basic assumptions related to, the process of spiritual development. Their contribution should therefore be the starting point of any new study of *bodhicitta*.

Together with the context, it is also important to focus one's attention on a group of relevant texts. In this respect, the *Bodhicaryāvatāra* of Śāntideva is, I believe, quite appropriate. This text deals with the Bodhisattva's path to awakening and, most important of all, the concept of *bodhicitta* is one of its central themes. It should therefore be an interesting case for understanding *bodhicitta* in relation to spiritual practice. Such a study, however, will not provide a comprehensive definition of *bodhicitta*—this objective might prove to be impossible, given the bulk of literature to assess—but it may suggest at least what Śāntideva had in mind when he used this concept in his *Bodhicaryāvatāra*. This study will be like trying to understand the strategy of a chess player by analyzing his or her various moves on the chessboard. What really interests me, however, are not the specific moves, but rather the strategy. This is where we can go beyond the text and venture a few ideas as to the nature of the spiritual path. Indeed, in Buddhist literature, one finds many accounts of religious and spiritual practices. Some of these practices emphasize the importance of devotion as a means of moral and spiritual improvement whereas others only advocate the practice of meditation. In some cases, it is of utmost importance to develop compassion toward all sentient beings while, in others, one should stay aloof from the world. Given this variety of practices, may this literature, dedicated to the means of spiritual progress, be considered homogeneous from the point of view of its understanding of what ought to be the basic model of spiritual practice or does it rather give evidence of a collection of spiritual approaches, each having its own structure and producing its own types of practices?

I think this type of study may allow us to better understand the development of the various spiritual practices of the Mahāyāna tradition and possibly of Buddhism as a whole. Indeed, with such an understanding we might be in a better position to analyze the process of assimilation or integration of the various social and cultural factors that marked the history of this tradition. Moreover, I believe its results might serve as a good starting point for a more in-depth discussion of the field of comparative religions and philosophies.

The *Bodhicaryāvatāra* as an object of study is appropriate for another reason. It exists in the Tibetan and Chinese versions, and it has at least nine commentaries. This text is very popular among the Tibetan Buddhists who still use it today as a source text of their tradition. Judging from the number of translations in European languages, it also has a certain appeal in the West, probably because of its apparent similarities with the well-known Christian spiritual text *Imitatio Christi* of Thomas a Kempis. Its popularity and especially its availability makes it an easy source of reference, and, by the same token, it allows the nonspecialists of Buddhist studies (those who do not have the philological background that would enable them to read original Buddhist scriptures) to participate in the discussion that may result from my study of *bodhicitta*.

This study puts forth two claims with regard to Buddhist religious or philosophical concepts such as *bodhicitta*. First, contrary to what has been argued by Michael Pye in his discussion of the doctrine of *upāya* (skillful means),[1] some Buddhist ideas and doctrines are more than just provisional means skillfully designed by the Buddha or the Bodhisattvas for the benefit of the unenlightened beings. To recall Pye's idea, "the 'answers' which Buddhism apparently offers, such as the teaching of cessation or *nirvāṇa*, are devised entirely in terms of the problem and they are not intended to have any particular meaning beyond the attainment of the solution."[2] And he further explains, "This is because every form of religious language, when conceived in terms of skillful means, is first allusive and then disposable."[3] This is supposed to "apply not merely to the preliminary suggestions of the religious system, but above all to its fundamental assumptions and final terms."[4]

This interpretation seems to overlook the fact that some Buddhist concepts did exist for a long time and, as it appears to be the case with *bodhicitta*, instead of being disposed of, were raised to a status of utmost importance within the Mahāyāna tradition. Of course, it could be argued that these concepts are maintained for the sake of the unenlightened and that they are discarded only at the moment of enlightenment. The difficulty with this argument is that it cannot be contradicted unless one has experienced enlightenment. I believe that it is nonetheless questionable because, while assuming (as Pye did) that there is some kind of consistency and unity at the level of the experience of enlightenment—and this should be true for all the paths and to a lesser extent to all the various means to enlightenment—it has been difficult to find a general consensus. Instead, what is more current in the various spiritual traditions is a consistency between the means to achieve their respective spiritual experiences and the ways in which to describe them. One does not see, in terms of the conceptual discourse, a marked difference between the descriptions of reality before and after the experience. For the followers of the Madhyamaka tradition, for example, the concept of *śūnyatā* (emptiness) is certainly an antidote to a person's mental and emotional attachment to the phenomenal world, but it is also their privileged way to describe reality as they ultimately view it. Therefore, I assume that religious language may be more than just a skillful means; it is also a standard or a measure of the authenticity of the religious experience. In other words, religious concepts are not quite without referents. Part of the goal of the present study is therefore to elucidate the definition of these concepts.

Secondly, the path to realization consists precisely in cultivating an awareness of these religious concepts. Not all religious concepts may serve as a basis for this cultivation: only those that are meant to encompass all aspects of one's dualistic experience of the world may do so. The idea that "All is Suffering (*sabbam dukkham*)," which is the First Noble Truth taught by the historical Buddha, is such a concept, because it is meant to cover every moment of existence. Realization of this truth means that one acquires a direct or intuitive knowledge of the three characteristics of reality as perceived, that is, causing suffering (*duḥkha*), impermanence (*anitya*), and being devoid of substance (*anātman*). This is usually brought about by cultivating or developing an awareness of these three characteristics. With this realization, in the context of the spiritual path of the Theravāda tradition, one knows that "the process of rebirth is exhausted, the religious life has been fulfilled, done is what had to be done, there is nothing more for the present state of becoming."[5] In other words, it is the final deliverance from suffering.

This work is divided into three parts. The first (chap. 1) is a brief survey of the modern and traditional views of *bodhicitta*. It starts with a discussion of the methodology I adopted along with a more detailed presentation of the text to be analyzed, the *Bodhicaryāvatāra*. A few biographical data on its author, Śāntideva, and on its main Sanskrit commentator, Prajñākaramati, are also provided.

The second part (chaps. 2 to 4) discusses the spiritual function of *bodhicitta*. It could be viewed, for example, as an exclusive commitment to a religious goal or simply as an object of concentration. I will argue that these two views are inappropriate. When *bodhicitta* is accepted as one's intrinsic nature to help all beings, it becomes the basis for the practice of the cultivation of awareness. Many examples in the Buddhist tradition speak in favor of this awareness as a valid model for the understanding of the path to realization, and indeed, this model appears to be the most adequate to explain the meaning and function of *bodhicitta* and of its relationship to the spiritual path described in the *Bodhicaryāvatāra.*

The third part (chaps. 5 to 7) is a discussion of the cultivation of awareness as such and of how *bodhicitta* serves as its basis in the context of the *Bodhicaryāvatāra.* This awareness has three aspects that I have identified as renunciation, conversion, and contemplation. Contemplation is defined as the maintenance of the awareness of the reality described by the concept of *bodhicitta*; renunciation is the acknowledgment of and the efforts to avoid the obstacles that are likely to disrupt that specific awareness; and finally, conversion is the act of turning one's mind toward it.

By writing the present work, I wish to contribute to our understanding of the nature and function of *bodhicitta* and of its relationship to the spiritual path suggested by Śāntideva in his *Bodhicaryāvatāra.* I think our present understanding of *bodhicitta* may reflect inappropriate assumptions regarding its spiritual context. I do not intend to provide a complete translation of *Bodhicaryāvatāra*, but only of the passages relevant to my argumentation. To clarify particularly difficult passages, I referred to Prajñākaramati's extensive commentary as well as to some of its translations in European languages.

1

Bodhicitta and the spiritual path of the Bodhisattva

1. Methodological considerations

Bodhicitta is a common technical term in Buddhist Sanskrit literature. Within the Mahāyāna tradition, it is closely related to the spiritual practice of the Buddhist aspirant to enlightenment (Bodhisattva). *Bodhicitta* is a Sanskrit compound composed of the words *bodhi* and *citta*. The feminine verbal noun *bodhi* usually means, in the Buddhist context, the state of being *buddha*, or the quality in virtue of which one is *buddha*, that is, awakened. In general, this term means: "perception," "comprehension," "knowledge," or "wisdom."[1] To modern translators it means either "enlightenment" or "awakening."[2] As for the Sanskrit term *citta*, the situation is a little bit more complex. This term has a long history dating back to the Vedic literature. It is also extensively employed in the Upaniṣads and in Buddhist canonical literature. *Citta* has consequently acquired various technical meanings in the course of the development of Indian philosophy and psychology. For the purpose of the present study, let us just mention its most basic and common meanings. These are: "mind," "thought," "attention," and also "desire," "intention," or "aim."[3] Similar to the English word *mind*, as in the expressions "to keep in mind" and "she changed her mind," *citta* has therefore either a cognitive or a conative connotation. Consequently, Buddhist scholars, depending on their interpretation of *bodhi* and *citta*, have suggested, among others, the following translations: "Thought of enlightenment,"[4] "Mind of enlightenment,"[5] "Desire for enlightenment,"[6] "Will of enlightenment,"[7] "Mind turned to Enlightenment,"[8] "Awakening mind,"[9] or "Desire for awakening."[10]

At this stage, it may be pointless to decide which translation is the most appropriate, because, no matter how accurate the linguistic analysis, I believe that one has to consider the context in which it is used in order to understand its meaning. In Chinese Buddhism, for example, *bodhicitta* has been rendered by *fa-hsin* or *ch'i-hsin*, or "arousing the mind." *Bodhicitta* has then been interpreted as "initiating the aspiration and determination to become awakened."[11] This interpretation seems to suggest a meaning that is not explicitly given by simply a literal translation of *bodhicitta*. Something has been added to it and to find out what it is, one would have to look at how and why Buddhist Chinese used the concept of *bodhicitta*. One may, for example, investigate whether *bodhicitta* is a means to enlightenment, a simple act of will, or a description of a mental state.

I assume that Buddhism is primarily a system of ideas and practices whose goal is to bring about a liberation from conditions recognized as unsatisfactory. Its doctrines are not speculative but rather soteriological. I use the word *soteriological* by way of extension from its usual meaning in Christian theology. It is the idea of being free from one's limited and unsatisfactory conditions that is emphasized and not the idea of salvation brought about by a savior. One can then speak of a soteriological system when referring to Buddhism by asking three basic questions. The first question deals with the description of the human situation, a situation that is deemed unsatisfactory. This question often reveals the most basic nature of human existence and of its destiny. It may also tell us about the intrinsic negative quality of this world. The second question relates to the means to overcome, to change, or to be free from an unsatisfactory condition. Finally, the third question, always implicit in the other two, has to do with a portrayal of the state to which the application of the means to solve the human problem leads. In other words, the soteriological context refers to the character, the structure, and the assumptions of any system whose main purpose is to effect a radical change of conditions of living or being.

The relevance of this context was pointed out to me by Charles J. Adams, a scholar of the Islamic tradition, who attempted to identify the fundamental differences between Islam and Christianity in an article entitled "Islam and Christianity: The Opposition of Similarities." The reason for using such an approach was that, since Christianity and Islam share many symbols such as the idea of sin or the role of prophecy, one may be misled by these similarities when trying to understand their exact significance. Besides, without an awareness of the differences between their spiritual and cultural contexts, there is always the possibility of interpreting the symbols of one tradition in terms of another soteriological system. The most important implication of this is the idea that, the words or the symbols being similar, they do not necessarily refer to the same thing. To give an example, to determine the meaning of the word *rendez-vous*, one has to know whether it is used in English or in French.

In Buddhism, we face the same situation. Some of its concepts have persisted over many stages of its historical and doctrinal development. The concept of *upāya* (skillful means) is perhaps such a concept. As it is presented in the simile of the Burning House of the Lotus Sūtra,[12] it advocates the idea that all Buddhist doctrines and practices are just provisional means skillfully designed by the Buddha or by the Bodhisattvas to help all unenlightened beings to attain enlightenment in ways that fit their own mental dispositions. From a certain point of view, one may argue, as Pye did, that "'Buddhism,' as a specific religion identifiable in human history, is a skillful means."[13] This affirmation is true as long as one makes no distinctions between the various means possible to achieve enlightenment. By overlooking these distinctions, one also downplays the importance of the identity or the characteristics of the various Buddhist traditions or schools that have indeed insisted on these distinctions by developing their own approaches to enlightenment. When one considers these various approaches, one may notice that the significance of *upāya* is likely to vary according to context. Thus, *upāya* has a different meaning whether one views enlightenment as a gradual process or as a sudden one. In the context of gradual approach, all means to enlightenment are skillful means; here the emphasis is on the word *means*, and the term *skillful* is to be understood as efficacious with respect to the goal to be achieved (*upeya*). In the sudden enlightenment approach, *upāya* refers to preliminary teachings that are in effect less important compared to the means that bring about enlightenment. In this case, the emphasis is on the word *skillful* that is interpreted as clever, ingenious, and even deceptive.[14]

In fact, the discussion concerning gradual versus sudden enlightenment involves many more issues than just the means to enlightenment. It affects all aspects of the soteriological context: does the experience of enlightenment, for example, admit degrees or is it indivisible? Is the human problem fundamentally an error in perception or is it woven throughout the whole fabric of the personality? All the possible answers to these questions will again depend on the structure and characteristics of the soteriological context in which ideas such as *upāya* are articulated.[15] Indeed, as it has been pointed out by Tao-sheng, a Chinese Buddhist monk (ca. 360–434 C.E.),[16] that *upāya*, being identified as an element of the gradual approach, can only lead to a state where the ties with this world are subdued and never eradicated.

I am aware of the fact that attributing importance to the soteriological context to understand the meaning of a concept might be violating some principles of the historico-philological method, because it is likely to leave out many details and exceptions in order to reveal only a broad picture. Nevertheless, I feel justified to adopt it because I believe that a comprehension of the general picture is what ultimately gives the true significance of an idea or a concept. The idea of a soteriological context could in fact be a very powerful hermeneutical tool. Just assuming that there is such a context already leads one to a different interpretation. It has been argued, for example, that the fundamental preoccupation of Diṅnāga and of his followers was metaphysical in nature. Others have said in this regard that his principal concern was with language. According to Richard Hayes, these views completely miss the point about Diṅnāga's philosophy because they overlook the fact that Buddhists' actions are oriented toward the goal of emancipation.[17] In other words, these views fail to bring to light the full significance of Diṅnāga's ideas because they are not articulated within a soteriological context.

Having discussed the approach I intend to use in order to analyze the significance of *bodhicitta*, I would now like to give a few details about the text I have chosen for my study of this concept as well as details about the background of its author, Śāntideva, and of its main Sanskrit commentator, Prajñākaramati.

2. Śāntideva's *Bodhicaryāvatāra*

The *Bodhicaryāvatāra* is a text of the Mahāyāna Buddhist tradition known to have been composed by Śāntideva, a Buddhist monk and philosopher who lived around the eighth century C.E.[18] It also exists in Tibetan, Mongolian, and Chinese versions. According to Hajime Nakamura, there are at least nine commentaries and summaries.[19] This text had little influence in later Chinese and Japanese Buddhism but became very popular in Tibet. Even today, the *Bodhicaryāvatāra* is considered an important source of spiritual information for Tibetan Buddhists.

In the West, the *Bodhicaryāvatāra* also aroused interest among scholars of Buddhism. It was first brought to their attention in 1889 by Minayeff, a Russian scholar. Since then, it has been translated, not always in its entirety, in modern European and Asian languages. To name the most important, we have the French translations produced by Louis de La Vallée Poussin (1892, 1896, and 1907) and by Louis Finot (1920). In English, there are the translations of Lionel D. Barnett (1909), of Marion L. Matics (1970), of Stephen Batchelor (1979), and the most recent are those of Parmananda Sharma (1990), Kate Crosby and Andrew Skilton (1996), and Vesna A. Wallace and B. Alan Wallace (1997). To these, one has to add the translations in German (Richard Schmidt, 1923; Ernst Steinkellner, 1981), Italian (Giuseppe Tucci, 1925; Amalia Pezzali, 1975), Japanese (Y. Kanakura, 1958), Dutch (J. Ensink, 1955), Danish (Christian Lindtner, 1981), and those produced in a few modern languages of India such as Hindi and Marāṭhī. It has been argued by Finot that this text has had a certain appeal to Western scholars because of its similarity with the *Imitatio Christi* of Thomas a Kempis, a well-known text of the Christian spiritual tradition. This comparison is valid as long as one considers the *Bodhicaryāvatāra*, as will be mentioned later, from the point of view of only one of its many aspects.

i. The text

According to Paul Williams, the *Bodhicaryāvatāra* "is, like the *Madhyamakāvatāra*, a statement of the Bodhisattva's path to Buddhahood, but distinguished by a poetic sensitivity and fervour which makes it one of the gems of Buddhist and world spiritual literature."[20] He also says that it is one of the great spiritual poems of humanity.[21] According to David Seyford Ruegg, this text has been predominantly perceived as a religious and devotional poem rather than as a philosophical treatise. However, he believes that it is hard to agree with such a view since it appears to overlook the importance of chapter 9 dealing with the Perfection of Wisdom. This chapter clearly places the *Bodhicaryāvatāra* in the main current of Madhyamaka thought; thus, "it becomes abundantly clear that the work is hardly more religious in any sense exclusive of philosophy than certain earlier works of the school attributed to Nāgārjuna."[22] Irrespective of this difference of perception concerning the nature of the *Bodhicaryāvatāra*, what is certain about this text is that it definitively deals with the spiritual practices of the Buddhist aspirant to enlightenment, the Bodhisattva, within the context of the Mahāyāna tradition. Whether it is a philosophical treatise or a devotional guide might not be an issue when looking at the soteriological context in which its philosophical ideas or devotional practices are articulated.

This context seems to be already alluded to in the title of Śāntideva's work. When comparing the various translations of the Sanskrit compound *bodhi-caryā-avatāra*, one sees various preferences. There is one type of translation that appears to take into consideration the title of the Tibetan version of Śāntideva's work, *Bodhisattvacaryāvatāra (Byang chub sems dpa'i spyod pa la 'jug pa)*, replacing thus the word *bodhi* by *Bodhisattva.* Examples of this type of translation are: *Introduction à la pratique des futurs Buddha*, *Exposition de la pratique des bodhisattvas* (both translations from La Vallée Poussin), or *A guide to the Bodhisattva's way of life* (Batchelor and Wallace and Wallace). A second type of translation, on the other hand, lays more emphasis on the notion of path. Examples of this type are *La marche à la lumière* (Finot), *The path of light* (Barnett), *In cammino verso la luce* (Tucci), and *Satori e no michi* (Y. Kanakura). What is noticeable in these translations is the fact that the word *avatāra*, in the expression *bodhicaryāvatāra*, has been disregarded. This point is, however, not true for all translations referring to the idea of path, for instance, *Der Eintritt in den Wandel in Erleuchtung* (Schmidt), *Eintritt in das Leben zur Erleuchtung* (Steinkellner), *La descente dans la carrière de l'éveil* (Pezzali), and *Entering the Path of Enlightenment* (Matics). The point I want to raise by presenting these translations is that it seems that the word *avatāra* as such gave some difficulty to modern translators. While some translators decided to omit the term altogether, others were split over the choice between two meanings. On the one hand, there is La Vallée Poussin who interpreted it in the sense of "introduction" or "presentation of a subject matter." This interpretation is confirmed by Apte's Practical Sanskrit-English dictionary. Analogously, *avatāra* can also mean "to explain" as "now, in order to raise the desire that causes the grasping of *bodhicitta,* [its] praising is to be explained, introduced or presented."[23] On the other hand, there are translators who interpreted it in a more literal sense, that is, as entering, descending, or going down into, thus alluding to some kind of happening. Similarly, the word *'jug*, which is the Tibetan rendering for the word *avatāra*, means "to go," "to walk in," or "to enter." This rendering is also supported by Prajñākaramati's commentary on the dedicatory verse of the *Bodhicaryāvatāra* where the word *avatāra* is glossed by *mārgaḥ* (path). It is further explained as that by which, having attained the stage of Bodhisattva, Buddhahood is reached, obtained, or secured.[24] Given this understanding, the idea of entry into may be, for example, compared to the first stage of the Theravādin's spiritual life that is incidentally called entering the stream (*sotāpanna*). This interpretation takes into consideration some aspects of the spiritual practice of the Bodhisattva. Indeed, it is said that a Bodhisattva's career begins with the production or arising of *bodhicitta.* As will be seen later, the Sanskrit term that is here translated by the word "production" is *utpāda*. This term is often used with the attainment of a mental state. In this circumstance, the title of Śāntideva's work could very well be rendered as "the attainment of a mental state making possible the practice to enlightenment" where the attainment of such a mental state is what it means to be a Bodhisattva. The validity of this interpretation can only be determined, as mentioned earlier, by examining the nature of the spiritual approach suggested by Śāntideva in his *Bodhicaryāvatāra*. For the moment, I just want to point out the possible clues with regard to Śāntideva's conception of the spiritual path of the Bodhisattva. Next, I would like to consider the structure of the text itself and see whether it may reveal other clues as to this spiritual path.

The original text of the *Bodhicaryāvatāra* in Sanskrit consists of ten chapters. These are (1) *Bodhicittānuśaṃsā* (The Praising of *bodhicitta*), (2) *Pāpadeśanā* (Confession of sins), (3) *Bodhicittaparigrahaḥ* (Acceptance of *bodhicitta*), (4) *Bodhicittāpramādaḥ* (Perseverance in *bodhicitta*), (5) *Saṃprajanyarakṣaṇam* (Guarding alertness), (6) *Kṣāntipāramitā* (The Perfection of patience), (7) *Vīryapāramitā* (The Perfection of endeavor), (8) *Dhyānapāramitā* (The Perfection of meditation), (9) *Prajñāpāramitā* (The Perfection of Wisdom), and (10) *Pariṇamanā* (Dedication).

It has been argued that chapter 10 of the *Bodhicaryāvatāra* was not part of the original text.[25] This affirmation is based on the fact that one of its major commentators, Prajñākaramati, disregarded it and that Tāranātha, a Tibetan historian of Buddhism (1575–1608),[26] doubted its authenticity. In this regard, P. L. Vaidya, a modern editor of the text, has drawn to our attention the fact that this chapter was extant in the various manuscripts that were used to prepare basic editions in the Sanskrit as well as in the Mongolian, Tibetan, and Chinese versions.[27] It would most certainly require extensive research—which is beyond the scope of this book—to determine which affirmation is exact. The interesting point about this chapter is, however, that it is considered an example of the Perfection of giving (*dānapāramitā*). Usually, this Perfection is the first of a series of six—the other five being *śīla* (discipline), *kṣānti* (patience), *vīrya* (endeavor), *dhyāna* (meditation), and *prajñā* (wisdom)—where each is often considered to be a prerequisite to the next. By putting the Perfection of giving at the end of the text, it may be seen as a result of having accomplished the goal of the spiritual path suggested in the *Bodhicaryāvatāra* rather than being its beginning or a prerequisite to it.

There is another interesting point to note concerning this text. A recension of the *Bodhicaryāvatāra* is reported to have lacked chapters 2 and 9.

In the *lDan-dkar-ma* Catalogue (no. 659), the extent of the *Bodhicaryāvatāra* is given as six hundred *ślokas* (stanzas) rather than as a thousand as indicated by Bu-ston, another Tibetan historian of Buddhism (1290–1364).[28] Bu-ston discussed the discrepancy and attributed it to the fact that chapter 2 had been omitted in this recension and that chapter 9 had been ascribed, according to some, to a certain Blo-gros-mi-zad-pa (Akṣayamati). Chapter 2 deals principally with the worship of holy figures of the Mahāyāna tradition. It is because of this chapter that the *Bodhicaryāvatāra* has somehow been compared to the *Imitatio Christi* and, consequently, perceived as a devotional breakthrough within the Buddhist tradition. In this regard Har Dayal, a scholar of Mahāyāna Buddhism, wrote that "the ideas of sin as an offense against higher deities, and of confession, repentance and extraneous protection were alien to the spirit of Buddhism during several centuries."[29] Also worth noting concerning chapter 2 is that Tibetan Buddhists, who extensively use this text as a source of spiritual inspiration, understand these devotional practices as preliminary steps in the cultivation of *bodhicitta*.[30]

As just mentioned, chapter 9 deals with Wisdom, that is, the realization of emptiness or of the Perfection of transcending discriminative understanding. This chapter is considered to be the accomplishment of the *Bodhicaryāvatāra* since it is argued that without Wisdom, all other Perfections are worthless. What is significant about this chapter is that *bodhicitta* is hardly mentioned and that the chapter itself could be considered as a separate entity from the rest of Śāntideva's work.[31] One finds herein the bulk of the philosophical ideas discussed in the *Bodhicaryāvatāra*. Perhaps for this reason, Tibetan Buddhists consider chapter 9 as the way to cultivate what they call "the ultimate *bodhicitta*."

Indeed, according to them, *bodhicitta* has two aspects: the conventional *bodhicitta* and the ultimate *bodhicitta*. The cultivation of the conventional *bodhicitta* is the means to develop compassion for all sentient beings. It consists in a variety of meditations where, for example, one imagines one's own mother and tries to extend the benevolent feelings one usually has for her to all sentient beings starting from one's own friends, then to people one is normally indifferent to, and finally to one's enemies. Cultivation of the ultimate *bodhicitta*, on the other hand, trains the mind to perceive the phenomenal world as impermanent and empty of intrinsic existence. By constantly entertaining the idea that everything is like a dream, even while eating, drinking, and doing all kinds of activities, one is likely to come to realize emptiness. This emptiness is beyond this world and cannot be formulated by concept or speech.[32] It is to be noted that, although this twofold conception of *bodhicitta* dated back to as early as the composition of the *Saṃdhinirmocana Sūtra*, a text of the Cittamātra tradition composed after Nāgārjuna (circa second century C.E.) and before Maitreya (ca. 270–350 C.E.), it is not discussed in the context of the *Bodhicaryāvatāra*.

The relevance of this discussion to the structure of the *Bodhicaryāvatāra* is that it may be possible to see chapter 2 (Confession of Sins), chapter 9 (The Perfection of Wisdom), and those dealing specifically with *bodhicitta*, that is, chapters 1, 3 to 8, and 10 as three autonomous and self-sufficient entities. In other words, the *Bodhicaryāvatāra* seems to offer three different spiritual approaches: the first focuses on the concept of *bodhicitta*, the second approach focuses on the idea of Wisdom (*prajñā*), and the third one is based on what one might identify as devotional practices. This means that such devotional practices, for example, are not some kind of preliminary exercises and that the realization of emptiness is not that which the entire *Bodhicaryāvatāra* is exclusively aiming at. From the point of view of the soteriological context, it could therefore be argued that these approaches lead to different spiritual experiences, each having its own definition of the human problem, each adopting the appropriate means to solve it, and each visualizing its own specific state to be attained.

ii. Śāntideva

In addition to being the author of the *Bodhicaryāvatāra*, Śāntideva composed the *Śikṣāsamuccaya*, an anthology with comments compiled on the basis of citations from various *sūtras* and a third text entitled *Sūtrasamuccaya*. This last text is not extant in any language and one knows of its existence from the fact that it is quoted in one verse (chap. 5–106) of the *Bodhicaryāvatāra*. On the basis of this fact, Bu-ston and Tāranātha have ascribed this work to Śāntideva. In this verse, however, Nāgārjuna, the author of another text also called *Sūtrasamuccaya*, also happened to be mentioned. Ruegg believes that it is ambiguous and argues that it is erroneous.[33]

What we know of Śāntideva is from biographies produced by three Tibetan historians: Bu-ston, Tāranātha, and Sum-pa mkham-po (1704–88). There is also a fourth source constituted from a Nepalese manuscript of the fourteenth century. According to J. W. de Jong,[34] this Sanskrit version and the Tibetan ones seem to go back to the same original source. Apart from these sources, we may rely, only as the dates of Śāntideva's life are concerned, on a few historical facts. It has been ascertained, for example, that I-Tsing, one of the Chinese pilgrims to whom we owe a lot of our knowledge on the history of Indian Mahāyāna Buddhism, left India in 685 C.E. In his account, there is no mention of Śāntideva nor of his works. One might assume from this that, at the very most, Śāntideva was not known before this time. Another significant event concerning Śāntideva is the first trip to Tibet of Śāntarakṣita (c. 725–88 C.E.) in 763 C.E. This is probably the latest date of composition of one of his works, the *Tattvasiddhi*, in which one verse of the *Bodhicaryāvatāra* is quoted. Given these details, it is believed that the productive life of Śāntideva is situated approximately in the period between 685 C.E. and 763 C.E. For the other details concerning the life of Śāntideva, one has to rely on these biographies that are in fact more legendary than historical. However, some details of his legend might be of interest.

According to tradition, Śāntideva, whose childhood name was Śāntivarman, was born in the southwestern part of India as the son of a royal chieftain named Mañjuśrīvarman. In his past lives, he served the various Buddhas and thereby accumulated the necessary merits that would later lead him to final liberation. His mother, who is said to be a reincarnation of the goddess Tārā, encouraged him to abandon the mundane life to become an ascetic. Another account claims that Śāntideva had a vision of Mañjuśri enjoining him to forsake the throne for the ascetic life. What should be noted here is that the tradition does not relate Śāntideva to the Brahmanic tradition but rather presents him as a true member of the Mahāyāna lineage.[35]

Having set forth to lead the ascetic life, Śāntideva met a teacher with whom he studied for twelve years. With his guru, he learned the science of Mañjuśri. We are told that Śāntideva was able to produce a vision of Mañjuśri by invoking him. After this period of training in the forest—chapter 8 of the *Bodhicaryāvatāra* praises dwelling in the forest and living the ascetic life—Śāntideva became a knight at the court of King Pañchamasiṃha. There, he was forced to display his wooden sword that caused the king's left eye to fall out of its socket because of the dazzling light it produced. It is believed that Śāntideva's wooden sword was special because it bore the seal of Mañjuśri. Thereupon, Śāntideva restored the king's eye and, acknowledging the suffering he had caused, decided to leave the mundane life once and for all.

It is probably at this moment that Śāntideva became a monk. He joined the monastic university of Nālandā where he was ordained by Jayadeva and received the name Śāntideva because of his quietness. There, the other monks despised him and, to them, it appeared that he did nothing but eat, sleep, and defecate. In reality, Śāntideva was meditating on the teachings during the night and sleeping during the day. As was the custom, each monk had to periodically give a discourse to the entire monastic community. When it came to Śāntideva's turn, the monks thought they had a good opportunity to humiliate him. Instead, when asked to recite something new, he began to disclose the *Bodhicaryāvatāra* thus showing that he was a real *paṇḍit.* Thereupon, he left for the south of India never to return to Nālandā. According to his biographers, Śāntideva left three manuscripts in his cell that correspond to the three texts that it is believed he had composed. This could be understood as an attempt by the tradition to settle the dispute over the authorship of the *Sūtrasamuccaya.*

Because Śāntideva is known to have performed miracles—for example, according to legend, he increased rice production to feed hungry people—and also due to the fact that a certain Bhusuku had been recognized as the composer of songs belonging to the Vajrayāna school of Tantric Buddhism, it has been argued that Śāntideva was an adept of Tantra or has been influenced by it.[36] It also appears, in the *Bstan 'gyur,* that a certain Śāntideva was the author of Tantric texts.[37] Despite these facts or coincidences, most scholars of Buddhism do not accept the idea that Śāntideva was connected in some way or another to the Tantric schools of Buddhism. According to Ruegg, he is considered a representative of the Madhyamaka school of Mahāyāna Buddhism, most probably its Prāsaṅgika branch.[38]

iii. Prajñākaramati

On the *Bodhicaryāvatāra,* as just mentioned, there exists a number of commentaries. Prajñākaramati's *Pañjikā* is probably the best known in Sanskrit. Not much is known about the life of this commentator. It is generally believed that he was an erudite Buddhist monk who lived at the monastic university of Vikramaśīla around the last quarter of the eighth century and the first quarter of the ninth. This assumption is based on the fact that, in his commentary, he quotes abundantly from earlier works such as the *Tattvasaṃgraha* of Śāntarakṣita.[39] Indeed, Prajñākaramati refers to more than seventy-three *sūtras* in his *Pañjikā.* It also appears that he had at his disposal more than one manuscript of the *Bodhicaryāvatāra* for his commentary.[40]

Having presented the text I intend to use as the data for my study of the concept of *bodhicitta,* as well as of its author and its most important Sanskrit commentator, I would now like to discuss the various interpretations of this concept provided by modern scholars of Buddhism. This discussion is in fact an analysis of their assumptions concerning the soteriological context in which *bodhicitta* is believed to be articulated.

3. Review of literature

In this section, I intend to look at two scholars of Buddhism. The first one is D. T. Suzuki, issued from the Zen tradition of Japan. His approach to the study of Buddhism is strongly influenced by the presuppositions of this tradition and by his long friendship with William James. The second, Sangharakshita, is in fact an English scholar who presents Buddhism as a practical system with a definite purpose: the attainment of emancipation. He attempts to give a comprehensive picture of the soteriological context in which the concepts and ideas of Buddhism are articulated. For this review of literature, I also relied on a third scholar, L. M. Joshi, who is not, as far as I know, identified with any schools of Buddhism and whose study of the concept of *bodhicitta* is probably the most comprehensive in terms of the textual sources analyzed.

i. Daisetz Teitaro Suzuki

Daisetz Teiraro Suzuki was probably one of the first non-Western Buddhist scholars to try to give a scientific explanation of the main concepts and practices of Buddhism. His contribution, especially in the area of Zen Buddhism, is without doubt impressive. He also translated and analyzed texts such as the *Gaṇḍavyūha* and the *Daśabhūmikasūtra*. Both texts deal explicitly with the practices of the Bodhisattva and with the concept of *bodhicitta*.

One of his basic assumptions concerning the development of the Buddhist tradition as a whole is that it began at some point in its history to evolve into two distinct directions. For him, as the idea of the Bodhisattva was being developed, "a sort of secular Buddhism came to replace the old school of ascetic and exclusive monasticism. This democratic social tendency brought about many great changes in Buddhist thought. One of them was to analyse in a practical way the process of enlightenment."[41] This assumption is not without consequences in Suzuki's interpretation of *bodhicitta*. According to him, the appearance of this concept was closely linked to the development of the Mahāyāna approach to spiritual fulfillment. Indeed, he argues, "When the actual process of enlightenment was examined, the Mahāyāna found that it consisted of two definite steps. In the beginning it was necessary to create for the sake of others an urgent longing for enlightenment, and then the attainment of the final goal would be possible." He further adds, "The motive determined the course, character, and power of the conduct. The desire for enlightenment intensely stirred meant, indeed, that the greater and more difficult part of the work was already achieved."[42]

In this context, *bodhicitta* refers to the driving force leading the Bodhisattva to his final goal. As such, it could be argued that this concept is not entirely new because, even though the term is not found in pre-Mahāyāna literature,[43] it is well-known that Gotama, the historical Buddha-to-be, after renouncing the household life, also resolved to put an end to all sufferings of existence. According to the Pāli tradition, we also know that the Buddha, after his experience of enlightenment, decided to preach to others the truth he had discovered out of great compassion for all sentient beings. Assuming that the spiritual career of the Buddha, including that of his previous lives, was taken by the early Buddhists as a model to emulate, there seems to be not much difference between them and the Mahāyānists from the point of view of the quality of their commitment. In other words, when *bodhicitta* is understood as an earnest decision to become enlightened, there is nothing that could later justify, that is, in Mahāyāna Buddhism, its promotion to the status of a technical term. Why then did the desire for enlightenment became pivotal to the path of the Bodhisattva whereas in early Buddhism there is no special emphasis on this idea? As mentioned in the preceding quote, this difference is to be attributed to a new understanding of the process of enlightenment. What then, according to Suzuki, is this process of enlightenment?

It is probably in the description of the *Satori* experience of the Zen tradition that Suzuki makes this process explicit. This experience is said to be brought about by an intense reflection on a *kōan*. A *kōan* may be considered a type of riddle given to a student to solve. A famous *kōan* is: "Two hands clap and there is a sound. What is the sound of the one hand?" What is interesting concerning the circumstances of its resolution, which is considered to be the experience of *Satori*, is that it "comes on in connection with the most trivial incidents such as the raising of a finger, uttering a cry, reciting a phrase, swinging a stick, slapping a face, and so on."[44] Suzuki interprets this experience in the following manner: "As the outcome is apparently incongruous with the occasion, we naturally presume some deep-seated psychological antecedents which are thereby abruptly brought to maturity."[45] To explain the nature of these deep-seated psychological antecedents, Suzuki analyzed the career of three early Zen masters.

The first example given is that of Hui-k' ê. He was a learned scholar dissatisfied with mere scholarship. He was earnestly searching for an inmost truth that would give peace and rest to his soul. It is believed that a long period of intense lucubration took place prior to his experience of *Satori.* The second example is that of Hui-nêng. Contrary to Hui-k' ê, Hui-nêng was not a scholar. The facts show, however, that he had some knowledge of several Mahāyāna *sūtras.* In his case also, Suzuki assumed that a great spiritual upheaval was going on in his mind, since, in spite of being assigned to menial work in the monastery, the purpose of his being there was to study Zen. The third example is that of Lin-chi who spent three years of silence under his master in order to grasp the final truth of Zen. In fact, he spent three years in silence because he did not know what to ask his master, thus pointing to an intense mental application and spiritual turmoil.

According to Suzuki, the common denominator of these three examples is that each aspirant to enlightenment cultivated an intense desire for its attainment. This cultivation is pivotal to the experience of *Satori.* As he explains, "The searching mind is vexed to the extreme as its fruitless strivings go on, but when it is brought up to an apex it breaks or it explodes and the whole structure of consciousness assumes an entirely different aspect."[46] According to Suzuki, this phenomenon is not exclusive to Buddhism; it is to be experienced whether one is pondering over a difficult problem or contriving a solution to an apparently hopeless situation. This phenomenon could be explained, as far as psychology goes, by the following law: "accumulation, saturation, and explosion."[47]

It is from the point of view of this understanding of the spiritual process or, as I called it, the soteriological context, that Suzuki interprets *bodhicitta. Bodhicitta* is therefore not a simple desire to become enlightened, as can be seen in pre-Mahāyāna Buddhism and in which case it has a relative significance, but rather, a strong commitment that is the primary cause of the experience of enlightenment. As Suzuki puts it, *bodhicitta* "is the becoming conscious of a new religious aspiration which brings about a cataclysm in one's mental organization."[48] This is essentially the reason why, according to Suzuki, the concept of *bodhicitta* is specific to the Mahāyāna tradition: only this tradition has recognized the value of desire as a spiritual catalyst, and this catalyst is best brought into function by *bodhicitta.*

To sum up Suzuki's understanding of *bodhicitta*, one may use an example taken from the physical world, namely, the process of lamination.

This process is used, among other things, to make gold sheets. Through successive striking on a gold ingot, one obtains very thin sheets of gold, so thin that no other method, such as cutting with precision instruments, can achieve this result. Furthermore, the result is sudden and unexpected. In this circumstance, the last blow that brought about the transformation of the ingot into sheets is no more important than all the previous blows. The last blow is like the trivial incident that brings about the experience of *Satori*. All other blows, like the intense desire stirred up by *bodhicitta*, produce an accumulation of pressure. In the case of the *Satori* experience, it is the structure of the mind, composed of false assumptions about reality, which is under pressure. In this context, *bodhicitta* is the instigator of a brute force, that is, the intense desire for enlightenment, and, as such, it is totally devoid of knowledge. In other words, *bodhicitta* has a definite conative connotation and therefore, the appropriate translation for it is, according to Suzuki, "Desire of Enlightenment."

Suzuki recognizes the fact that *bodhicitta* has acquired other connotations in the course of the development of the Buddhist tradition. In an earlier work, he defined it as "intelligence-heart." Thus *bodhicitta* is understood as a form of the *tathāgatagarbha* (Buddha-womb) or *ālayavijñāna* (substratum-consciousness). As such, *bodhicitta* is hidden in each being and constitutes its essential nature. It is something which, similar to the Buddha-nature or Buddha-essence, one ought to be awakened to. Many Mahāyāna *sūtras* and Buddhist philosophers in general confirmed this connection between *bodhicitta* and the description of metaphysical realities. For example, in the *Treatise on the Formless Enlightenment-Mind*,[49] *bodhicitta* is free from all characteristics; it is universal and is the highest essence.[50] Sthiramati, an author of the Cittamātra (Mind-only) school of Mahāyāna Buddhism, in his Discourse on the *Mahāyānadharmadhātu*, also said that *bodhicitta* is the Cosmic Body of the Buddha (Dharmakāya) or Reality as such (Bhūtatathātā).[51] It is, however, within the Tibetan tradition that *bodhicitta* has acquired the strongest connections with metaphysical realities.

In the Vajrayāna school of Esoteric Buddhism, for example, a school that had been founded in India around the third century C.E. and that eventually became popular in Tibet, *bodhicitta* is understood as the final unification of *śūnyatā* (emptiness; also called *prajñā* [Wisdom]) and *karuṇā* (compassion; also called *upāya* [skillful means]). This term also very often refers to the Great Delight (*mahāsukha*) itself.[52] *Mahāsukha* is related to a practice of Esoteric Buddhism involving rituals connected with the enjoyment of meat, intoxicating liquors, and sexual intercourse. In the *Guhyasamājatantra*, a text produced by the Esoteric Buddhist tradition at its last stage, the great Bodhisattvas, headed by Maitreya, pay homage to *bodhicitta* in the same manner in which Nāgārjuna has paid homage to the *prajñāpāramitā* (the Perfection of Wisdom). *Bodhicitta* is, consequently, described as born of the emptiness of things, complementary to the Buddha's awakening, beyond imagination and without support.[53] In this text, an interesting definition of *bodhicitta* is given: "The *bodhicitta* is the unity of voidness and compassion; it is beginningless and endless, quiescent and bereft of the notion of being and non-being."[54] And, in another text of the same tradition, the *Prajñopāyaviniścayasiddhi* (composed about 650–800 C.E.), *bodhicitta* is considered the eternal, luminous, pure, abode of the Conquerors, made of all *dharmas* (phenomena), divine, and the cause of the whole universe.[55] And later in the text, the same homage as that just mentioned is paid to *bodhicitta.*[56]

According to Suzuki, all of these metaphysical connotations must be regarded as a degeneration of pure Mahāyāna Buddhism.[57] The reason for this shift of meaning is that the "historical connection between the compound *bodhicitta* and the phrase *anuttarāyāṃ samyaksaṃbodhau cittam utpādam*—*bodhicitta* ought to be considered as the abbreviation of this phrase that means "to cherish a spiritual aspiration for the attainment of supreme enlightenment"[58]—was altogether forgotten so that the Bodhicitta came to be treated as having an independent technical value."[59]

The view that there are two different meanings for the concept of *bodhicitta* has also been advocated by L. M. Joshi in a short paper surveying the literature of the Mahāyāna and of the Tantric Buddhist traditions.[60] According to him, *bodhicitta* is understood in Mahāyāna "as a strong resolution to work for the spiritual benefit of all creatures; . . . it is nevertheless, a mere thought or will (a strong will, no doubt) turned towards *samyaksaṃbodhi* [perfect enlightenment]." With regard to the Tantric tradition, he adds, "*bodhicitta* is not a way of Bodhi or *nirvana*, but it is *nirvana* itself. It is the supreme Reality."[61] Concerning the question of how this change of meaning was brought about, Joshi only says that it occurred gradually but, contrary to Suzuki, he does not attribute it to some kind of degeneration. At this point, it might be appropriate to look at Sangharakshita's ideas on *bodhicitta.*

ii. Sangharakshita

Sangharakshita is probably among the first Westerners who devoted their life to the practice as well as to the spreading of Buddhism. His major contribution is without doubt his attempt to translate the ideas and practices of this Eastern spiritual tradition into Western languages. For that purpose, Sangharakshita has not shied away from borrowing concepts from the field of science. As such, he could be compared, in his enterprise, to Pierre Teilhard de Chardin, a Catholic philosopher and paleontologist, who tried to explain religious phenomena in terms of scientific language.

Sangharakshita has been a very prolific writer, translator, and practitioner of Buddhism. One of his books, *A Survey of Buddhism* is still a valid source of information, even for non-Buddhists. One of his major preoccupations was to demonstrate the unity of Buddhism's metaphysical ideas as well as of its diverse spiritual approaches. It is therefore in the context of his vision of the unifying principle of Buddhism that he discussed *bodhicitta*.

According to Sangharakshita, the practice of Going for Refuge to the Buddha, the *dharma*, and the *saṅgha* is the central and definitive Act of the Buddhist life and the unifying principle of Buddhism itself.[62] Moreover, in his opinion the language of Going for Refuge provides the most helpful model of spiritual life.[63] Before looking at Sangharakshita's understanding of *bodhicitta*, it is therefore necessary to explain this model of spiritual life based on the practice of Going for Refuge.

Going for Refuge can be defined as the expression of one's commitment to the ideals of Buddhism. Sangharakshita explains that this practice has, in the course of time, in effect lost this meaning. Going for Refuge has more or less become a formality. "In some 'Buddhist countries' virtually the entire population will recite the formula when they go to temples, but few will do so with much consciousness of what the words really mean."[64] Because of this, Sangharakshita therefore argues that other means of expressing the essential act of commitment had to be developed. One of these expressions came to be known as "the arising of *bodhicitta*."[65] In this way, *bodhicitta* could be understood as an alternative to the practice of Going for Refuge. Eventually, in the course of the development of the Buddhist tradition, other forms such as the Tantric initiation of Vajrayāna appeared because even the arising of *bodhicitta* degenerated into a mere ritual. To be more precise, Sangharakshita did not say that these new forms of expressing this essential act of commitment were exactly like the original Going for Refuge, but rather, he argued that the development of these new forms resulted in making more explicit certain dimensions of Going for Refuge. For example, the arising of *bodhicitta*, which is interpreted as a deep urge to go forward on the path for the benefit of all beings,[66] came to reveal its altruistic dimension. However, it is essential to realize that, for Sangharakshita, the arising of *bodhicitta* brings nothing new to the basic act of commitment encompassed in the Going for Refuge: "The spiritual path [based on Going for Refuge] is of its very nature altruistic, a growth in harmony, friendship, and compassion."[67]

The act of Going for Refuge can be done, according to Sangharakshita, at five different levels. These are the Cultural, the Provisional, the Effective, the Real, and the Absolute. Although this classification is his own, it is not without basis in the canonical literature of Buddhism. These levels represent the various degrees of commitment to the ideals of Buddhism. The first level, the Cultural Going for Refuge has the least spiritual significance and probably plays the most prominent social role. Here, the formula of Going for Refuge is an affirmation of cultural and national identity; it is a characteristic of the tradition one vows allegiance to. The second level is called Provisional because it refers to an act which, although marked by strong feelings of devotion and reverence toward the ideals, falls short of being a true commitment. At this level, one is still torn by competing interests and ambitions. At the third level, the Effective Going for Refuge, these interests and ambitions are still there but one "is sufficiently drawn to the Three Jewels to be able to commit oneself to making systematic steps towards them. It is really at this point of 'Effective' Going for Refuge that the spiritual life begins in earnest. Here, the decisive reorientation from the mundane towards the transcendental is made."[68]

As mentioned earlier, these levels represent degrees of commitment. Sangharakshita has also provided a model to explain the succession of levels; he calls it the principle of Higher Evolution. The idea of evolution is one of these concepts used by Sangharakshita to make certain ideas of Buddhism easier to understand by a Western audience. It is to be considered a metaphor. The principle of Higher Evolution is to be contrasted to the Lower Evolution: where the latter corresponds to the scientific principle of evolution used to explain the developments of the biologic world, the former is used to describe the developments of the spiritual life. The Lower Evolution is cyclic and does not require consciousness to happen whereas the Higher Evolution evolves like a spiral and requires personal commitment and sustained effort. The image of the spiral is used by Sangharakshita because along this path toward greater commitment one experiences a deepening of self-awareness, that is, an increase in transcendental consciousness. As long as efforts are sustained, one moves upward along the spiral toward enlightenment. This progression, however, does not seem to be linear.

At the fourth level, the Real Going for Refuge, one gains a transforming insight that brings one onto the transcendental path. "It is the point on the path of the Higher Evolution where transcendental consciousness arises and one becomes a true individual."[69] This transition is a point of no-return; it is considered the first goal of spiritual life. In the Buddhist tradition, there are many images used to describe this moment: Stream Entry or the Opening of the Dhamma-Eye in the Pāli tradition, the attainment of the eighth *bhūmi* called Acalā in Mahāyāna, or entering the Path of Vision in Tibetan Buddhism. At this point, one is assured of gaining enlightenment. In other words, at this level the act of commitment has become a second nature for the aspirant to enlightenment. Finally, there is the Absolute or Ultimate Going for Refuge. This is the point of full Enlightenment. Here, "the cyclic trend of conditionality is completely exhausted and there is only a spontaneous unfolding of the spiral trend in unending creativity. Here, even Going for Refuge is transcended, since one has oneself become the refuge. In fact, in so far as all dualistic thought has been left behind, there is no refuge to go to and no one to go to it."[70]

To sum up, the progression from one level of Going for Refuge to the next corresponds to a more radical turning toward the Three Jewels. "It is Going for Refuge that drives one to leave behind what one has presently achieved and to seek yet greater heights. Going for Refuge therefore takes place within the context of the Higher Evolution, of which it is the vital fuel and spark."[71] The relevance of this idea for the concept of *bodhicitta* is that to Sangharakshita Going for Refuge is the expression, within the context of Mahāyāna Buddhism, of a general principle. This principle that Sangharakshita refers to as the "Cosmic Going for Refuge," is "considered the universal principle that underlies the entire evolutionary process."[72] This interpretation of *bodhicitta* has been corroborated by Marion L. Matics, a modern translator and commentator of Śāntideva's *Bodhicaryāvatāra*. According to him, [*bodhicitta*] "is the force of the thought which thus turns one's life completely upside down (as any thought is a force insofar as it results in action). Consequently, Bodhicitta (like Citta) partakes of a quasi-universal aspect, because in the latter sense, it is a force let loose in the universe to work for the good of all."[73] What this means is that the commitment for enlightenment does not only depend on one's individual will, but rather, it could be stirred up by a cosmic force. The best way to get attuned to this force is through the practice of Going for Refuge. As Sangharakshita explained, "The individual's spiritual efforts are not merely the efforts of an individual entirely isolated from everything else: they take place within a vast context."[74] It is probably at the fourth level, the Real Going for Refuge, that one has the experience of being carried off by this cosmic force.

Sangharakshita's understanding of *bodhicitta* is not devoid of interest. Earlier in my introduction, I drew a parallel between him and Teilhard de

Chardin. The comparison was not gratuitous. This Jesuit scholar also saw in the phenomenon of evolution a principle of spiritual growth, a force leading it to a spiritual finality. According to him, the evolution is "une cosmogenèse en mouvement dans laquelle, de lentes maturations en brusques explosions, quelque chose se fait, de la matière à la vie, de la vie au phénomène humain et jusqu'à, préparé et attendu, un ultra-humain. (a cosmogenesis in movement, in which, by dint of slow maturation and sudden explosions, something is brought forth; from matter to life, from life to the human phenomenon and even—prepared for and awaited—a beyond-the-human.)"[75] This "phénomène humain" is a crucial moment of the evolution because it is the point where consciousness starts to grow in complexity. In Sangharakshita's language, this is the beginning of the Higher Evolution.

When one compares Suzuki with Sangharakshita, one can see that they stand at the opposite ends of a spectrum with regard to the significance of *bodhicitta*. Suzuki understands this concept as purely motivational and does not recognize the validity of its metaphysical connotations. The abstract and technical meanings that developed in the Tantric tradition, for example, must be regarded, as mentioned earlier, as a deviation from the original meaning of *bodhicitta*. On the other hand, Sangharakshita's understanding of this concept, based on his vision of the soteriological context in which it is found, renders it, at the motivational level, somewhat redundant and obsolete. As he himself says, "I think it is all the more necessary to fall back on the Going for Refuge as the basic Buddhist act, not on the arising of *bodhicitta* and becoming a Bodhisattva—which is the archetype of Going for Refuge, on a cosmic scale."[76] In a way, Sangharakshita has, if one allows me the analogy, given to the concept of *bodhicitta* a seat in the House of Lords knowing that in fact things really happen in the Commons. In this context, although *bodhicitta* is translated as "Will to Enlightenment," this "will" should not be understood as the usual mental event of volition but rather as the description of a metaphysical reality.

Despite these two opposing views, I am of the opinion that it is possible to find a middle way, that is, to elaborate a soteriological context that would allow both aspects of *bodhicitta*, the functional and the metaphysical, to have a role to play in the process of spiritual transformation. As a matter of fact, this concept also has an important ethical aspect. In many instances, the person in whom *bodhicitta* arises is considered a son or a daughter of the Buddha. In the *Bodhicaryāvatāra*, for example, it is said that "the moment *bodhicitta* arises in a wretched man who is attached to existence, he becomes a son of the Buddhas and is praised by both men and gods."[77] This event is viewed as a life-transforming experience and is characterized by the acquisition of an attitude or spontaneous feeling of compassion toward all beings. Such a person is also said to be instantaneously freed from negative mental tendencies. In other words, this ethical aspect is related to the behavior or state of being of the person in whom *bodhicitta* has arisen. In this circumstance, I believe that any suggested soteriological context should take these three aspects into consideration.

As the next step of my study, I would like to investigate the possible functions that *bodhicitta* might assume in the context of a spiritual path. One function, as we have already seen, is *bodhicitta* as a desire for enlightenment, where the desire is to be understood literally, that is, as an act of the will and by extension as a commitment. A second function is *bodhicitta* as an object of concentration. Here, the emphasis is on the experience of calmness of the mind. The third function, the one that will lead me to the elaboration of what I believe to be an appropriate soteriological context for the understanding of *bodhicitta*, is *bodhicitta* as a basis for the cultivation of awareness.

2

Bodhicitta as a desire for enlightenment

From the analysis of Suzuki's conception of the spiritual path of the Bodhisattva, it is quite clear that desire plays a crucial role in its development. To state the obvious: in order to attain enlightenment, one has to desire it. But when we looked at Sangharakshita's understanding of the path, the idea of desire became a bit more complex. In addition to assimilating it to a conventional mental event, Sangharakshita, with his idea of Cosmic Going for Refuge, added a new dimension. As mentioned earlier, he feels that the individual's spiritual efforts are not merely the efforts of being entirely isolated from everything: they are somehow interconnected with a wider context that he called the Higher Evolution. It is most probably at the fourth level of Going for Refuge that this interconnection is observed. At this point, the desire for enlightenment appears to require less effort; the act of commitment has become, so to speak, a second nature for the aspirant to enlightenment.

The difference between Suzuki and Sangharakshita's view of the notion of desire is basically that, for the former, desire is exclusively a voluntary act requiring intense efforts and motivation. It is a brute force of the will allowing one to cross the sea of *saṃsāra*. Using an adapted version of the well-known simile of the raft, desire would be the fuel of an engine that one has attached to the raft for a more rapid crossing. What matters is the quantity, and probably the quality, of fuel one disposed of in order to reach the other shore. For Sangharakshita, on the other hand, desire, in the course of the spiritual progression, seems to detach itself from the necessity of willpower. Using the same modified simile of the raft, an engine is still needed to move it across the sea of *saṃsāra*, but, at some point, it enters into a stream or is pushed by a strong wind so that its speed is maintained or even increased, and above all, it no longer requires fuel to progress along its path. This means that progression on the path is not always directly proportional to the intensity of efforts put in by the aspirant to enlightenment. Sangharakshita's view of the desire for enlightenment is for this reason a somewhat more sophisticated than that of Suzuki. As will be seen later, I am of the opinion that it is also more faithful to the nature of the spiritual path as conceived by Śāntideva in his *Bodhicaryāvatāra*.

In the present chapter, I will therefore look at the possible connotations of the idea of desire and evaluate their appropriateness for a definition of *bodhicitta*. It is especially the notion of voluntary efforts that will be investigated. As for the interpretation suggested by Sangharakshita, I will demonstrate that *bodhicitta* can be more than a mere expression of a metaphysical principle. Implicitly, I will be criticizing Sangharakshita's interpretation of the historical development of *bodhicitta*. For instance, I do not think that *bodhicitta*, even as the expression of a ritual of initiation, is to be assimilated to the Cultural Going for Refuge, that is, to a simple social event. This means that even at the moment of initiation, *bodhicitta* could be seen as the basis of a spiritual approach in its own right and, consequently, it is not to be understood in terms of the terminology and concepts of another approach such as that of the Going for Refuge. My arguments in this regard will be expounded after I have discussed what I consider to be an appropriate soteriological context to understand the meaning of *bodhicitta*.

1. The idea of desire

When viewing desire exclusively as an act of the will, one inevitably has to discuss the notion of the goal. The goal is the incentive, the basis of one's motivation, that for which efforts are made. It is also that which allows one to make decisions and choices: some choices lead one away from the goal while others bring one closer to its attainment. This idea is quite straightforward because one can easily relate to it.

In Mahāyāna Buddhism, the goal of the spiritual practice of its aspirants is *bodhi*. As mentioned earlier, this term has been translated either as "enlightenment" or "awakening." In the literature of this tradition, one also finds expressions such as *saṃbodhi* (enlightenment), *samyaksaṃbodhi* (perfect enlightenment), or *anuttarā samyaksaṃbodhi* (unsurpassed perfect enlightenment). All of these expressions refer to the final experience of the path of the Bodhisattva. In the Pāli canon, however, there seems to be a distinction between these expressions. Indeed, *bodhi* is used to express the lofty knowledge of an ascetic and the stage of enlightenment of the *paccekabuddhas*, those who attained enlightenment by their own means, whereas the final experience of the Buddha is identified as *sammāsaṃbodhi*.[1]

The relevance of this observation is that, from the early beginning of the Buddhist tradition, one began to make distinctions as to the nature and content of this final goal. The Mahāyāna Buddhists were not exempted from this trend and indeed argued that their goal was superior to that of the non-Mahāyānists. Its superiority was mainly justified on the basis of the idea of desire.

According to the *Abhisamayalaṅkara*, the thought of Enlightenment is the desire for supreme enlightenment in pursuit of the welfare of others.[2] In the *Vajradhara sūtra*, also a text of the Mahāyāna tradition, the Bodhisattva, overflowing with compassion, says, "It is my resolution to save all sentient beings, I must set all beings free, I must save all the universe, from the wilderness of birth, of old age, of disease, of rebirth, of all sins, of all misfortunes, of all transmigrations, of all pains caused by heretical doctrines, of the destruction of the skillful Dharma, of the occurrence of ignorance, therefore I must set all sentient beings free from all these wildernesses."[3] In Mahāyāna Buddhism, the desire to help all beings is the reason for which one seeks enlightenment. On the basis of this implication, a distinction was made between the aspirants who were engaged on the Mahāyāna path to enlightenment and those who were not. Indeed, according to Atiśa (982–1054) in his *Bodhipathapradīpa*, beings can be classified in terms of their aspirations into three types: the lesser, the average, and the superior. To the lesser type belong those who have no religious aspirations. The average seekers act to bring about their own pacification, that is, to attain enlightenment as an Arhat. Those of the highest, superior type are the Bodhisattvas as they seek to bring a complete end to all the sufferings of others.[4] This distinction on the basis of one's aspiration seems to have been carried over in the analysis of modern Buddhist scholars such as L. M. Joshi. Indeed, he affirms the fact that the altruistic and self-negating attitude of the Bodhisattva, instilled by *bodhicitta*, "stands out in sharp contrast to the dictum of the Theravada tradition wherein we read, 'One should not sacrifice one's own interest, one ought to devote to one's true interest.' "[5]

The significance of this discussion concerning what I would call the apologetic function of desire is that it contributes to a tightening of the connection between desire and act of will. Among the Mahāyānists, it is believed that the desire for enlightenment, because it is motivated by the desire to help all sentient beings, renders one who embrace its ideology a superior aspirant. As long as one wishes to justify a distinction between the Mahāyāna and non-Mahāyāna paths to enlightenment, one has no other alternative than to maintain that desire is exclusively a voluntary act, an act involving a specific choice, that is, to follow the Mahāyāna path and no other. If one were to argue, on the other hand, that the experience of enlightenment is beneficial, then the reasons for which one seeks enlightenment become secondary and, consequently, any distinction between aspirants to enlightenment on the basis of these reasons would be senseless. In other words, if, for example, the experience of enlightenment means the realization of one's own compassionate nature and, as a result of which, as the *Aṣṭasahasrikā Prajñāpāramitāsūtra* puts it, one "radiates great friendliness and compassion over all beings,"[6] then there is no reason to exclude the non-Mahāyāna Buddhists since they too must be endowed with this nature. As will be discussed later, I believe that this interpretation of the desire to work for the welfare of all beings is quite plausible. For the moment, I would just like to point out the fact that historical and cultural circumstances may have led one to adopt an interpretation that reinforces the link between the desire to help all other sentient beings and an act of will on the part of the aspirant to enlightenment.

There is another reason why one may believe that the desire for enlightenment is assimilated to a voluntary act of will. There are many passages in the Mahāyāna scriptures that stress the importance of this idea. In the *Śikṣāsamuccaya* of Śāntideva, for example, it is said that "the Bodhisattva makes a courageous effort with all the forces of his body, speech and mind to appease all bodily and mental sufferings of all beings, both present and future and to produce bodily and mental happiness present and to come."[7] The twenty-fourth verse of this anthology cannot be more explicit: "Having first made firm with efforts your determination and intention, having adopted compassion, you should strive so that merits increase."[8]

Efforts are also necessary for being faithful to the resolve taken. In many passages, the Bodhisattva is enjoined never to desert it. In the *Lalitavistara*, for example, it is said that Bodhisattva Siddhārtha was reminded of his resolution to obtain *bodhi* and to liberate the creatures of the world from sorrow.[9] In the *Rāṣṭrapāla*, it is said that the Bodhisattva must remember the following verse for the purpose of counteracting despondency: "In many millions of ages a Buddha sometimes arises, someone [who works] for the welfare of the world, a great sage. For the one who desires emancipation, now a great opportunity has come, today he must reject indolence."[10] After reflecting on the meaning of this verse, he further motivates himself by saying, "Thus persevere in and always strive for the Perfections, the spiritual Stages, the Powers; never relax your vigor until you are awakened to the most excellent enlightenment."[11]

To sum up the present discussion of the idea of desire, it appears that there are two main reasons why *bodhicitta*, which is the desire for enlightenment for the sake of all beings, may be considered exclusively as an act of will. The first deals with the fact that the Mahāyāna tradition tried to distinguish its ultimate experience from that of other Buddhist traditions; this is what I called the apologetic function of the idea of desire. The major implication of this function is to firmly establish the notion of the individual who makes decisions and who acts upon them. The second reason is based on scriptural passages highlighting the importance of efforts for progressing on the path. On the one hand, there is a certain understanding of the spiritual path in which efforts and commitment play a key role in the Bodhisattva's spiritual practice and, on the other hand, one has a prominent concept within the Mahāyāna literature that can easily be translated as "desire for enlightenment." In this circumstance, it is natural that *bodhicitta* becomes the privileged means to express the Bodhisattva's spiritual commitment.

The issue I would like to address now is whether *bodhicitta* has to be understood in terms of commitment. I do not want to deny the importance of this idea but rather to evaluate its exact nature in the context of what I believe to be an appropriate view of the spiritual path of the Bodhisattva. Like the laws of Newton that have been integrated into Einstein's theories of relativity, I believe that the idea of commitment can be seen from the perspective of a wider context thereby reassessing its character and its significance.

It has been shown earlier that *citta* in the compound *bodhi-citta* has been interpreted as desire, that is, as having exclusively a conative connotation. In the Mahāyāna sources, however, when it comes to expressing the desire or the resolution of the Bodhisattva, apart from the context of the expression *anuttarāyāṃ samyak-saṃbodhau cittam utpādam* (the arising of the thought [desire] of unsurpassed perfect enlightenment), *citta* is, as far as I know, rarely employed. Instead, one encounters the terms *praṇidhāna* as in *sarvasattva-uttāraṇa-praṇidhānaṃ mama* (it is my resolution to save all creatures);[12] *kāma* as in *yadi moktu-kāmaḥ* (if one wishes release);[13] *artha* as in *tasmāt mayā bodhi-arthikena bhavitavyam* (Therefore I must be desirous of enlightenment);[14] *āśaya* and *adhyāśaya* as in *āśayu yeṣa prasādiviśuddhaḥ teṣa adhyāśayu uttama śreṣṭhaḥ* (For the one who has intention, there is complete composure; for the one who has determination, there is the very best desire);[15] or *abhilāṣa* as in *ayaṃ ca saṃvaraḥ strīṇām api mṛdukleśānāṃ bodhi-abhilāṣacittānāṃ labhyate* (And this discipline is attained even in the case of women, when their mental tendencies are soft and their minds are characterized by a longing for enlightenment).[16] The last example is not without interest because of the simultaneous occurrence of the words *citta* and *abhilāṣa* in the compound *bodhi-abhilāṣa-citta*. This compound is in fact made up of two other compounds: the first is *bodhi-abhilāṣa*, which is a *tatpuruṣa* (desire for enlightenment) and the second, *abhilāṣa-citta*, could be viewed as a *upamāna-pūrvapada-karmadhāraya*.[17] In this case, *abhilāṣa* denotes a quality or characteristic of *citta*. The meaning of this compound could then be "a mind whose characteristic is to desire."

The relevance of this discussion is to draw to one's attention the fact that *citta* may refer to a state of mind having such and such qualities. This renders the psychological process of desiring a bit more complex because the desire appears to be not a willful act but rather a consequence of a certain state of mind. In other words, one does not have desires, but rather, one is in a state of mind that desires. This distinction may appear to be superfluous at first sight, but I am of the opinion that it makes all the difference in the way in which one understands *bodhicitta*. In the next section, I will therefore look at the various semantic applications of *citta* and try to justify why it is possible that it may refer to a state of mind.

2. Criticism of *bodhicitta* as an act of will

i. *Citta* (mind)

Previously, I maintained that to have a comprehensive picture of the meaning of a concept such as that of *bodhicitta*, one has to take into consideration the soteriological context in which it is articulated. Such a context, however, is never created out of a vacuum; it has itself its own history. Part of this history may be revealed by the various semantic applications its key concepts or terms have assumed or are still assuming. In the case of *citta*, for example, because it is related to a mental process that could have a direct bearing on one's state of being, a knowledge of its semantic applications may inform us on the type of means required or appropriate to influence or modify this mental process.

The present discussion of the various semantic applications assumed by *citta* is not meant to be exhaustive, but rather, it is to be considered an attempt to trace the origin of the various meanings that it has assumed in the course of its history of application and to evaluate the consequences this may have for understanding *bodhicitta*.

In chapter 1, while discussing the possible interpretations of *bodhicitta*, I mentioned the fact that *citta* can have either a cognitive or a conative connotation. These two interpretations are well supported in most of the philosophical traditions of India including Buddhism. From the point of view of its etymology, these two meanings are also confirmed. Indeed, *citta* comes from the verbal root √*cit* that gives us the verbs *cetati* (1P) and *cetayate* (10Ā). Both have a wide range of meanings. Vaman Shivaran Apte gives the following translations among others: (1) to perceive, notice, or observe; (2) to know, understand, or be aware or conscious of; (3) to regain consciousness; (4) to aim at, intend, or design; (5) to desire or long for; (6) to be anxious about, care for, be intent upon, or be engaged in; (7) to resolve upon; (8) to appear or to shine; (9) to be regarded as; (10) to make attentive or remind of; (11) to teach or instruct; (12) to form an idea, be conscious of, understand, comprehend, think, or reflect upon, and (13) to be awake.[18] The form *cittam*, which is the neuter past particle of the verb *cetati*, therefore, means (1) perceiving; (2) understanding; (3) regaining consciousness; (4) aiming at or intending; (5) being intent upon, and so forth. Sometimes, *cittam* is glossed by *cetanā* as in the following example taken from the *Bhāvanākrama* of Kamalaśīla: *prārthanākārā cetanā tat praṇidhicittam* (the aspiration-mind is the intention that has the form of a desire).[19] According to Apte, the feminine noun *cetanā* means (1) sense or consciousness; (2) understanding or intelligence; (3) life, vitality, or animation; and (4) wisdom or reflection.[20] As shown in the last example, this term is also used in the sense of intention and volition.

One can therefore see that the derivatives of the verbal root √*cit* occur in relation to various mental faculties. Already in the literature of the *ṛg Veda*, these derivatives assumed a wide range of meanings and connotations. According to Ross N. Reat, who studied the various psychological concepts of early Indian thought, "used with the term *manas*, √*cit* indicates mental perception or intellectual thought. With *hṛd* (heart) it refers to emotional or intuitive thought. With √*dhī* it refers to imaginative, visionary thought. With *kratu* it refers to volitional thought."[21] The important point to notice in this analysis is that derivatives of √*cit* denote simply mental activity in general. The purpose of this mental activity was, in the context of the Vedic culture, to maximize the efficiency of sacrifices. These sacrifices were performed in order to obtain boons or a place in heaven. As Ross Reat says in an attempt to summarize this worldview, "Roughly speaking, the entire human psychological complex, as represented in the *ṛg Veda*, may be conceived in terms of electronic communications." He further explains, "In such model, *hṛd* would be the transmitting room, *manas* the transmitter itself, and derivatives of √*cit* would be the various forms of current and electrical activity in the transmitter. *Kratu* would be the antenna, which focuses and directs the signal, and *dhī* would be the message sent, hopefully to be received by the Gods."[22]

The Vedic tradition, however, is not the only source of meaning for the various concepts used in the context of the philosophical and psychological thinking of India. One also has to take into consideration the non-Vedic, or more specifically, the yogic worldview. Yoga is one of the six orthodox systems of Indian philosophy. It has been systematized by Patañjali (ca. second century B.C.E.) in a text called *Yoga Sūtra*. According to him, Yoga is a methodical effort to attain perfection, through the control of the different elements of human nature, both physical and psychic.[23] The very idea of controlling human nature already sets this approach apart from the Vedic system of thought. Probably before the arrival of the Vedic culture in India there were ascetics strolling the country in search of immortality and permanent happiness, something that the Vedic gods themselves would never have been able to grant. Indeed, the favors granted by the gods were usually proportional to the extent of the sacrifices. To obtain immortality, that is, an unlimited stay in heaven, would therefore require an unlimited sacrifice or a sacrifice whose extent is beyond imagination.[24] The Yoga system, on account of its goal and aspiration, could therefore be considered an offshoot of this tradition of seekers.

At the very outset, Yoga is declared to be the restraining of the modifications of *citta*.[25] In this context, *citta* is the mind-stuff that undergoes modifications or fluctuations when it is affected by objects through the senses. These modifications are called *vṛtti* and may be likened to the impressions left on material like wax when some force acts upon it. These impressions are left on the *citta* and as such are called *vāsanās*. Another metaphor used to describe *citta* is that of the lake whose surface is agitated by the strong winds that are the *vṛtti*. When the disturbing winds are absent, one can see through the calm surface of the lake which is, in the case of Yoga, the pure Self or *puruṣa*. One can see from these two metaphors that the basic image behind the notion of *citta*, in the context of the Yoga system, is that of a repository of habits, memories, and dispositions acquired through one's experience with the phenomenal world. This idea of repository is not without precedents in the Buddhist tradition.

In this tradition, there is the concept of *viññāṇa* (Pāli) or *vijñāna* (Sanskrit) (consciousness) that seems to play this role. Not the *viññāṇa* that arises from contact of the senses and sense-objects, but rather, the one that appears as a member of the doctrine of dependent origination (*pratītyasamutpāda*).[26] According to this doctrine, the karma-formations (*saṃskāra*), which have been accumulated in the preceding lives due to ignorance, condition the arising of a new consciousness (*viññāṇa*) in the womb, on the basis of which a new psychophysical complex (*nāma-rūpa*), equipped with the six-senses-bases, comes into being. Contact between any of these and sense-objects produces feeling, which in turn leads to craving. This *viññāṇa* was considered a transmigratory entity and could be compared to a stream or a series of *viññāṇa*-moments (*kṣaṇa*) that is modified according to the nature of its relationship with the environment, that is, the objects of consciousness.

This attempt to account for the continuity between one's actions and the ripening of their consequences has been thus formulated by the Theravādins. There are also other attempts within the Buddhist tradition. Some avoided altogether the concept of *viññāṇa*—this is the case of the Vātsīputrīyas with their idea of the indefinable person (*pudgala*)—while others, like the Yogācārins and their concept of substratum consciousness (*ālayavijñāna*), made *vijñāna*, not only the repository of one's past actions but also of the whole phenomenal world. Despite these variations, however, the basic understanding behind this idea of repository remains nevertheless the same. Referring back to the soteriological context, this idea directly addresses the human problem: it is then because one has accumulated and reinforced certain dispositions and tendencies that one has such and such responses. And these tendencies have to be stored somewhere to produce their effects later; hence the importance of the idea of repository.

In Buddhism, *citta* also seems to play this function of repository. According to W. S. Karunaratna, who wrote an article on *bodhicitta* in the *Encyclopedia of Buddhism*, "As a psychic factor *citta* carries the traces of the experiences of the individual. *Citta*, therefore, may be viewed as the storehouse of each man's psychic heritage transmitted through the cycle of birth and rebirth."[27] As such, this term is more or less synonymous with *manas* (mind), but often used much like *heart* in English.[28] The word *heart* usually refers to the whole personality including its intellectual as well as its emotional functions or traits. It is also considered, as one's innermost character, feelings, or inclinations.[29]

Citta by itself appears to have no moral connotation; it is rather the words it is associated with, as just mentioned, which denotes its quality. For example, we are told in the *Bodhisattvaprātimokṣa* that the Bodhisattvas do not have a despondent mind *(līna-citta)*[30] or, in the *Ratnamegha Sūtra*, that he (the Bodhisattva) does not cause an angry thought *(pratigha-citta)* to arise.[31] These tendencies of the mind are not necessarily negative; they could be beneficial as well. An aspirant for enlightenment, for example, should have a mind desiring *(abhilaṣita-citta)* the practice of the Bodhisattvas,[32] a mind eager *(abhilaṣita-citta)* [to respond] to all requests[33] or a mind that has no consideration *(anapekṣa-citta)* for his own body.[34] Again, *citta* seems to refer to a state of mind that has such and such qualities, one of which could be the tendency to desire or even to abandon as in "on account of the force or impulse of a mind [inclined] towards renunciation (tyāga-citta), there is abandonment of all possessions."[35]

Coming back to the analysis of *citta* in the context of the discussion of *bodhicitta*, it appears that these two semantic applications, namely mental activity and repository, have not really been taken into consideration. When trying to decide whether *citta* is either cognitive or conative, one has assumed that it refers exclusively to a mental activity. One has failed to notice that this term has, so to speak, an active connotation as well as a passive one. For the sake of clarity let us take, for example, the Sanskrit word *saṃskāra*.

According to Ross Reat, this word, as used in Buddhist psychology, represents a concept unfamiliar to the Western mind.[36] In this regard, it is said in the Pāli-English dictionary, that it is "one of the most difficult terms in Buddhist metaphysics, in which the blending of the subjective-objective view of the world and of happening, peculiar to the East, is so complete, that it is almost impossible for Occidental terminology to get at the root of its meaning in a translation."[37] It has been difficult to translate into European languages because its semantic applications cover ideas that are normally considered distinct in Western thinking. On the one hand, *saṃskāra* is characterized by the tendency to accumulate or to build up. This is what may constitute memory. Like memory, its function is to store elements of past experiences. On the other hand, *saṃskāra* accounts for the basic mechanism of karma, that is, the actions of the mind, speech, and body. As such, it could be translated as *cetanā* (volition). The idea of volition, in most Western systems of thought, is usually understood as being quite different from the process of memorizing or that of the accumulation of habits.

It is for this reason that I believe that *citta* refers to a state of mind that may respond in such and such a way depending on the situations. From this point of view, one may say that one has no control over *citta* as in "I have no control over my mind to make it give up";[38] it dictates one's behavior and makes one a passive subject. But when one considers the possibility that one of its qualities could be the desire for enlightenment, then the connotation of passiveness is no longer valid; it is somehow blended with a notion of activity. This idea should not be, despite its unfamiliarity, so difficult to understand. One is well familiar with the phenomenon of procrastination. From the point of view of motivation, one is waiting for the moment when the interest or the will to do what should be done arises. This attitude is quite different from that where one forcibly goes against one's emotions and mood to do what is to be done.

While presenting D. T. Suzuki's understanding of *bodhicitta*, I mentioned that, according to this author, this concept should really be considered the abbreviation of the expression *anuttarāyāṃ samyaksaṃbodhau cittam utpādam*. Consequently, *citta*, in the compound *bodhicitta*, should be understood as *citta-utpāda* which, according to him, refers explicitly to an act of will. There has been some debate in the Buddhist tradition over this interpretation of *citta* as *citta-utpāda* and therefore, I would like to now consider its validity.

ii. *Citta-utpāda* (arising of the mind)

Suzuki's main contention concerning *bodhicitta* is that it should not, as mentioned earlier, be interpreted as a thought. To translate the phrase *anuttarāyāṃ samyaksaṃbodhau cittam utpādam* by "to awaken the idea of enlightenment" would be, according to him, incorrect and misleading. To support his interpretation, Suzuki argues that *anuttarāyāṃ samyaksaṃbodhau cittam utpādam* is equivalent to *anuttarāṃ samyaksaṃbodhim ākāṅkṣamāṇa* (longing for supreme enlightenment), or to *anuttarāyāṃ samyaksaṃbodhau praṇidhānaṃ parigṛhya* (cherishing an intense desire for supreme enlightenment). Both of these passages are taken from the Lotus Sutra.[39] He also quotes passages from the *Gaṇḍavyūha* where one finds expressions that convey the same idea: *vipula-kṛpa-karaṇa-mānasa paryeṣase 'nuttamāṃ bodhim* (raising a far-reaching compassion, you seek for supreme enlightenment); or *ye bodhiprāthayante* (those who desire enlightenment).[40] His most important argument is probably the idea that the phrase *anuttarāyāṃ samyaksaṃbodhau cittam utpādam*, the abbreviated form of which being *bodhicittotpāda*, is also equivalent to *anuttarāyāṃ samyaksaṃbodhau praṇidadhanti*.[41]

Praṇidadhāti should be given special consideration according to Suzuki. It means "to give one's entire attention to something," that is, "to resolve firmly to accomplish the work." He further explains that, "the Bodhisattva's Praṇidhāna is his intense determination to carry out his plan of universal salvation. Of course, it is necessary here to have an adequate knowledge of the work he intends to accomplish, but a Praṇidhāna is far more than this. Mere intellectuality has no backing of the willpower; mere idealism can never be an efficient executive agency." He then concludes, "Cittotpāda is a form of Praṇidhāna."[42] That is why *citta*, that is, *citta-utpāda* is not an "arising of a thought" but rather the "cherishing of a desire." Consequently,

"*Cittotpāda* is a volitional movement definitely made towards the realization of enlightenment."[43]

This interpretation of *citta-utpāda* seems to be well supported in Sanskrit literature. According to the Buddhist Hybrid Sanskrit dictionary, it is rendered as *production of intention* or *resolution* as in *antaśa ekacittotpādenāpy anumoditam idaṃ sūtram* (by even so much as a single deliberate mental act this *sūtra* has been approved),[44] or *śobhanas te citta-utpādaḥ* (an excellent resolution of yours or a fine idea).[45] In Pāli, this expression is also translated as "intention" or "desire" as in *theyya cittaṃ uppādesi* (he had the intention to steal).[46] In the context of the Mahāyāna literature, it has been pointed out that "most of the philosophers who accept the definition of *bodhicitta* as one leaning towards aspiration, wish and devotion, prefer to use the term *cittotpāda* instead of *bodhicitta*."[47] In particular, this is the case of the Buddhist philosophers such as Asaṅga. Indeed, according to Tsong-kha-pa, a Tibetan scholar of the fourteenth century (ca. 1357–1419), Asaṅga claimed in his *Bodhisattvabhūmi* that *cittotpāda* has to be understood as an aspiration *(praṇidhi/smon lam).* In support of his affirmation he says that the Bodhisattva's best aspiration is the *citta-utpāda*.[48]

Contrary to Asaṅga and Suzuki, Ārya Vimuktisena, a Buddhist scholar of the eighth century, considers it as being composed of two different words that ought to be interpreted literally. For him, *utpāda* means "production" and it refers to the bringing into existence of a consciousness (*citta*) composed of, or supported by, in the case of *bodhicitta*, wholesome phenomena. In other words, *utpāda* identifies a result, something that has been brought into being, and as such, it could be used independently to express the production or the bringing into function of any kind of mental activity. For example, it is used to express feelings as in *asmin putre 'tiriktataraṃ prema-utpādayāmi* (I feel excessive affection for this son),[49] or as in *spṛhām utpādayanti* (they cause arrogance to arise).[50] It could also refer to the process of thinking as in *punaraparaṃ bodhisattvaḥ sarvadharmeṣu parakīya-saṃjñām utpādayati* (Again, the Bodhisattva, in relation to all things, thinks that this belongs to others).[51] The point of this discussion is to say that the use of *utpāda* is not to be necessarily understood metaphorically to designate an act of will but that it could be looked upon as description of a mental process that is the production of a mental state.

While discussing the meaning of *citta-utpāda*, Suzuki explicitly said that it is to be considered as a form of *praṇidhāna*. By the same token, *bodhicitta*, being its synonym, has to be interpreted as a commitment or as a strong resolution. The problem with this view is that *praṇidhāna* is in fact only one aspect of *bodhicitta*. Indeed, the Mahāyāna tradition advocates the idea of a twofold division of *bodhicitta*. According to the *Bhāvanākrama* of Kamalaśīla, the *Śikṣasamuccaya*, and the *Bodhicaryāvatāra* of Śāntideva, there are two types of *bodhicitta*. The first type is called *bodhipraṇidhicitta* and can be translated as "the resolution to attain Bodhi" and the second, *bodhiprasthānacitta*, as "progression toward the attainment of Bodhi." From the point of view of an understanding of *bodhicitta* as commitment, this twofold division has been interpreted in the following manner: the Bodhisattva must first resolve to become awakened then implement his resolve. In the light of what has been suggested in the analysis of *citta* and *citta-utpāda*, I am of the opinion that it could be interpreted otherwise. This is what I would like to consider next.

iii. The two types of *bodhicitta*

The first reference to this twofold division of *bodhicitta* seems to have been in the *Gaṇḍavyūha*, a Mahāyāna text that precedes the works of Kamalaśīla and Śāntideva. In this text, we are told that it is very difficult to find in the world beings who have made the resolve for supreme enlightenment; and those who are proceeding toward it are even more rare to come by.[52] For the purpose of the present discussion, let us look at what Śāntideva is telling us about the two types of *bodhicitta*. In chapter 1 of his *Bodhicaryāvatāra*, he says, "Then, in short, one should know that *bodhicitta* is two-fold: the mind having made a resolve for *bodhi* and the actual proceeding towards *bodhi*."[53] This division of *bodhicitta* is made more explicit with a simple analogy, "Just as a difference is perceived between the one who desires to go and the one who is going, so a difference between both [types of *bodhicitta*] is acknowledged by the wise men."[54]

As just mentioned, one way of interpreting this division of *bodhicitta* is to say that first there is a wish for enlightenment, then the making of efforts for its implementation. From the point of view of ordinary experience, this is common sense, but from the perspective of spiritual endeavor, this situation is a little bit odd. Why would someone, for example, put a lot of energy in strengthening his desire and commitment, then fall short of implementing it? Such a person is comparable to a racing car spinning its tires to increase adherence to the road and which, with all the fuel consumption it requires and the noise and smoke it causes, never crosses the starting line. Either this person is not serious in his decision or is dishonest. This is how one would judge a person who says "I am going to that place," but never goes.

There are therefore a few problems with this interpretation of this division of *bodhicitta*. First of all, it diminishes the value of the first type of *bodhicitta*. As Parmananda Sharma, a translator of the *Bodhicaryāvatāra*, says, commenting on this last verse, "the secret of the attainment of bodhi is the practice aspect and not merely a pious wish."[55] What Sharma implies is that a pious wish achieves practically nothing; this is, however, contrary to what the Mahāyāna scriptures are telling us. In the *Maitreyavimokṣa*, for example, it is said that "even when broken the diamond-gem is distinguished above all others and is superior to a golden ornament, and as such, does not lose the name of diamond-gem; it averts all poverty. So also the diamond of the production of the thought of perfect enlightenment, even though divorced from good intention and conduct, is superior to the gold ornament of the virtues of mere *śrāvakas* and *pratyekabuddhas*, and does not lose the name of thought of enlightenment."[56] Concerning this view, Śāntideva adds, "even without practice the thought of enlightenment is to be recognized as a helpful thing."[57]

The interpretation suggested by Sharma also assumes the idea that a thought, if not carried out, has no spiritual value. Still commenting on the passage just quoted from the *Bodhicaryāvatāra*, he says that "he who thinks, stays; he who ventures, reaches."[58] Suzuki seems to argue along the same lines when he says, "'To conceive an idea' or 'to awaken a thought' is one thing, and to carry it out in action is quite another, especially when it is carried out with intensity and fervency."[59] In a way, the present problem concerning this interpretation of this division of *bodhicitta* is directly related to its underlying philosophical presuppositions: an intention must be supported by some sort of commitment to be effective. Again, there are passages in the Mahāyāna literature that seem to suggest another view on the significance of thoughts in the process of spiritual development.

In the *Saddharmapuṇḍarīka*, it is said, "The wise man must always be thinking: 'May I and all other beings become a Buddha!' This is for me the means to attain all happiness."[60] The most explicit examples confirming the spiritual importance of just having a thought are probably related to the recollection of the Buddhas and of their qualities. In the *Dharmasaṅgīti Sūtra*, it is mentioned that "Thus he calls them [the Blessed Buddhas] to mind; and thus having called them to mind he remains established in his "vision" of them in order to develop their virtues. This is what is meant by calling the Buddhas to mind."[61] In fact, this practice of recollecting the Buddhas and their qualities (*buddha-anusmṛti*) is one important spiritual approach developed by the Buddhists. I would like to deal with it in more detail later. For the moment, I just want to challenge the idea that a thought alone has no spiritual value, as assumed or implied by this interpretation of this division of *bodhicitta*.

There is probably a second problem concerning this interpretation that is worth noting. This interpretation presupposes two decisions: the first is to attain enlightenment and the second is to actually move toward it. Such a distinction is possible if one views the first decision, granted that it is done in good faith, as a kind of ritual that has lost, in the course of time, its spiritual significance and the second, as the expression of a true wishful attitude. According to the Mahāyāna tradition, a Bodhisattva is called upon taking a series of vows and making a few commitments in front of a suitable master and the community he is about to join. There is an elaborate ceremony surrounding this event whose climax is, according to Atiśa, for the aspirant to repeat three times the following vow: "May all the Buddhas and Bodhisattvas abiding in the ten directions deign to take notice of me! May the master deign to take notice of me! I, named so-and-so, . . . generate a thought towards supreme, right and full great awakening."[62] It is usually taken for granted that such a vow is a sufficient condition to engage into the practice of the Bodhisattva unless, as observed by Sangharakshita, this ritual of the arising of *bodhicitta* assumed only a social meaning. In such a case, one has to renew one's commitment, usually at a personal level. As mentioned before, it is possible that a Bodhisattva relaxes his commitment at some point in his career—that is why he may sometimes have to be reminded about his vow—but I do not believe that the reason for advocating a twofold division of *bodhicitta* was meant to draw one's attention to this type of situation. As far as I know, these two ideas are never presented or discussed together in the Mahāyāna literature. It is also probably anachronistic to see in the treatment of this division of *bodhicitta* a discussion related to the degeneration of the ritual surrounding the arising of *bodhicitta*.

This interpretation of this division of *bodhicitta* rests on the understanding of the words *praṇidhi* and *prasthāna*. *Praṇidhi* has been rightly rendered by "desire" or "resolution." In this regard, one may recall the following passage from the *Śikṣāsamuccaya*, "It is my resolution to save all creatures."[63] What I would like to discuss here is not the meaning of this word proper, but rather the significance of the fact that it is combined with *citta*. Earlier in this chapter, while discussing the simultaneous occurrence of *citta* and *abhilāṣa* in the compound *bodhi-abhilāṣa-citta*, I maintained that the compound *abhilāṣa-citta* could be viewed as a *upamāna-pūrvapada-karmadhāraya* where *abhilāṣa* denotes a quality or characteristic of *citta*. I am of the opinion that this reasoning also applies to the expression *bodhipraṇidhicittaṃ*. Indeed, Prajñākaramati, in his commentary of the verse introducing this division of *bodhicitta*, says, "The mind which arises (*utpanna*) on account of entreaty that is the resolution-mind."[64] Again, the use of *utpanna* seems to point out the fact that the mind described is a state of mind. Another passage, this time from the *Śikṣāsamuccaya*, seems to confirm the same idea: "They [the Bodhisattvas] emit the Ray Incombustible. By this, vicious persons incited become established in purity of conduct, and they conceive the thought 'May I become a Buddha.' In the skillful and purified path of action, they undertake good conduct by solemn vow, which awakens the minds of many persons: thus the Ray Incombustible is accomplished."[65] Regardless of the circumstances of its arising, the resolution-mind is a state of mind that is characterized by the ability to express the vow or the intention to become a Buddha. Consequently, it appears that not all states of mind are conducive to expressing this wish.[66] Although this state of mind does not yet proceed toward enlightenment—in this regard, Prajñākaramati says that it is "devoid of the practice of the Perfections beginning with giving"[67]—it has nevertheless beneficial spiritual consequences. The arising of this state of mind could be compared to an experience of conversion or "a call of God." As will be discussed later, this experience could be provoked by one's own decision as well as by someone else thus being also gratuitous. In this regard, one might quote the *Bodhicaryāvatāra*, "Just as lightning produces a momentary illumination during a dark night, so also sometimes people may have a brief thought for what is beneficial through the power of the Buddhas."[68] Again, despite its spiritual significance, this event is not yet enlightenment: another spiritual event has to occur and I believe that it is what is implied or referred to by *bodhiprasthānam*.

In the previous discussion, *prasthāna* has been rendered by progression toward or proceeding. These translations are supported by the lexicographers such as Apte who gives (1) going or setting forth, departing, moving, or walking; (2) coming to; (3) sending away or despatching, and (4) proceeding or marching.[69] This word comes from the root *pra+√sthā* that gives the verbs *prasthīyate* (1Ā) and *prasthāpayate* (10Ā). These verbs mean respectively (1) to set out or depart; (2) to advance or march toward; (3) to walk or move; and (4) to send away, dismiss, or despatch.[70] In this circumstance, the idea of movement is not to be denied. But what exactly is the nature of this movement?

In addition to the idea of moving forward, *prasthīyate* also assumes a connotation of being stationary. Indeed, it is translated as "to stand firmly and to be established."[71] It might therefore be plausible to interpret *prasthāna* as a basis or perhaps as a point of departure. Moreover, it might be possible to relate this term to the word *upasthānam* that is used in the expression *smṛti-upasthāna* (establishing of mindfulness), a meditative practice common to both Mahāyāna and early Buddhism. In this context, *upasthānam* has been interpreted as "foundation"[72] or "establishment."[73] According to Apte, this word usually means (1) presence, proximity, or nearness; (2) approaching, coming, appearance, or coming into the presence of; (3) worshiping; (4) attending to or guarding; (5) an abode; and (6) a sanctuary or a sacred place.[74] In some way, *upasthānam* could be seen as a kind of refuge in which the main happening is watching or guarding. According to R. M. L. Gethin, who made a significant contribution to the study of the *bodhi-pakkhīyā dhammā* (the factors of enlightenment), "the *satipaṭṭhānas* (Pāli translation of *smṛti-upasthāna*) always constitute the *bhikkhu*'s refuge—they guard and protect him."[75] It is exactly this idea of refuge that leads to a more in-depth understanding of the second aspect of *bodhicitta*. Indeed, this image of refuge is not foreign to *bodhicitta* in general. For example, Vasubandhu, in his *Bodhicittotpādaśastra*, compares the production of *bodhicitta* to the earth that provides shelter to all creatures irrespective of their nature. So also *bodhicitta* provides refuge to all beings.[76]

I am aware of the fact that it may be difficult to establish the link between *prasthāna* and *upasthāna* from the historical and philological point of view. In this regard, Har Dayal said that "Buddhist Sanskrit *smṛty-upasthāna* is a wrong back-formation[77] and for this reason "the Mahāyānists have interpreted it, not as *prasthāna*, but as *upasthāna*, and they have recklessly changed the sense in order to get an intelligible Sanskrit word"[78] His position has been refuted by Gethin, thus confirming the validity of *upasthāna*.[79] Apart from these remarks, I have not come across any discussion of this matter. Therefore, as just hinted, it is rather from the perspective of the spiritual context that I assume a connection between these two terms. For this reason, I believe that a closer look at the semantic implications of *upasthāna* might give us some clues about what is going on when someone is "proceeding" toward enlightenment.

According to Buddhaghosa, in the *Satipaṭṭhāna-saṃyutta*, one basic use of *satipaṭṭhāna* is that it is the field or pasture of mindfulness (*sati-gocara*) like a resting place for elephants and horses.[80] There is a second use of *satipaṭṭhāna*, which is significant for our understanding of the second aspect of *bodhicitta*. Again, Buddhaghosa says that it also means "a standing forth" (*patiṭṭhāti*), "a coming forth and leaping forward it proceeds."[81] What is interesting to notice in these two ways of understanding *satipaṭṭhāna* is first of all the use of *patiṭṭhāti* (in Sanskrit *pratitiṣṭhati*) which means both to rest and to stand forth and secondly, the tendency to relate this verb to *paṭṭhāna*. According to Gethin, there seems to be some amount of play with *satipaṭṭhāna* and it "should be regarded as arising directly out of an ambiguity inherent in Middle Indo-Aryan *satipaṭṭhāna*."[82] If one were to argue in favor of a connection between *prasthāna* and *upasthāna* from the historical and philological point of view, I believe that this is the closest one can get in terms of proof. But, as mentioned earlier, it is from the perspective of the spiritual context that such a connection could be more convincingly established.

The explanation given by Buddhaghosa for *satipaṭṭhāna* seems to suggest, as mentioned earlier, the idea of refuge but also of growth. This second idea is also related to *bodhicitta*. For example, in the *Gaṇḍavyūha*, it is said that "*bodhicitta*, noble son, is the seed of all qualities of the Buddhas; it is the field for growing all the white qualities of all the world; it is the earth which is the refuge of all the world."[83] It also appears that this growth occurs by the simple fact of being there and not by doing specific actions. This is, I believe, the most relevant aspect of the *bodhiprasthānacitta*: a place where one should be so that transformation occurs. At this stage, an act of will or a commitment, as mentioned earlier, does not have any role to play; as a matter of fact, it might be counterproductive because it reinforces the distinction between subject and object. In a way, the idea that *citta* is a state of mind, where something is happening, avoids the pitfall of dualism. What is happening at this stage is the subject matter of the next section.

iv. The ethical aspect of *bodhicitta*

In chapter 1, I mentioned that *bodhicitta*, in addition to its metaphysical connotations, also had an ethical aspect. This means that, for example, the efforts given to help all sentient beings are not the product of a desire but rather the result of having reached a certain spiritual stage. What this means for someone to have reached such a stage is described by the following passage of the *Bodhicaryāvatāra:*

> May I become the protector of those without protection, the guide for those on the path, the boat, the bridge and the causeway for those wishing to go to the other shore.
>
> May I become a lamp for those desiring a lamp, a bed for those desiring a bed, a slave for all beings desiring a slave.

> May I become the wish-fulfilling gem, the miracle urn, a successful mantra, a universal remedy, the wish-fulfilling tree and the wish-fulfilling cow for all beings.[84]

These verses, and many others, describe what it means to be an accomplished Bodhisattva: a person who is, in all aspects of the spiritual as well as material life, of benefit for all sentient beings. There is another important idea related to the ethical aspect of *bodhicitta*. Because of its radical implications it may be viewed as a metaphor, but, giving this understanding of the spiritual path, that is, the passage from one state of mind to another (*citta-utpāda*), I believe that it could be taken literally. This idea is that of the Bodhisattva's self-sacrifice.

In addition to the well-known birth-stories (*jātaka*) of the Buddha in which the latter sacrifices his body to feed some beings in need such as the female tiger and her offspring, there are many passages in the Mahāyāna literature related to the spiritual practice of the Bodhisattvas that mention this idea. In the *Akṣayamati sūtra*, for example, we are told by a Bodhisattva the following, "I must wear out even this body of mine for the benefits of all sentient beings. And as these four great elements, that is, earth, air, fire and water, go to the varied enjoyment of beings through many directions and turnings, supports, appliances and uses: so I purpose to make this body of mine, itself an aggregation of the four great elements, fit for the enjoyment of all beings through the many directions and other means."[85] And in the *Vajradhvaja sūtra*, it is said, "So indeed the Bodhisattva, giving himself amongst all sentient beings, by aiding all roots of happiness, regarding all creatures in their roots of happiness, offering himself as a lamp amongst all creatures. . . ."[86] What transpires from such passages is not the idea of strong will or intense motivation on the part of the Bodhisattva, but rather, an attitude of readiness. This readiness does not seem to be the result of an active effort of renunciation similar to that given by a smoker trying to stop smoking, but, on the contrary, it appears to be a natural disposition of the mind. It is something that is or ought to be done quite effortlessly. In the *Nārāyaṇa-paripṛcchā*, for example, it is said that

> one must not hold to anything of which one will have no thought of renouncing, no understanding of renouncing; no such acquisition is to be acquired as to which he [the Bodhisattva] would have not the heart to let go. He must not take articles of which there arises in him, when asked by beggars, the thought of possession. Nor must he hold

to kingdom, enjoyments, treasure, . . . or anything whatever which would make the Bodhisattva unready to give it up.[87]

The idea of readiness is further emphasized by the fact that it is not the Bodhisattva who initiates the action of giving but rather those who are in need. In the text just mentioned, one is told, for instance, "I [the Bodhisattva] will give hand, foot, eye, flesh, blood, marrow, limbs great and small—my head itself to those who ask for them"[88] or "Whoever wants them [various possessions], I will give them to him for his benefit,"[89] and finally, "Let all sentient beings take them [parts of my body] as they require them, a hand, for such who needs it, or a foot, for such who needs it."[90]

Given these examples, I am of the opinion that it would be wrong again to interpret the generous attitude of the Bodhisattva on account of his willpower or even his commitment to the final goal. Instead, his readiness to give up parts of his body for the sake of others could be explained by the fact that he or she has attained a state of mind characterized by the absence of a lack of motivation. At first sight, this might be viewed as a twisted way of describing the behavior of the Bodhisattva, but it makes sense when considering that, at this stage, there is also the absence of fear.

The presence of fear is probably the most important inhibiting factor for those who are reluctant to give up any of their possessions. Indeed, in the *Bodhicaryāvatāra*, one is reminded that the prospect of loosing one's possessions is the cause of fear and consequently, of suffering,

> "I am rich, honored and desired by many," a person boasting thus is overcome by fear when confronted with death.
>
> Whenever the mind deluded by pleasure gets attached, it faces a thousand-fold suffering which it has caused.
>
> That is why the sage ought not to desire because from desire fear is produced; this desire goes away by itself when faced with a steady mind.[91]

In this circumstance, fear and attachment are closely interdependent and the absence of one inevitably leads to the nonoccurrence of the other. In other words, fear is a sign of attachment. For this reason, the Bodhisattva, by producing a mind free from distress directed toward fearlessness, will be in a position to sacrifice parts of his body and even himself to those who ask for them or for him.[92]

If fear is a sign of attachment, then the state of fearlessness is an important characteristic of spiritual achievement. For this reason, it is something that is eagerly sought.

> Having transgressed your word and because now I see fear, I seek your [the Bodhisattva Vajrapāni] refuge, do take away this fear immediately from me who is afraid.[93]

> Who would grant me fearlessness and how will I escape from it, certainly I will cease to be, how can my mind be well-established?[94]

The last verse is not devoid of interest because *susthita* has also been translated as "peace of mind,"[95] "composed mind,"[96] or even as "esprit joyeux."[97] The significance of this point is that the state of fearlessness, which makes it possible for the Bodhisattva to have the self-sacrificing attitude, is also characterized by feelings of contentment and joy. Indeed, Śāntideva is quite clear on this point.

> The Bodhisattva, sacrificing his own body, offering his blood to those begging for it, he whose *bodhicitta* is delighting (*praharṣita-bodhicittaḥ*), desiring to follow the path of the Bodhisattva, not casting away a thought that was made clear to him, ready and eager for all who are begging, not hated by any one who receives, practicing the path of renunciation of all the Bodhisattvas, not regarding his own body because of unconquerable joy and contentment, offering the blood from his own body, devoted to the Mahāyāna path as the abode of knowledge, with mind unspoiled in the Mahāyāna path, agreeable, pleased, delighted, joyful, friendly, happy, contented, and becoming joyful, pleased, and content, sacrificing the very marrow from his body for those begging for it.[98]

The fact that feelings of joy and contentment are related to the self-sacrificing attitude of the Bodhisattva is, in my opinion, another argument in favor of the idea that his behavior is possible because he attained a state of mind where the absence of a lack of motivation is one of its main characteristics and not, as assumed from the perspective of a soteriological context giving emphasis on spiritual commitment, a product of strong will. This latter mental activity is never done without stress, as described by Suzuki in his interpretation of the antecedents to the *Satori* experience, and for that reason, I believe that it is incompatible with feelings of contentment and joy.

To sum up the present section, I argued that the concept of *bodhicitta*, in addition to its metaphysical connotations, is also related to realities or phenomena pertaining to the behavior of the Bodhisattva, that is, to his ethics or rules of conduct. And for that reason, I am of the opinion that one has to reject any soteriological context defining *bodhicitta* as motivational, as advocated by D. T. Suzuki. In this regard, I would like to present one last passage taken from the *Maitreyavimokṣa*. "Just as, sir, the great Nāga kings with the magic jewels in their royal tiaras did not fear the enemy's approach, so also the Bodhisattvas, with those magic jewels which is the thought of enlightenment [*bodhicitta*] and great compassion, fastened in their royal tiaras, do not fear the hostile approach of misery and unhappiness."[99] It goes without saying that an interpretation of this concept as exclusively metaphysical is also to be rejected. Despite the fact I criticized Suzuki's understanding of *bodhicitta*, I am not going as far as Sangharakshita who argues that, as a Cosmic Going for Refuge, it requires no involvement on the part of the aspirant to enlightenment. I believe that *bodhicitta* plays an important function in his practice; what remains then to be determined is this function and consequently, the nature of his involvement.

3. Conclusion

The purpose of the present chapter was to discuss *bodhicitta* as an act of will or commitment. It also discussed the validity of assimilating *citta* to the notion of desire instead of thought. The basic problem with this view is that it reinforces the distinction between subject and object. The way to avoid this problem is, I believe, to argue that *citta* is a state of mind where the desire for awakening is one of its qualities or characteristics. This means that, for one to be able to express the vow to become a Buddha, it also requires a certain degree of mental transformation or a type of conversion involving a spiritual experience. This is supported by the fact that one refers most of the times to the experience of *bodhicitta* as the "arising of *bodhicitta*." The expression *arising* is not to be taken as a simple metaphor for expressing the idea of desire or intention, but rather, it is to be understood quite literally, that is, to mean that something arises or is produced. This model for explaining mental activity is not devoid of precedents; it confirms the basic Buddhist understanding of causation that is found in the doctrine of dependent origination (*pratītyasamutpāda*). Applied to *citta*, it means that, when certain elements are present, a certain state of mind arises. When they are absent, it does not. In a way, *citta* is like a living being: it has to be fed to be maintained or it could be starved to death.

Earlier in this chapter, I mentioned the fact that *upasthānam* could be seen as a kind of refuge in which the main happening is watching or guarding. Taking into consideration the suggested understanding of *bodhiprasthānacitta*, it means that this state of mind, where skillful things are happening, has to be maintained and guarded against what might disrupt it. What is the nature of this activity? Is it an exercise of concentration with the purpose of inhibiting all mental activity? The Buddhist literature offers many reasons that could lead one to such an interpretation as a way to understand the concept of *bodhicitta*. This will be the topic of the following chapter.

3

Bodhicitta as an object of concentration

In the preceding chapter, I challenged the attempt to assimilate *bodhicitta*, often rendered as a "desire of enlightenment," to an act of will and, by extension, to a commitment. The purpose was not to negate the importance of these ideas for the attainment of enlightenment, but rather to situate them in their proper perspective. For this I had to introduce the idea that Indian philosophical and religious concepts constitute a blending of passive and active characteristics. These passive characteristics were more or less related to the phenomena of memory and accumulation of habits or latent mental tendencies. The active characteristics, on the other hand, accounted for mental activity in all its forms, that is, perception, reflection, imagination, and volition, in other words, the mental tendencies in action. Consequently, the desire for enlightenment should not be viewed as a pure act of volition in which there is a subject reaching out for an object, but rather, as the product of having reached a particular state of mind where the occurrence of this desire is possible.[1] Moreover, I argued that not only the desire for enlightenment but also the actual progression toward it depends on having undergone a change of state of mind. Perhaps, the praising of a human rebirth as opposed to being born as an animal or a hungry ghost, is metaphorically describing the importance of having attained certain states of mind to progress spiritually.

In chapter 2, I also said, while discussing the significance of *bodhiprasthānacitta*, that the progression toward enlightenment was characterized by an activity that could be described as watching or guarding. The exact nature of this activity, however, remains unclear. Is it, for example, an attempt to pay attention to things as they actually are, or is it rather the fixing of attention onto an object of the mind? In the first case, a cognitive experience is sought for whereas in the second, one is aiming and striving exclusively at an experience of complete cessation of mental activity or of a perfect peace of mind.

These two alternatives seem to reveal a major difference of perspective at the level of the soteriological context. As Paul J. Griffiths pointed out, "there appears to be some tension between a view which regards dispassionate knowledge of the way things are as a *sine qua non* and constituent factor of enlightenment, and a view which sees complete unconsciousness, the cessation of all mental functions, as essential to, or even identical with, enlightenment."[2] Griffiths called these two approaches to enlightenment respectively the analytic and the enstatic approach.[3] According to him, the first approach corresponds to the practice of cultivation of insight (*vipassanā-bhāvanā*) and the second, to the cultivation of tranquillity (*samatha-bhāvanā*). As he further explains, the practice of cultivation of insight "is concerned with repeated meditations upon standard items of Buddhist doctrine—the four truths, the 12-fold chain of dependent origination and so forth—until these are completely internalized by practitioners and their cognitive and perceptual systems operate only in terms of them." The cultivation of tranquillity, on the other hand, is "designed to reduce the contents of consciousness, to focus awareness upon a single point and ultimately to bring all mental activity to a halt."[4]

According to the Hindu Yoga system of thought, a system also aiming at the cessation of mental activity (*cittavṛtti-nirodha*), this single point upon which one's attention is focused need not necessarily be a physical object like the tip of the nose or the rhythm of the breath; on the contrary, it could also be something quite abstract like the ideas of friendliness, compassion, and complacency.[5] In fact, it appears that, from the perspective of this spiritual approach, any idea, concept, piece of knowledge, or belief could be used for the purpose of calming the mind. Even doctrines that are pivotal to a particular tradition could be used for that purpose. In the case of the Buddhist Madhyamaka tradition, for example, it might be legitimate to interpret its key doctrine of dependent origination (*pratītyasamutpāda*) in such a way. Referring to the introductory verses of Nāgārjuna's *Mūlamadhyamakakārikā*, it is said that "I salute him, the Enlightened One, the best of speakers, who preached the non-ceasing, non-arising, non-annihilating, non-permanent, non-identical, non-different, non-appearing, non-disappearing co-dependent origination (*pratītyasamutpāda*) which is the cessation of discursive thought (*prapañca-upaśamam*) and which is auspicious."[6] In fact, given the parameters of this soteriological context, the whole endeavor of a thinker may be interpreted as a way of bringing mental activity to a complete standstill.

The question I would like to address at this point is whether *bodhicitta*, in the context of the Buddhist literature dealing with the path of the Bodhisattva, including the *Bodhicaryāvatāra*, is used as a means of reducing all mental activity in order to subdue the mind and eventually to attain a state of perfect peace of mind. In other words, similar to the idea of the stick used to stir up a fire which, by the same process, consumes itself, it could therefore be argued that *bodhicitta*, defined as the desire for enlightenment for the sake of all beings, is used as a means of bringing the mind to a complete state of desirelessness. In this circumstance, this desire to act for the benefit of all beings is not to be considered as a genuine altruistic attitude, but rather as a skillful means (*upāya*) designed to lead one to the final goal or to the various stages of the spiritual path. There are a few clues in this literature that may lead one to such an interpretation. This is what I intend to consider in the next section.

1. Arguments in favor of *bodhicitta* as an object of concentration

The first clue or argument has to do with the terminology used in relation with *bodhicitta*. As will be shown later, this terminology is not without ambiguities. The soteriological context just presented could, however, provide a way to harmonize these ambiguities.

i. Derivatives of the Sanskrit verbal roots √*grah* (to take) and √*dhṛ* (to hold)

In the *Sāgaramati*, one is told that the repelling of a mind perverted toward worldly objects, concentration, restraint, entire quietude, and discipline are called grasping the good law (*sad-dharma-parigrahaḥ*).[7] What is of interest here is the importance if not the predominance of the activity described by *parigrahaḥ*. In the *śrīmālāsiṃhanāda sūtra*, one reads: "All the aspirations of the Bodhisattvas, countless as the sand of the Ganges, are included and comprehended in one great aspiration—namely, the grasping (*parigrahaḥ*) of *dharma*. This, then, is the great object."[8] A second point to notice is its value for spiritual growth and achievement. In the *sutra* just mentioned, it is also said that "just as, Lady, a small blow inflicted on a mighty man, if it is in a vital part, is painful and harmful, so the grasping (*parigrahaḥ*) of *dharma*, even though it is feeble, causes pain, sorrow, and lamentation to Māra, the Evil One. I cannot regard any other good act so effective against

Māra as grasping (*parigrahaḥ*) of *dharma*, be it so little."[9] One can read further: "Just as Sumeru, the King of Mountains, shines forth supreme in loftiness and extent, surpassing all mountains, so when a follower of the Mahāyāna, having no regards for life and limbs, with a non-grasping mind grasps the *dharma* (*sad-dharma-parigrahaḥ*), this action outweighs all the good principles of the Mahāyānists who are careful for their life and limbs, and have newly set forth on the new [Mahāyāna] path."[10] Judging from the last passage, *saddharma-parigrahaḥ* clearly involves some kind of event of spiritual significance because of, among other things, the absence of fear for self-sacrifice.

When *parigrahaḥ* is compounded with *bodhicitta*, the activity it describes also seems to refer to something of spiritual importance and value that occurs after reaching a certain state of mind. Indeed, chapter 3 of the *Bodhicaryāvatāra*, which described the characteristics of what it means to be an accomplished Bodhisattva, is entitled *bodhicitta-parigrahaḥ*. Moreover, in many passages of the *Bodhicaryāvatāra*, the beginning aspirant to enlightenment is enjoined to act in order to bring about these events of spiritual significance so that he or she may progress further on the path, and the expressions used to describe this act are often formulated in terms of another derivative of √*grah*. For example:

> Having taken this impure form, it [*bodhicitta*] transforms it into the priceless form of a *Jina* [an accomplished Bodhisattva]; it is like a gold-making elixir. So, hold fast (*sudṛḍhaṃ gṛhṇata*) to what is called *bodhicitta*.
>
> It has been considered as having an immense value by those of immeasurable intellects and guides of this world. Oh you, you used to dwell in the foreign counties and cities which are the six destinies, hold fast (*sudṛḍhaṃ gṛhṇata*) to the jewel which is *bodhicitta*.[11]

Given these examples, I believe that one can say with confidence that the derivatives of √*grah* may be employed as technical terms describing some aspects of the spiritual experience of the Bodhisattva similar to the expressions issued from the prefix *ut* and from √*pad*. Because of that, however, the exact meaning of these terms might be difficult to establish just on the basis of what the lexicographers are telling us.

Indeed, according to Vaman Shivaran Apte, for example, *gṛhṇāti* could mean: (1) to seize, take, take or catch hold of, catch, or grasp; (2) to receive, take, or accept; (3) to apprehend, stop, or catch; (4) to affect or seize or possess (as a demon or spirit); (5) to assume or take; (6) to learn, know, recognize, or understand; (7) to regard, consider, believe, or take for; (8) to catch or perceive (as by an organ of sense); (9) to master, grasp, or comprehend; (10) to wear or put on (clothes, etc.); (11) to conceive; and (12) to undertake, undergo, or begin.[12] More specifically, *parigrahaḥ* means, among other things: (1) seizing, holding, taking, grasping, or taking or entertaining a doubt; (2) surrounding or enclosing; (3) putting on or wrapping round (as a dress); (4) assuming or taking; (5) receiving, taking, or accepting; (6) grace or favor; (7) comprehending or understanding; (8) undertaking or performing; and (9) subjugating.[13]

It may be remarked that, when the derivatives of √*grah* have a physical object as in the phrase *aśucipratimām imāṃ gṛhītvā*, in which case *gṛhītvā* is glossed as *ādāya* (having taken this impure form, i.e., the body), there is no ambiguity as to their meaning. On the other hand, however, when their objects are abstract concepts such as *bodhicitta*, as in the phrase *sudṛḍhaṃ gṛhṇata bodhicittasaṃjñam* (hold fast to what is called *bodhicitta*), or *saddharma*, as in *evaṃ mahāviṣayo saddharmaparigraha iti* (the accepting of *dharma* is thus our great object), one is not clear as to the exact significance or nature of the activity described by these derivatives. Let us look at other terms and expressions used in the same context to see if this situation can be clarified.

Chapter 3 of Śāntideva's *Śikṣāsamuccaya* begins with the following verse: "In this regard, what is the protection of oneself? It is the avoidance of evil."[14] This avoidance of evil is discussed in the *Gaganagañjasūtra* by the Bodhisattvas who are diligent in preserving (*dhāraṇa*) the true *dharma.*[15] In the text just mentioned, one is told that "at that evil time we will hold fast (*dhārayiṣyāma*) to the True *dharma*, sacrificing our body and life for the sake of sentient beings."[16]

The noun *dhāraṇa* and the verb *dhārayiṣyāma* are both issued from √*dhṛ*. According to Apte, it can mean: (1) to hold, bear, or carry; (2) to hold or bear up, maintain, support, or sustain; (3) to hold in one's possession, possess, have, or keep; (4) to assume or take (as a form or disguise); (5) to wear or put on (clothes or ornaments); (6) to hold, in check, curb, restrain, stop, or detain; (7) to fix upon or direct toward; (8) to suffer or undergo; (9) to hold or contain; (10) to observe or practice; (11) to preserve or maintain; (12) to seize or lay hold of; (13) to hold out or on or endure; (14) to fix, place, or deposit; and (15) to intend in mind.[17] When it is used in association with terms referring to the mind such as *manas*, *matiḥ*, *cittam*, and *buddhiḥ*, it means to bend the mind to a thing, fix the mind upon, think of, or resolve upon.[18] Similarly, the neutral substantive *dhāraṇam* is translated as: (1) holding, bearing, carrying, preserving, sustaining, protecting, having or assuming; (2) observing or holding fast; (3) retaining in the memory; (4) maintaining a steady abstraction of the mind; (5) keeping or maintaining; and (6) restraining.[19] And, as a feminine noun, it means: (1) the act of holding, bearing, supporting, preserving, and so forth; (2) the faculty of retaining in the mind, a good or retentive memory; (3) memory in general; (4) a collected mind, the art of holding one's breath suspended, or steady abstraction of the mind; (5) fortitude, firmness, or steadiness; (6) a fixed precept or injunction, a settled rule, or conclusion; (7) understanding or intellect; and (8) conviction or abstraction.[20]

Again, it is to be noticed that these translations, as was the case with the derivatives of √*grah*, manifest a blending of passive and active characteristics. Consequently, the spiritual activity referred to by these may describe either an active event where a subject is holding firm to an object of the mind or a passive happening in which a subject is established in some kind of knowledge. The point of this discussion, on the basis of the terminology used to describe the activity of watching and guarding alone, is that both interpretations can be supported. Even when looking at how Prajñākaramati glossed *gṛhṇīta*: "when it is obtained, it does not go or move again. *gṛhṇīta* [to be understood in the sense of] obtained. This rendering is according to the tradition,"[21] it is still difficult to decide since the idea of stability of the mind is common to both situations. Given this circumstance, it is, I believe, legitimate to argue that *bodhicitta* is an object of concentration. It is therefore possible to reconcile these two alternatives by saying that, whatever knowledge is involved, it is for the sake of making the activity of concentration as intense as possible. This means that, in this practice, it is the activity of fixing that is dominant and consequently, the object being fixed upon is secondary. Later in the present chapter, I intend to analyze the implications of this view. For the moment, however, let us consider other arguments in favor of interpreting *bodhicitta* in terms of an object of concentration.

ii. The practice of meditation

In chapter 1, while discussing the significance of the *Bodhicaryāvatāra*, I mentioned that according to the Tibetan Buddhists, there are two types of *bodhicitta*: the conventional *bodhicitta* and the ultimate *bodhicitta*. The conventional *bodhicitta* consisted essentially in various meditations used to develop compassion whereas the ultimate *bodhicitta* was the realization of emptiness. This practice of developing compassion was above all a way to pacify the mind. As one Tibetan Buddhist teacher said, "At present our mind is unsettled and biased; instead of looking at all beings equally with an eye of compassion, we feel very partial towards some and very distant from, or even hostile towards, others. In such an unbalanced state it is very difficult to recognize all beings as our mothers so if our meditation is to be successful we must first try to remove our prejudices by cultivating an attitude of equanimity."[22] It is assumed that this attitude of equanimity is synonymous to peace of mind since, by being impartial to all beings, one is not drawn into making distinctions between these beings. This peace of mind, still according to the Tibetans, should lead one to the final realization of *bodhicitta*, which is emptiness. In a way, the Tibetan Buddhists, by these two types of *bodhicitta*, have reconciled the two spiritual approaches discussed earlier by Paul Griffiths. It would, however, exceed the scope of my research to evaluate the merits of this treatment of *bodhicitta*. The reason why I am referring to this practice of cultivating compassion, though, is to draw to one's attention the fact that the content of the meditations need not be true, that is, something established on account of strict logic and hard facts. Indeed, this practice of cultivating compassion is based on the idea that each and every being, of the past, present, and future, has been at least once one's own mother. This idea itself is based on the doctrine of rebirth, which is more a question of faith than the result of scientific evidence. But from the point of view of the result to achieve, this is of no consequence. In fact, everything is possible as attested by a Tibetan monk who said, upon being asked why it was possible for him to believe that the sun is going around the earth, "Despite the fact that the knowledge that the earth goes round the sun might be a scientific truth useful for the development of modern techniques, it was not useful for the inward belief, for the realization of the Ultimate Truth."[23]

There are many passages in the *Bodhicaryāvatāra*, especially in chapter 8, which is devoted to the practice of meditation, which show this interaction between ideas and stabilization of the mind. One such meditation, which has perhaps a lengthy history within the Buddhist tradition, has as its main theme the impurities of the body and its impermanence. Indeed

> It is no wonder that you do not realize the body of others to be excrement; but that you do not understand your own body to be excrement is amazing.[24]

> This body of mine will become so putrid that even jackals will not be able to approach it because of its stench.[25]

The principle underlying this kind of meditation is to create the mental conditions that would neutralize one's tendency to be attached to one's own body and to that of the others and consequently, to get rid of the fear issued from the worries concerning their fate. In a way, this kind of meditation is an exercise in mental creations. Many passages of the *Bodhicaryāvatāra* are the basis of mental pictures, almost comparable to *maṇḍalas* that are visualized and internalized in the mind of the meditator. These images are like fruits containing a taste of the absolute peace. They are pressed by means of visualization and reflection to extract their juice. Once the juice is extracted and consumed, the skin of the fruit is thrown away. So much is the value of what has been used to create the mental picture.

This principle of neutralization could most probably be best exemplified by the meditative practice of exchanging the self for others. This meditation is mentioned in chapter 8 of the *Bodhicaryāvatāra* and it could be seen as a culmination point of all previous meditations. In short, it consists in viewing oneself as being the other and the other as being oneself. In this regard, Śāntideva says,

> Whoever wishes to quickly rescue himself and others should practice the most secret path: the exchange of his own self with others.[26]

> There is certainly no accomplishment, no Buddhahood, or even happiness in the realms of rebirth, for the one who does not exchange his own happiness for the sorrow of others.[27]

> That is why that for the sake of tranquilizing my own sorrow, and for the tranquilizing of others' sorrow, I give myself to others and I accept others like myself.[28]

Due to its drastic nature, Marion Matics, a modern translator of the *Bodhicaryāvatāra*, has considered this meditation as a "curious doctrine" and as "exercises belonging primarily to the realm of trance."[29] He justifies his affirmation since this transference of selves is practically impossible. As he says, "A saint like Francis of Assisi could pronounce the Bodhisattva vow and appropriately undertake *parātma-parivartana* (exchange of selves) as a symbolic expression of his moral intention; but as a mere humanitarian, however holy, he cannot execute his intention in literal practice." He further adds, "He cannot get into another's skin and there experience the pains of the other; he cannot interpose himself, literally, between the sin of the other and the judgment which the sinner merits; he cannot renounce the good qualities which are the attributes of his Franciscan soul and give them away, like alms to the poor, no matter how he tries. He cannot really even begin to try, for these are things which can be accomplished only on the level of trance."[30] This level of trance has been previously described by Matics as a form of *ṛddhi* or "meditative power." Examples of such powers are the ability to prolong one's life or the ability to create a kingdom without slaughter. Therefore, according to Matics, without *ṛddhi*, "there can be no literal transference of selves."[31]

I believe that there is a simpler way to explain this practice of exchanging the selves. It is not necessary to have recourse to the notion of supernatural powers in order to make it plausible. This meditation is not the only curious and out of the ordinary thing that is mentioned in the *Bodhicaryāvatāra*. Indeed, in chapter 2 one learns that the Bodhisattva, in an outburst of devotion, offers to the Buddhas and to the great Bodhisattvas all kind of extraordinary things:

> I shall offer to the Compassionate Ones palaces bedecked with hanging garlands of costly gems, shining in all directions and resounding all over with chants of prayerful hymns.[32]

> I shall offer to the great sages umbrellas with jewels and golden handles and exquisitely embellished rims, stretching up-right and with shapes beautiful to look at.[33]

It is unlikely that the Bodhisattva materializes these fabulous objects through some kind of powers in order to offer them in his *pūjas*. What is more plausible is that this exercise of devotion is performed mentally. In fact, this assumption is confirmed by the *Bodhicaryāvatāra* itself: "These I offer mentally (*buddhayā*) to the eminent sages (*muni*) and their sons [the Bodhisattvas]."[34] What Matics is not realizing is that, in the case of the practice of exchanging the selves, its literalness is an issue whereas it is not in the case of the devotional practices. From the point of view of the spiritual approach aiming at bringing the mind to a complete standstill, however, both practices are explained by a common principle that could be called the principle of neutralization.

Earlier I mentioned that the Bodhisattva might meditate on the fact that the body is composed of impure and impermanent elements. One of the goals of this meditation could be to neutralize his physical attraction to other people's body. In this case, however, the goal to achieve is very limited; being free from such attachment, the Bodhisattva is not yet off the hook: there are other tendencies he or she should care to destroy. Instead of finding a new theme of meditation for each of his tendencies, which in itself might be a task more demanding than the actual practice of meditation, he might rather settle for a theme that would work as a kind of universal antidote. The practice of exchanging the selves could be such an antidote because its limits are those of the selfish ego that is in effect the main obstacle to perfect peace of mind. In other words, the meditation based on the exchange of the selves could be perceived as a mental exercise whose goal is to neutralize all tendencies resulting from attachment to the egoistic self. To use a metaphor, this meditation is like producing the mental antibodies that neutralize the viruses created by the ego.

The point of this discussion is to argue that there is a relationship between the nature of the object of concentration and the quality of the spiritual experience. If the object is limited, like the decaying body, the fruit is also limited: the neutralization of the tendency that consists in being attracted to beautiful bodies. On the other hand, if the object expands to the limits of the reach of what causes mental instability, meditation on such an object should result in achieving mental stability. In a way, this is the basic logic of the practice of sacrifice that has marked Eastern thoughts from the early beginning: the fruits to be awarded are proportional to the extent of what is sacrificed. This is also the basic principle underlying the doctrine of karma.

It is therefore possible to define *bodhicitta* according to the same principle. Indeed, *bodhicitta*, as the desire to help all sentient beings is, so to speak, an object that is limitless because there is no end to this enterprise. In fact, this idea ought not be taken literally for the obvious reason that all those who had become Bodhisattvas would never be enlightened. On the contrary, like the practice of the exchanging of selves, it is done at the mental level. Consequently, meditation on such an object should produce an unlimited reward, as the following verse from the *Bodhicaryāvatāra* seems to imply, "All other wholesome results lose their effects, like the plantain tree which begins to decay after its fruition. But, the tree of *bodhicitta* produces fruits and does not decay. It even bears fruit perpetually."[35] In this circumstance, it is legitimate to believe that the experience of enlightenment, which is the calming down of mental activity, is not a limited process. It could be viewed as a perpetual deepening of the experience of peacefulness, which, following the principle of Higher Evolution discussed by Sangharakshita, is similar to the deepening of commitment to the ideals of Buddhism. To sum up the present discussion, I would like to look at some of the implications of having *bodhicitta* assimilated to an object of concentration.

iii. Implications related to the idea of *bodhicitta* as an object of concentration

One of the major implications related to defining *bodhicitta* as an object of concentration, as already alluded to earlier in this chapter, is to say that any ideas, concepts, or beliefs, having a doctrinal status or not, are true insofar as they fulfill the purpose of bringing the mind to a standstill. Consequently, these ideas or concepts are important for this ability only and not for being an expression of some kind of ontological truth. In other words, if one understands *bodhicitta* according to the soteriological context just discussed, one has to assume a pragmatic theory of truth. This assumption has moreover a direct incidence on the very nature of religious language and on other forms of religious expressions.

In fact, this view of religious language is exactly what has been implied by the doctrine of skillful means (*upāyakauśalya*) propounded by the Lotus Sutra and by the simile of the Burning House.[36] On the basis of this doctrine, it has been argued by Michael Pye, a modern scholar of Buddhism, "that religious language is essentially indirect, allusive, based in cultural circumstance, and subject to qualification and to criticism."[37] This means that religious concepts such as that of *bodhicitta* are not supposed to have any particular meaning beyond the attainment of the solution of the problem they are meant to solve. In other words, religious concepts are disposable. Consequently, if one were to view *bodhicitta* as an object of concentration, one would have to say that whatever cognitive element is related to it, it is of no consequence from the perspective of ontology for the simple reason that it is not meant to describe any ultimate reality, whatever this may be.

While discussing the relevance of *bodhicitta* as an act of will, I mentioned that this concept was related to metaphysical realities. I did not, however, analyze the full significance of this statement. Despite the implications of the doctrine of skillful means, I believe that one can observe, within the different spiritual traditions of Buddhism, a certain consistency between the means to achieve their respective spiritual experience and the ways to describe it. As mentioned in the introduction, for the followers of the Madhyamaka school, for example, the concept of emptiness is certainly an antidote to a person's mental and emotional attachment to phenomenal and ideal entities, but it is also their privileged way to describe reality as they ultimately view it. Consequently, I assume that religious language may be more than just a means to achieve a religious experience; it is also a standard or a measure of the authenticity of that experience. In the next section, I intend to look at the importance of viewing the concept of *bodhicitta* as a metaphysical reality in order to criticize the idea of *bodhicitta* as an object of concentration.

2. Criticism of *bodhicitta* as an object of concentration

There is a short passage taken from the *Bodhicaryāvatāra* which, I believe, may serve as the basis for a criticism of *bodhicitta* as an object of concentration. I would now like to provide a fresh translation of this passage and make some comments with the help of Prajñākaramati's Sanskrit commentary.

> The teachings [of the Buddha] are the foundations of the practice of the monk [aspirant to enlightenment]. This practice is, however, poor and *nirvāṇa* is impossible for those whose mind is holding on to props.
>
> If liberation is caused by the destruction of the tendencies [desire, hatred, pride, etc.], then it should occur immediately afterwards [i.e., when the tendencies are destroyed]. It has been, however, observed that they [certain monks mentioned in the tradition] retained a propensity for actions although their tendencies were absent.
>
> If it has been ascertained that there is no attachment as far as there is no craving, why then is there not a non-afflicted craving for them? [The answer is: Such craving is] like confusion [i.e., without clear understanding].
>
> Feelings are caused by craving and they have feelings. A mind which holds on to props remains attached whatever [the object of concentration].
>
> Without emptiness the mind may remain subdued but it is bound to become active again. Similar to those who meditate to the point of reaching a state of absence of consciousness, [their mind is reactivated as soon as they come out of this state]. Therefore, emptiness [should be cultivated].[38]

The point that is being made in this passage is that it would be an inaccurate application of the teachings of the Buddha, that is, that which is to be practiced for the attainment of Buddhahood,[39] to use them as props for the mind or as objects of concentration. The teachings of the Buddha are the thirty-seven factors of enlightenment (*bodhipakṣa-dharmas*) as well as the Four Noble truths. Thus, if the practice of the monk is bogged down in mere contemplation of the Four Noble Truths, for example, without an understanding of emptiness, then this practice or approach is bound to yield poor results.[40] For this reason, it does not lead to liberation.[41]

The reasons given to support this affirmation are essentially the idea that, despite the fact that the practice of contemplation may quieten down the tendencies, the tendency to act, either in a good or a bad way (*śubha-aśubha-lakṣaṇa*), is still present. At this point, some clarifications are perhaps called for. The word that has been translated by "tendency" is *kleśa*. According to the *Abhidharmakośa*,[42] there are six *kleśas*: desire (*rāga*), hatred (*pratigha*), pride (*māna*), ignorance (*avidyā*), wrong view (*kudṛṣṭi*), and doubt (*vicikisā*). Taking into consideration the blending of passive and active characteristics of Indian concepts, the ambiguity could be resolved thus: the *kleśas* refer to such actions as desiring, as well as to the latent potentiality to desire. Consequently, the practice of contemplating the Four Noble Truths, for example, is efficient in curbing the action of desiring but it is insufficient to eradicate the latent tendency to desire. For that purpose, an understanding of emptiness is necessary. In other words, despite the fact that the mind has been brought to a complete standstill, ignorance, which is the cause of the latent tendencies, is still present.[43]

Two examples are given by Prajñākaramati in support of his argumentation. The first example is the case of two disciples of the Buddha, the Venerables Maudgalyāyana and Aṅgulimāla, who, having attained a state where the working of the tendencies were subdued (*kleśa-sahakāri-rahita*), still retained the propensity (*sāmarthyam*) to perform actions (*karman*). According to Parmananda Sharma, a translator of the *Bodhicaryāvatara*, these two disciples had, as a result of their spiritual achievement, the power to grant wishes. But this power "was also a kind of craving and, therefore, enough to cause a redescent into *saṃsāra*."[44]

The second example deals with those who have attained a state where there is absence of consciousness (*asaṃjñisamāpatti*). This example is not devoid of interest because it refers us to the quote from Griffiths at the beginning of this chapter. The state of complete cessation of mental functions is known within the Buddhist tradition as Absorption into the Cessation of Notions and Sensations (*saṃjñā-vedayita-nirodha-samāpatti*). This state is characterized, in contrast to death, by the fact that "life-force (*āyus*) is not yet exhausted, bodily heat (*uṣman*) is not yet extinguished, the sense-faculties are unimpaired, and *vijñāna* [consciousness] has not withdrawn from the body."[45]

This spiritual experience creates doctrinal problems for the Buddhists themselves. For one, what is the nature of the consciousness that remains, given the Buddhist understanding of the traditional sixfold consciousness that says that, in order to arise, there must be an object and a contact between this object and a sense-organ? Consequently, in a meditative state in which there is absence of perception, how can there be consciousness? The second problem, which has been dealt with by Griffiths, has to do with the relationship between the mind and the body, as conceived by Buddhist thinkers. If one reaches a state where there is absence of perceptions, what is the mechanism that allows a meditator to come out of this state? In this regard, the Vaibhāṣikas provided the beginning of an answer by asserting that

> i. there are no mental events in the attainment of cessation, ii. the emergence of consciousness from attainment of cessation must have an immediately antecedent and similar condition, iii. the immediately antecedent and similar condition of any event may be temporally separated from that event and finally, iv. the immediately antecedent and similar condition for the emergence of consciousness from the attainment of cessation is the last moment of consciousness to occur before entering that attainment.[46]

It is precisely the implications of this view that have been criticized in the passage just quoted. If there is no difference between what is going on in the mind before entering the state of cessation and at the moment of coming out of it, then this type of meditation has no real effect with regard to obtaining permanent spiritual fruits.

To sum up the point of this passage, one can use a simile. Let us imagine a ship that is about to shipwreck. The captain of this ship must supervise the rescue of the passengers. He does so by coordinating the activities of his crew. Once the passengers are rescued, he personally orders his crew to leave the ship. Then finally, when everyone is safe, he also must go. But, because he makes things happen only by giving orders to others and cannot give himself the order to leave the ship, he remains on it and never succeeds in saving all the people, that is, every person including himself. Similarly, the practice of meditation based on the contemplation of an object can succeed in eliminating all tendencies but never the idea that there is a meditator, the last tendency caused by ignorance. Referring back to the meditation of exchanging the selves, there would always remain a self thinking of being the other self.

Similar to the criticism of *bodhicitta* as an act of will, to reduce this concept to an object of concentration, with the implications it entails, would reinforce the distinction between subject and object. The only difference here is that one may be fooled by the peace of mind that could result out of this type of meditation. In this regard, Buddhists have said that such achievement is nevertheless a failure to understand what they called the emptiness of emptiness, if emptiness is used as a prop. An interesting story from the Zen tradition illustrates this point.

> There was an old woman in China who had supported a monk for over twenty years. She had built a little hut for him and fed him while he was meditating. Finally she wondered just what progress he had made in all this time. To find out, she obtained the help of a girl rich in desire. "Go and embrace him," she told her, "and then ask him suddenly: 'What now?' " The girl called upon the monk and without much ado caressed him, asking him what he was going to do about it. "An old tree grows on a cold rock in winter," replied the monk somewhat poetically. "Nowhere is there any warmth." The girl returned and related what he had said. "To think I fed that fellow for twenty years!" exclaimed the old woman in anger. "He showed no consideration for your need, no disposition to explain your condition. He need not have responded to passion, but at least he should have evidenced some compassion." She at once went to the hut of the monk and burned it down.[47]

Poor monk! He missed it both ways.

The expression used in the passage to describe those who used the teachings of the Buddha as props for the mind is *sāvalambana-citta* that literally means: "those whose mind is with a prop or support (*avalamba*)." Those who are not trapped by this kind of practice are called *nirālambana-citta* (those whose mind is without a prop) and for them, the practice is not fruitless.[48] What does it mean then to have such a mind? In other words, how can one think about concepts without making them objects of one's attention? In the *Āryavajracchedikā*, the Buddha said to Subhuti, "That is why, Subhuti, the magnanimous Bodhisattva should cause to arise a mind which is not permanently fixed (or abiding in trance), never should he cause a mind which is permanently fixed to arise, a mind which is permanently fixed onto a form, a sound, a smell or a tactile sensation. That is why emptiness has been established as the path to enlightenment."[49] This passage only deals with the objects of the senses, but it is clear, given the fact that it has been quoted by Prajñākaramati in his commentary of the previous passage, that it also includes mental objects. Then, what is the nature of the activity described earlier as watching and guarding? How is the relationship between the "one who watches" and "that which is being watched," that is, emptiness, *saddharma*, or *bodhicitta*? The answer to these questions would define the spiritual function of the concept of *bodhicitta*. In chapter 1, I defined this function as being a basis for the cultivation of awareness. The analysis and the argumentation in favor of this idea will be the topic of the next chapter. For the moment, however, I would like to show how it might be possible to have a situation in which concepts are "apprehended" by someone whose mind is without support (*nirālambanacitta*) and discuss the implications that such possibility might have for one's understanding of the nature of religious language and consequently, of the doctrine of *upāya* that defines all concepts and doctrines as provisional and disposable.

Michael Polanyi, a scientist and philosopher, has advocated the idea that all activity is characterized by two kinds of awareness. For example, describing the action of driving a nail, he says,

> When we use a hammer to drive a nail, we attend to both nail and hammer, *but in a different way*. We *watch* the effect of our strokes on the nail and try to wield the hammer so as to hit the nail most effectively. When we bring down the hammer we do not feel that its handle has struck our palm but that its head has struck the nail. Yet in a sense we are certainly alert to the feeling in our palm and the fingers that hold the hammer. They guide us in handling it effectively, and the degree of attention that we give to the nail is given to the same extent but in a different way to these feelings. The difference may be stated by saying that the latter are not, like the nail, objects of our attention, but instruments of it. They are not watched in themselves; we watch something else while keeping intensely aware of them. I have a *subsidiary awareness* of the feeling in the palm of my hand which merged into my *focal awareness* of my driving in the nail.[50]

This idea of two kinds of awareness led him to distinguish between what he called tacit and explicit knowledge. Explicit knowledge refers to one's perception of objects and ideas. This knowledge would be *sāvalaṃbana*. Tacit knowledge is something that is never directly apprehended. In this regard, Polanyi gives another example:

> Consider the act of viewing a pair of stereoscopic pictures in the usual way, with one eye on each of the pictures. Their joint image

> might be regarded as a whole, composed of the two pictures as its parts. But we can get closer to understanding what is going on here if we note that, when looking through a stereo viewer, we see a stereo image at the focus of our attention and are also aware of the two stereo pictures in some peculiar nonfocal way. We seem to look through these two pictures, or past them, while we look straight at their joint image. We are indeed aware of them only as guides to the image on which we focus our attention. We can describe this relationship of the two pictures to the stereo image by saying that the two pictures function as *subsidiaries* to our seeing their *joint* image, which is their joint meaning.[51]

This is, according to Polanyi, the typical structure of tacit knowing. This way of knowing might be what has been meant before as *nirālambana.*

There is perhaps another way of explaining this tacit knowledge. One way of apprehending objects, mental or physical, could be by being asked "when," "where," or "what." To some extent, these objects are perceived as having an existence independent of any context, framework, or background. In contrast to this, we have concepts such as "long" or "short" and these concepts never pinpoint objects as such. What is long or short is always perceived in relationship with a context. In other words, when one looks at a long object, one apprehends the object as well as the context in which it is found. A rope, for example, is long in relation to another short object. These concepts are not identified by asking "when" or "where," but rather "how" or "what." These questions always refer to the quality of the objects, and as such, require an awareness of a context to be answered.

Let us take, for example, a man and his wife. The man introduces his wife to his friends. At first, she might be perceived by them as just another woman—an explicit knowledge—but as soon they become aware that she is their friend's wife—a tacit knowledge—that woman assumes an entirely new meaning. This is tacit because it is not directly apprehended. This awareness is also the context that defines that particular woman as their friend's wife.

It is in this sense that one may understand the significance of religious concepts such as that of emptiness. They are not to be apprehended as objects of the mind, but rather as contextual backgrounds. Objects are focused on, but their background is also perceived. This background could be defined in terms of *svabhāva*, that is, the idea that objects have an independent existence, or in terms of emptiness, namely, the idea that objects have no independent existence. Like the well-known example of the vase and the two faces of the cognitive theories of Gestalt, both backgrounds can never be perceived at the same time. To hold onto the idea of emptiness would therefore mean to cultivate an awareness of the fact that the ultimate meaning of all objects is that they do not have an independent existence. To cultivate such awareness is comparable to keeping in mind the fact that, to use this example, this woman is the friend's wife, something that is apprehended tacitly and not explicitly. In the next chapter, I will discuss how this can be done.

One can now see why an idea such as that of emptiness can be viewed as a metaphysical reality. It is that which gives the meaning of all things. Such ideas and concepts are therefore a true description of reality because the moment they are understood, everything, including the attempt and the event of understanding them, is perceived as a manifestation of the reality they are meant to describe. Thus, they are not provisional and never disposed of. In fact, to consider religious concepts as simply provisional, as suggested by *upāya*, only leads us to a dead end. Indeed, if these concepts are provisional, when are they gotten rid of and by whom? As just discussed, the notion of *upāya* is dependent on the idea of *upeya* (goal) and as such, it maintains the duality between what is the goal and what is not, and above all, it leaves unchallenged the *upāyin* (he who appropriates and applies the means). In support of this interpretation of *upāya*, the simile of the raft, which is mentioned in the Pāli canon, has often been used. In the light of the present argumentation, it would not be an example of the provisional nature of the teachings of the Buddha, but rather of the necessity to view them as a description of a background defining all phenomena and not as objects of the mind. This simile is a warning against maintaining a fruitless relationship between the "one who watches" and "that which is being watched." In this circumstance, the paradox between the idea of right view and that of no view could be resolved thus: right view becomes no view when the right view is perceived as the background of all views. With regard to *bodhicitta*, this affirmation means that *bodhicitta*, as the desire for enlightenment for the sake of all beings, is itself a true description of things as they are. Taking into consideration what has been said in chapter 2, *bodhicitta* is also a description of what it means to be an accomplished Bodhisattva as well as being the means to attain this state of ethical and cognitive perfection. Cultivation of *bodhicitta* would therefore mean cultivation of the idea or awareness that one's true nature is to search for enlightenment for the sake of all beings. *Bodhicitta* is therefore the means to an end as well as the end itself.

4

Bodhicitta as cultivation of awareness

In chapter 2, I demonstrated that the spiritual activity leading to enlightenment or awakening consisted in "watching" or "guarding." Chapter 3 analyzed the possibility of viewing this activity as an exercise in concentration or in fixing one's attention on real or mental objects. In this circumstance, *bodhicitta*, as the desire for enlightenment for the sake of all sentient beings, could be viewed as a way to expand the boundaries of the egoistic self, thereby neutralizing all of its tendencies such as passion and hatred. This approach, however, was criticized on the ground that the state of nonconscious meditative equipoise that was achieved by it could only quieten down the tendencies in their active manifestations but not in their latent state. For example, when someone comes out of this nonconscious meditative equipoise, he or she is bound to resume the activity happening just before entering it. This spiritual experience thus becomes only an interruption of the tendencies without transforming them. From the point of view of the continuity of karma, this experience is comparable to the passage of death to rebirth where all the latent tendencies are carried over from one life to the other.

This criticism was based on the interpretation of a short passage of the *Bodhicaryāvatāra*. According to this passage, the distinction between fruitful and fruitless practice could be made on the basis of the type of mind adopted by the meditator, that is, by the one who is watching. For those whose minds are holding onto props (*sāvalambanacitta*), the practice is deficient, and for them, *nirvāṇa* is impossible. On the other hand, those whose minds are not holding onto props (*nirālambanacitta*), they are on the right path to enlightenment. It is therefore primordial to understand the significance of this type of mind if one wishes to comprehend what is going on during the activity characterized by watching. Since *bodhicitta*, as mentioned earlier, is directly related to this activity, it is also that which is likely to define the spiritual function of this concept.

Chapter 3 was therefore an attempt to understand the meaning and the implications of this type of mind called *nirālambanacitta*. For that, I introduced Michael Polanyi's idea of twofold awareness. Basically, this idea points to the fact that, while perceiving an object, one is also aware of something else, that is, a background or a context in which this object is found. This object is the content of one's explicit knowledge because it can always be pointed to. Its meaning, on the other hand, is the content of one's tacit knowledge. It is the focus of one's attention while its support, the object proper, is perceived subsidiarily. To some extent, this idea of twofold awareness is the conceptual foundation of my thesis in the present study of *bodhicitta*.

If concepts such as that of emptiness are to be perceived by a mind not relying on props (*nirālambanacitta*), then it means, given the idea of twofold awareness, that emptiness is a description of the background from which everything finds its meaning; it is reality as experienced by the enlightened being. For the unenlightened, this background could be defined, for example, by the idea that all things have an inherent existence (*svabhāva*). Consequently, the path to enlightenment could be viewed as the attempt to change one's understanding of the background defining all things. At first sight, one could say that enlightenment is essentially a cognitive transformation, that is, the acquisition of a liberating insight. But when one considers the fact that the way in which one views the background of all things has a direct influence on one's behavior—to understand it in terms of emptiness releases one from all forms of attachment—then efforts to change one's behavior are equally as important as the efforts to acquire the liberating insight. In fact, both approaches could be seen as the two sides of the same coin. Both these approaches are part of what I called the cultivation of awareness. This is what I intend to discuss in the present chapter.

The idea of twofold awareness also has some incidence on the ways in which one understands the nature of religious language. In the preceding chapter, I argued that the interpretation of *upāya*, which advocates the view that religious concepts are provisional and disposable, was not an appropriate way to describe the function of religious language. The main argument was that this interpretation maintains unchallenged the notion of a user of the skillful means (*upāyin*). As such, it could also be said that some form of craving is maintained; in the case of *bodhicitta* as an object of concentration, it is a craving for peace of mind. What is needed is therefore something that would allow the dissolution of the idea of doer and consequently, the foundation of all craving. The idea of cultivating an awareness of a background that defines the person cultivating this awareness seems to be that which would allow this dissolution. In other words, when the means is what constitutes the goal, then, because the former is no longer distinct from the later, there is no path to follow and consequently, no one to follow it. At this point, this statement may appear a little bit obscure, but, I believe that it could make sense given a certain understanding of the nature of religious language. For this reason, I believe that it would be appropriate to present this understanding before looking at the cultivation of awareness.

1. The nature of religious language

Previously, I argued that the idea of the blending of the passive and the active was a key element in one's understanding of the concepts of the Indian religious and philosophical traditions. I would now like to introduce a second blending with regard to these concepts and to religious language in general. Indeed, I am of the opinion that religious concepts or truths could be viewed from three different perspectives. These are the functional, the ethical, and the metaphysical. The Buddhist concept of *dharma*, for example, seems to be viewed from these three different perspectives. Indeed, according to Kong-sprul Rinpoche's vast encyclopedia of Buddhism, the *Shes-bya kun-khyab*, *dharma* means "phenomena," the "Path," *nirvāṇa*, "mental objects," "the meritorious," "life," "the teachings," "the process of becoming," "the religious life," and "customs."[1] Thus, *dharma* as phenomena, *nirvāṇa*, mental objects, and the process of becoming could refer to metaphysical realities; the meritorious, life, the religious life and customs, to ethical realities and finally, the teachings and the path to the functional aspect of this concept. It should be noted that this distinction does not mean that each aspect has an existence apart from the others; the reason why religious concepts can be viewed from these three perspectives is that they describe or imply something that is considered true with regard to the three components of any soteriological context, that is, the reality it presupposes (metaphysical aspect), the means of salvation it suggests (functional aspect), and the state of salvation it aims at (ethical aspect).

i. The functional aspect of religious language

The functional aspect is what is considered to be the means to attain or to bring about a certain spiritual experience. These means are valid because of their recognized efficiency to lead one to the final goal. They are usually enshrined in some kind of oral or written tradition and are consequently available to every generation of spiritual aspirants. As such, they are also part of the very fabric of the identity of any given spiritual tradition. In this regard, it might be interesting to note Michael Pye's observation concerning the Japanese Buddhists who have the tendency to regard their teachings and practices as true while those of other sects are seen as skillful means. As he further remarked, this is not in accord with the main usage in the early Mahāyāna *sutras.* According to these *sutras*, he adds, "all expressions of Buddhism are in principle somehow located in human culture and consciousness, and all are therefore understood in the terms of the dialectic between skillful means and insight."[2] All this may well be true with regard to the origin or the source of religious concepts, but it has nothing to do with how these concepts are appropriated and used by a living tradition at a given moment in its history. At this level, other factors enter into play, the most important being personal commitment to a specific tradition and group identity. If Pye had looked at the developments of the various Buddhist schools and sects, I don't think he would have wondered at the behavior of the Japanese Buddhists. Indeed, there are other examples of this type of behavior or attitude within the Buddhist tradition.

The first example deals with the distinction between the two kinds of discourse held by the historical Buddha. This distinction led to the classification of the *suttas* of the Pāli tradition into two categories: the *nītattha-suttas* or those of the direct meaning and the *neyyattha-suttas* or those of the indirect meaning. The *nītattha-suttas* are to be taken literally whereas the *neyyattha-suttas* need to have their intended meaning drawn out. From the point of view of hermeneutics, the former type of *suttas* describes reality as it is whereas the latter refers to mere conventions. One effective example of this distinction is perhaps the doctrine of no-self (*anattā*): discourses of the Buddha advocating the nonexistence of the self are to be interpreted as *nītattha-suttas* while expressions such as "I," and "self" used by the Buddha in the course of his conversations are to be taken as *neyyattha-suttas.* Such expressions are not to be taken as a valid description of things as they actually are.

From the perspective of their ability to bring about a spiritual experience, one might compare this distinction between the *nītattha-suttas* and the *neyyattha-suttas* with the knowledge required to conduct a successful experiment and the knowledge used to prepare or train someone so that he or she may be able to understand the instructions necessary for conducting the experiment successfully. In other words, the *neyyattha* knowledge is a kind of prerequisite that has its validity only as such. For example, one could argue that the acceptance of the Buddhist doctrine of karma, as expounded in the *Sāmaññaphala sutta* of the *Dīgha-nikāya* is such a prerequisite because it provides a foundation for the practice of the path toward enlightenment. Without this prerequisite, all the teachings of Buddhism have no efficiency. It is for this reason, I believe, that the Buddha disapproved of Pūraṇa Kassapa's view of karmic retribution in the *sutta* just mentioned, a view that states that no evil is done by, among other things, killing sentient beings and that there is no merit in giving, self-control, and so on. It is obvious that, with such a view, one would have no incentive to follow the teachings of the Buddha.

Because of this crucial distinction, it was considered of the utmost importance for the early Buddhists to identify which *sutta* corresponds to which type. Failure to do so, as it is confirmed in the *Aṅguttara-nikāya*, would lead one to misunderstand the teachings of the Buddha.[3] Despite this warning, it appears that the means or guidelines making possible such discrimination were left to the discretion of the commentators of the Buddha's discourses. According to K. N. Jayatilleke, "no examples are given in the Canon of the two kinds of Suttas referred to, and we have to seek this information in the commentaries."[4] It would exceed the scope of the present work to look into what the commentators suggested as guidelines. Instead, what interests me at this point, is to show that this distinction between the two types of *sutta* led to the organization of the various teachings of the Buddha into some kind of a hierarchy, something that contradicts the spirit of *upāya* as interpreted by Pye, but that very well describes the behavior of the Japanese Buddhists just mentioned. Indeed, still according to Jayatilleke, "the very fact that one is called a nītattha Sutta, whose meaning is plain and direct and the other a neyyatha—in the sense that its meaning should be inferred in the light of the former, gives the former a definite precedence over the latter."[5]

The same preoccupation could be seen among the Chinese Buddhists who elaborated the system of *p'an-chiao* (judging the teachings). At first, this system was employed simply to determine the historical place of the particular *sūtras* and doctrines taught by the Buddha. It was a way to verify the authenticity of his teachings on the basis of historical evidence. Indeed, the Chinese Buddhists felt that there were many contradictions and apparent discrepancies between the Mahāyāna teachings and those identified as Hināyāna. For this reason, they wanted those contradictions and discrepancies reconciled in order to put an end to confusion and dispute. Later, however, *p'an-chiao* degenerated into mere value judgments of the doctrines and philosophical concepts expounded in the *sūtras* and treatises; it became a way of establishing a supremacy of one over the other.[6]

The reasons for establishing a hierarchy was, as was the case with the distinction between the *nītattha-suttas* and the *neyyattha-suttas*, mainly attributed to an evaluation of the efficiency of the teachings. According to the Chinese Buddhists, this efficiency was evaluated in the light of the debate between sudden and gradual enlightenment. For them, the teachings of the Buddha could be classified into two broad categories: (a) teachings of the half word (imperfect teaching) and (b) teachings of the full word (perfect teachings). It was held that to people of superior intellect, the Buddha preached teachings producing instantaneous enlightenment, while to people of lesser intellect he preached teachings producing gradual enlightenment in order to raise them to a higher plane. The sudden teachings were direct, not mediated, whereas the gradual teachings were gradual because they resorted to expedients (*upāya*) as a means to accommodate the Buddha's enlightened insight to the understanding of unenlightened beings. As mentioned in chapter 1, *upāya* consequently came to qualify a type of teaching that had a lesser significance. Again, judging from Pye's observation, this distinction seems to have prevailed among the Buddhists of Japan.

To sum up the present discussion of the functional aspect of religious language, the point I want to make is that these concepts could be considered true within a particular tradition because the latter acknowledges them as the best expression of what is the most efficient means to attain the goal set out by its spiritual path. One could agree that Buddhists, as a general rule, did not indulge in fruitless speculations about things unrelated to what is beneficial for the aspirant to enlightenment—this is one important argument used in support of Pye's view of religious language—nevertheless, this did not prevent them from engaging in debates over various points in the teachings of the Buddha. They did so precisely because of their differences in appreciating what is beneficial and what is not from the point of view of their respective spiritual path. In other words, the reasons underlying these differences are their implicit or explicit understanding of what is worth committing oneself to. This commitment is incidentally what establishes the specific characteristics of their own identity as a group of aspirants to enlightenment. In a way, one may say that even if it is argued that Buddhists used a pragmatic theory of truth, as Pye maintained in the light of his interpretation of *upāya*, it does not mean that there should not be any debate among them, something that Pye would prefer. On the contrary, given the idea of the functional aspect of religious concepts just suggested, one can see that there will always be some debates, that is, a distinction will always have to be made between right and wrong views. I believe that a survey of the historical developments of the Buddhist schools and sects confirms that point rather than the view that Buddhists are impartial to doctrinal diversity because "there exists a concept, namely this very concept of skillful means, for recognizing that partial expression of truth elsewhere is valid."[7] In fact, it seems that Pye, with his interpretation of *upāya*, is confusing two different issues: on the one hand, there is the issue concerning the interpretation of religious documents, that is, hermeneutics, and on the other hand, the attempt to understand the behavior of a living Buddhist tradition that is influenced by various factors such as the historical, sociological, and even political environment, namely, phenomenology. Its relationship toward the documents of its own tradition is one such factor. It will be a mistake to assume that it is the only one.

ii. The metaphysical aspect of religious language

The metaphysical aspect refers to what is said about the cognitive content of a given spiritual experience. As mentioned previously, it is, for a given group of spiritual seekers, their privileged way to describe what has been and what is to be experienced. From this perspective, a religious concept is true because it is a confirmation of the authenticity of the spiritual experience. In other words, religious concepts, in addition to being a means to a goal, are also a description of that goal. In this regard, one might consider again the implications of Pye's understanding of the nature of religious language: "The Buddhist concept of skillful means suggests that it is of the nature of a developed religious teaching to be extended through a series of forms building upon each other and even criticizing each other, while sharing an inner consistency that cannot be directly stated. It suggests that absoluteness should be ascribed to the teaching of no one sect, even though Buddhists sometimes forget this themselves."[8] The difficulty with this view is that it cannot be contradicted objectively: to verify it, one has to undergo the experience for which a given set of religious ideas and concepts are meant to bring about. Nonetheless, I believe that it can be challenged.

Firstly, it is interesting to notice that Pye once more wonders at the "deviant" behavior of the Buddhists. I believe that what he describes as an exception is in fact the rule. Indeed, it has been so far difficult to find an agreement on this idea of inner consistency from people who claimed to have had attained the final goal of their respective spiritual path.

Secondly, the view propounded by Pye does reiterate the idea that the ultimate reality is beyond conceptualization. There are indeed many passages in the literature of Mahāyāna Buddhism that could easily support this view. For example, in the *Bodhicaryāvatāra*, one learns that "there are two truths: the conventional and the ultimate truths. The ultimate reality is beyond the range of conceptualization; conceptualization [belongs] to the conventional world."[9] In this circumstance, it could be argued that all metaphysical claims are necessarily false with respect to the ultimate reality. As Pye himself says, "Skillful means cannot be a direct expression of truth, and in some sense therefore is always false."[10] This means that for him, skillful means belongs entirely to the conventional world whereas the ultimate reality is what he described as the inner consistency that cannot be directly stated. While this view may solve some problems with respect to explaining why there is an extreme diversity of teachings within the Buddhist tradition, it raises, however, new questions at another level.

If the ultimate is beyond conceptualization, what are the criteria for distinguishing salutary teachings from perversion? If the conventional truth serves as a pointer toward the ultimate, as argued by Nāgārjuna in his *Mūlamadhyamakakārikā*,[11] then, is there anything common between these two truths? Because it seems that Pye's interpretation of *upāya* leaves these problems without a solution, I believe that his view concerning the nature of religious language is not adequate. Given this affirmation, the onus is now on me to interpret these passages. As just alluded, I am of the opinion that the conventional truth is also an expression of the ultimate, that, to some extent, it participates in the reality of the ultimate truth. I wish to now explain the nature of this participation.

I would like to use two similes to explain how a reality beyond conceptualization can still be expressed with language. First, let us imagine that some people are given a picture of a city. They then decide to go to that city. The only information they have to reach it is the picture. On the basis of that picture only, they evaluate the most probable choices, make hypotheses and, assuming that they also have unlimited resources to travel, they move around the world to find it. Eventually, they succeed in reaching the city. Then, at that moment, what is the relationship between the picture they have in their hands and the actual experience of being in the city or close to it? This picture, although it is a very limited representation of the city sought for, remains nevertheless a true representation of its existence. Upon seeing that picture, any person who knows the city is likely to recognize it as a representation of that very city and not of another. It is therefore in that sense that religious concepts could be viewed as a confirmation of the authenticity of the spiritual experience and consequently, that religious language, in addition to being a means to a goal, is also a description of that goal, hence its metaphysical aspect. In other words, religious concepts are like snapshots of the ultimate reality, and as such, although capturing only one moment of it, they are nevertheless valuable because they are clues leading to it. At this point, it is worth noting that, referring to this simile, no picture can fully describe the experience of being in the city. A picture is always something limited with respect to the actual experience of being at the place it depicts. This limitation is, I believe, what is meant when one says that the ultimate reality is beyond conceptualization.

In this way, religious concepts, which are part of the conventional world, always maintain a certain presence at the level of the ultimate reality, and for that reason, I believe that it is not appropriate to say that they are disposable like a map, once one has arrived at a destination. Instead of being disposed of, which would mean that all connections with the ultimate reality are severed, and consequently that there are no criteria for distinguishing salutary teachings from perversion, it is their function that changes or rather their relationship with the apprehending subject that is redefined. Indeed, from being the only available picture of the reality it represents, it is now integrated into the reality it is meant to describe. At this moment, it becomes one event, among an infinity of other events, which could be used as a guide to, as well as a description of, the place sought for. In other words, it becomes part of the background alluded to in the preceding chapter. This change of status is what it means to transcend the world of conventions. To make this more explicit, I would like to suggest a second simile.

Let us imagine that one has to assemble a puzzle. At first, all the pieces that lie apart are almost meaningless. With one piece only, it is sometimes possible to guess what the whole puzzle looks like once assembled. On the basis of these guesses, one searches for other clues, and manages to join more pieces together up to the moment when one can really see the picture that the puzzle is meant to represent. At this moment, it becomes very easy to find the position of the remaining pieces. The question I would like to address at this point is which piece of the puzzle is responsible for bringing about the vision of the complete picture?

One may assume that there was one piece that triggered the experience of seeing the global picture, but one has to say that, given other circumstances, that is, a different course of event in assembling the pieces, another piece could have been responsible for it. Moreover, once the puzzle is completed, all the pieces, by the very fact that they are now integrated into the whole picture, equally contribute to, or participate in, the formation of this whole picture. One may get rid of a few pieces without disturbing the picture, but this should not mean that they are disposable. On the contrary, what it means is that they are just not indispensable. In this way, even if I argue that religious concepts say something about the ultimate reality, there is still some flexibility and diversity with regard to which concepts may be used as a means. Only this time, contrary to what Pye's interpretation of religious language suggests, there are certain limitations as to what may be chosen. These limitations are imposed by the ability of these concepts to describe or to represent parts of the ultimate experience they are meant to bring about. In a way, it is because religious concepts are limited with respect to the ultimate reality that they may be used as means to reach that ultimate reality. Similar to the situation in which they have no connections whatsoever with the ultimate reality, if they were encompassing the entire reality, then one would also have no sense of direction. Like being everywhere at the same time, one can go nowhere.

iii. The ethical aspect of religious language

The ethical aspect refers to what is said about the emotional and behavioral content of a given spiritual experience. In chapter 2, I gave a few examples of what the fruits of undergoing such an experience could be. First of all, there is an absence of fear that results in a self-sacrificing attitude and in the acquisition of an earnest and spontaneous desire to help all sentient beings. This state of fearlessness is further characterized by a stable mind as well as by feelings of contentment and joy. The most important of these fruits, however, is probably the acquisition of a perfect peace of mind.

In chapter 3, I made a few references to the importance of this peace of mind. In fact, it is so important that, as Paul J. Griffiths explained, it has become identical with enlightenment itself. In that chapter, I also questioned the validity of any spiritual approach that considers this experience of peace of mind as an end in itself. I argued that, in the context of such a spiritual approach, any ideas or concepts ought to be viewed as disposable means. This view was rejected, from the perspective of the quality of the resulting spiritual experience, that is, on the ground of its inability to transcend the duality of the subject and the object and, from the historical point of view, on the ground of its inappropriateness to account for the behavior of living Buddhists with regard to their evaluation of the various means to enlightenment.

Contrary to this view, it could be argued that the experience of perfect peace of mind is only a result of acquiring some kind of knowledge or wisdom. As Griffiths pointed out, as an alternative to the spiritual approach just suggested, enlightenment consists in seeing things the way they actually are. If one is attached to things and consequently suffers because one is separated from them, it is fundamentally because one does not see the real nature of these things. The tendencies such as desire and hatred that arise in relation to the objects of the phenomenal world are in fact only secondary: one has to first overcome the ignorance that is causing these tendencies. Given this view, the acquisition of the liberating knowledge is the first priority or the final objective and consequently, the practice of moral discipline and mental restraint are considered prerequisites for this acquisition.

This view, as R. M. L. Gethin says, is "basically a manifestation of the principles of the consecutive stages of the path or of the hierarchy of *sīla*, *samādhi* and *paññā*."[12] In this regard, Sangharakshita argues that "according to the Threefold Way, spiritual life begins with *śīla* or morality, then proceeds to *samādhi* or meditation, and concludes with *prajñā* or Wisdom. Ethics is only *śīla* in the Buddhist sense if it is a step on the path. Since the path leads towards the goal of Buddhahood, moral action is not merely the expression of skilful states of mind but has Buddhahood as its ultimate object."[13] This means that ethics or rather the criteria of what it means to behave ethically are not to be seen as some kind of ultimate truth, that is, as a code that is structured on the revelations of a God as a law-giver, but rather as guidelines for developing the mental states conducive to the higher practices of the spiritual path. As Sangharakshita says, "The primary terms of ethical evaluation are not 'good' and 'bad' but 'skilful' and 'unskilful.' "[14]

This Threefold Way is, according to the Buddhist tradition, a way to subsume the Eightfold path (*ariya-aṭṭhangika-magga*) which is the fourth Noble Truth taught by the Buddha in his first discourse at Bārāṇasī, that is, the truth concerning the path leading to the cessation of suffering (*dukkha-nirodha-gāminī-paṭipadā*). This idea has been confirmed by Etienne Lamotte, an eminent scholar of Buddhism: "La quatrième vérité sainte . . . a pour objet le chemin conduisant à la destruction de la douleur (*duḥkhanirodhagāminī pratipad*). Le noble chemin à huit branches défini dans le sermon de Bénares comporte trois éléments: la moralité, la concentration et la sagesse." (The fourth Noble Truth is the path leading to the destruction of suffering. The Eightfold path as defined in the discourse of Benares consists of three parts: morality, concentration, and wisdom.)[15] This Eightfold path consists of (1) Right View (*sammā-diṭṭhi*), (2) Right Thought (*sammā-saṅkappa*), (3) Right Speech (*sammā-vācā*), (4) Right Action (*sammā-kammanta*), (5) Right Livelihood (*sammā-ājiva*), (6) Right Effort (*sammā-vāyāma*), (7) Right Mindfulness (*sammā-sati*), and (8) Right Concentration (*sammā-samādhi*). Consequently, according to the Threefold Way, *sīla* would consist in factors 3 to 5, *samādhi*, factors 6 to 8, and *paññā*, factors 1 and 2. It is to be noticed that the standard sequence of the Eightfold path does not give the normative progression of *sīla*, *samādhi*, and *paññā*, but instead, of *paññā*, *sīla*, and *samādhi*. According to Maurice Walshe, "this is because, while some preliminary wisdom is needed to start on the path, the final flowering of the higher Wisdom follows after the development of morality and concentration."[16] To some extent this is true; however, it seems that this change of order reveals something more. At this point, I would like to introduce Gethin's illuminating discussion, taken from his book *The Buddhist Path to Awakening: A Study of the Bodhi-Pakkhiyā Dhammā*, on the nature of this Threefold Way.

Lamotte's statement that was just quoted is following the *Cūḷavedalla sutta*'s method of classifying the eight factors in terms of *sīla*, *samādhi*, and *paññā*. According to Gethin,[17] scholars have tended to ignore a key passage in the *sutta* that immediately precedes it: "My lady, are the three aggregates of [*sīla*, *samādhi* and *paññā*] included in the ariyo *aṭṭhaṅgiko maggo*, or is it the ariyo *aṭṭhaṅgiko maggo* that is included in the three aggregates?" "The three aggregates are not, Visākha, included in the *ariyo aṭṭhaṅgiko maggo*, but it is the *ariyo aṭṭhaṅgiko maggo*, Visākha, that is included in the three aggregates."[18] What is to be intended here is made explicit in the commentary of the *Visuddhimagga*: "In the present case, because the *maggo* [path] is specific and the three aggregates are all inclusive, it is therefore comprised, on account of its specificity, by the three all inclusive aggregates like a city by a kingdom."[19] Gethin is here asking, "So why is the *ariyo aṭṭhaṅgiko maggo* comprised by the three *khandhas* but not vice versa?"[20] He suggests the following answer: "The triad of *sīla*, *samādhi* and *paññā* implies a comprehensive graded description of the stages of the spiritual path. In terms of content it comprises the successive stages in full, and while reflecting the overall general nature of the actual stages of the path, it does in part represent something of an ideal scheme."[21] The reason why it is considered an ideal scheme is because it is generally understood, within the Buddhist tradition, that if one tries to develop *paññā*, it becomes apparent that some measure of *samādhi* is required and if one tries to develop *samādhi*, some degree of *sīla* is needed. What this means in practice, as Gethin says, "is that it is understood that someone can have developed *sīla* but need not necessarily have developed *samādhi* and *paññā*; someone can have developed *sīla* and *samādhi*, but not necessarily have developed *paññā* to any great degree. However, the converse cannot be so."[22]

In theory, this hierarchy of spiritual achievements may make sense, but in practice, the relationship between *sīla*, *samādhi*, and *paññā* seems to be a little bit more subtle than that. Indeed, in the *Soṇadaṇḍa sutta*, one is told by the Brahmin Soṇadaṇḍa, "Just as, Gotama, one hand may wash another hand, or a foot another foot, so *paññā* is cleansed by *sīla*, and *sīla* is cleansed by *paññā*; where there is *sīla* there is *paññā*, where there is *paññā* there is *sīla*; one who has *sīla* has *paññā*, one who has *paññā* has *sīla*; *sīla* and *paññā* together are declared the most excellent thing of the world."[23] Although this passage considers the stages of the path by way of just *sīla* and *paññā*—the context was a discussion of what is required for one to be a true Brahmin—it could be assumed that *samādhi* is to be included in this scheme as well. Indeed, in the *Mahāparinibbāna sutta*, it is said, "*samādhi* when imbued with *sīla* leads to great fruit and profit. *Paññā* when imbued with concentration leads to great fruit and profit."[24] Therefore, what this passage presumably means "is that the intent to develop *sīla* is seen as bound up with *paññā* and that the development of *sīla* naturally tends to the development of *paññā* and *samādhi.* The latter two in turn tend to the development of *sīla.*"[25] Consequently, the hierarchy just referred to should "not mean that when the novice at the initial stages of the path establishes *sīla*, he does not also in some way and to some degree begin to develop *samādhi* and *paññā*, or that when the adept at the advanced stage of the path develops *paññā* he does not need *sīla* or *samādhi.*"[26] Indeed, as Tong Ba Mai, a monk and a scholar of Buddhism, argued, "they [*sīla*, *samādhi*, and *paññā*] are dependent on each other to arise. They are regarded as three classes of eight paths and therefore each of them can be a primary path and support the others. The fulfillment of knowledge, ethical conduct or meditative practices cannot be obtained independently; each of them is inaccessible if treated separately." He further adds that "they can be considered as three aspects of an element or three qualities of Nibbāna. *Sīla*, *samādhi* and *paññā* are so related with each other that when this arises the other naturally arises; there is no need to make effort to have the other arise."[27] In support of his last affirmation, he quotes the following passage taken from the *Aṅguttara-nikāya*: "Monks, for one whose body is calmed, there is no need to think, 'I feel happiness.' This, monks, is in comformity to the nature of things (*dhammatā esā*) that one whose body is calmed feels happiness. . . ."[28]

With regard to the Eightfold path then, it implies that it is not to be understood primarily as a description of the successive stages of the path. Indeed, according to Saddhatissa, a Buddhist monk and translator often writing for nonspecialists, the path leading to the release from suffering is said to be eightfold. These are not consecutive steps. The eight factors are interdependent and must be perfected simultaneously, "the fulfillment of one factor being unlikely without at least the partial development of the others."[29] I shall come back to this idea of interdependence when discussing the role of the *pāramitās* or "Perfections" in the context of the cultivation of *bodhicitta.* Indeed, as with the Eightfold path and its threefold division into *sīla, samādhi, and paññā,* there is also a tendency to view the various *pāramitās* as successive stages of spiritual achievements. For the moment, I would like to finish the present discussion of the significance of the *ariyo aṭṭhaṅgiko maggo.*

While the scheme consisting in the triad of *sīla, samādhi,* and *paññā* may be seen as a general picture of the various aspects of the path, the *ariyo aṭṭhaṅgiko maggo* as a whole represents, according to Gethin, "an actual manifestation of all three aspects so that the *ariyo aṭṭhaṅgiko maggo* can be seen as the essential distillation of the aggregates of *sīla, samādhi* and *paññā.*"[30] In other words, the *ariyo aṭṭhaṅgiko maggo* is the consummation of the development of *sīla, samādhi,* and *paññā.* As Gethin further explains, "it is the path or way of life that issues from that development. Its end is a reflection and crystallization of the way one has come. In other words, the development of *sīla, samādhi,* and *paññā* in all its various aspects culminates in right view, right thought, right speech, right action, right livelihood, right striving, right mindfulness, right concentration—*paññā, sīla* and *samādhi,* the three essential aspects in perfect balance."[31] In support of his affirmation, Gethin essentially argues that the Eightfold path is where one wishes to arrive as well as the way one must go in order to get there. In other words, "the *ariyo aṭṭhaṅgiko maggo* is the transformation of view, thought, speech, action, livelihood, striving, mindfulness and concentration into right view, right thought, right speech, right action, right livelihood, right striving, right mindfulness, right concentration."[32] How then could the Eightfold path be seen not only as a means but also as the goal of spiritual endeavor? Gethin gives the following arguments.

First of all, the Buddhist tradition seems to view the *ariyo aṭṭhaṅgiko maggo* as a kind of yardstick against which all spiritual practice could be compared. Indeed, in the *Mahāparinibbāna sutta,* when Subhadda asked the Buddha whether teachers such as Pūraṇa Kassapa have realized the truth, the Buddha responded,

> Enough, Subhadda, do not bother about all those who claim to have realized the truth, or about all those who do not, or about some of those who do and some of those who do not. I shall teach you *dhamma,* Subhadda. Listen and pay careful attention, I shall speak. In whatever *dhamma-vinaya* the noble eight-factored path is not found,

> there too the ascetic [Stream-Attainer] is not found, there too the second [Once-Returner], the third [Non-Returner], and the fourth [Arhat] are not found. But in the *dhamma-vinaya* where the noble eight-factored path is found, there too these ascetics are found.[33]

As such, the *ariyo aṭṭhaṅgiko maggo* seems to be viewed not as a specific path, but rather, as something encompassing some kind of principle that is the essence of all spiritual paths. The understanding of this principle, rather than going through the different stages it refers to, appears to be the solution to the basic problem of suffering. In other words, the *ariyo aṭṭhaṅgiko maggo*, as the fourth Noble Truth, is something one is awakened to, not only the fourth Noble Truth, but the entire scheme of the four Noble Truths. This might explain why the realization of these Noble Truths is seen, in the *Sāmaññaphala sutta* of the *Dīgha-nikāya*, as an accomplishment of the practice of the four *jhānas* or "meditations." If the *ariyo aṭṭhaṅgiko maggo* were to be considered simply as a path, then one would face a paradox: how could it be possible to follow a path whose accomplishment results in understanding the path to follow? This idea that the *ariyo aṭṭhaṅgiko maggo* is seen as the content of spiritual experience might become clearer when considering Gethin's second argument.

This argument addresses the significance of *ariya* in the expression *ariyo aṭṭhaṅgiko maggo*. This term has been analyzed in the context of the *Abhidhamma* but, according to Gethin, its usage has been somewhat overlooked when considering early Pāli literature such as the *Nikāyas*. In this regard, Gethin believes that "the Nikāyas' technical usage of the term *ariya* must be considered in broad agreement with, although not always as clear cut as, the usage in the *Abhidhamma/Abhidharma* literature."[34] This therefore means that *ariya/ārya* "is applied to anything that is directly associated with the world-transcending (*lokuttara*) knowledge of the stream-attainer, the once-returner, the non-returner and the *arahant/arhat*—the 'noble persons' (*ariya-puggala/ārya-pudgala*)." Gethin further adds, "By way of contrast we have the 'world' *(loka)*: the sphere of the five senses *(kāmâvacara)*, the *jhānas* of the form sphere *(rūpâvacara)* and the formless sphere *(arūpâvacara);* in short, the 'world' accessible to the ordinary man *(puthujjana)*."[35] What this means is that "there are strong grounds for thinking that the *ariyo aṭṭhaṅgiko maggo* should be particularly associated with the notion of *sotāpatti* (the stage of stream-attainer).[36] Indeed, a passage taken from the *Saṃyutta-nikāya* confirms this: "When the word "stream" is mentioned, Sāriputta, what stream is meant?" "The stream, Sir, is the noble eight-factored path, that is, right view. . . . " "Good! Sāriputta, when the expression 'stream-attainer' is mentioned, what stream-attainer is meant?" "Sir, one who is endowed with this noble eight-factored path he is said to be a stream-attainer. . . ."[37] The significance of *ariya* is therefore to identify, whatever knowledge or behavior is associated to it, something that is possible only after a certain spiritual breakthrough has occurred. This means that *sīla*, which is right speech, right action, and right livelihood, is not a prerequisite for the acquisition of *samādhi* and *paññā* but rather it is a characteristic of what it means to undergo that spiritual breakthrough. In this regard, Gethin relates a simile, taken again from the *Saṃyutta-nikāya*, which illustrates quite well the conception of the spiritual progress associated with the *ariyo aṭṭhaṅgiko maggo*:

> Let's imagine, *bhikkhus*, that a person wandering in a forest, in a jungle were to see an ancient path, an ancient road which had been followed by ancient people. He follows it, and, having followed it, he would see an ancient city, an ancient royal town, with delightful parks, gardens, lotus-ponds with high walls, which had been inhabited by ancient people. And then, that person would tell the king or his minister: "You should surely know, Sir, that while wandering in the forest, in the jungle, I saw an ancient path. . . . Claim that city, Sir!"[38]

Gethin suggests that we consider this simile from the point of view of the king. He is without doubt likened to the aspirant to enlightenment who has been instructed by the Buddha about the existence of a path leading to cessation of suffering. The king must find the path in the jungle himself. For that, he has to first accept on trust the existence of such a path. This path, which is somewhere in the jungle, is not something easily accessible. Therefore, the search for it may involve some wandering; doubts may also arise as to its existence, and so forth. But as soon as he comes across the path he was eagerly searching, one may assume that he experiences great relief because, having seen the way to the delightful place, the possibility to reach it is now a certainty. Similarly, the aspirant to enlightenment may work with ordinary views and practices; at this point he or she may doubt the existence of a path leading to the cessation of suffering but then, comes across the Eightfold path and follows it. What it means to follow this path is what I discussed in the context of *bodhiprasthānacitta*, that is, to go along a stream in which motivation, as an act of the will, even for enlightenment, is absent and in which mental factors that allow spiritual progression are present.

I believe that it is now obvious why I feel that religious language could be true from an ethical perspective. It is because there is no difference between the way to describe a behavior that is induced by such a concept or its implications, at the worldly level, and that that results from assimilating or integrating it, as a kind of spiritual breakthrough. Before the experience, the change of behavior may be a conscious act requiring efforts; after the experience, the desired behavior has become spontaneous, like a second nature. This idea of truth from the ethical point of view also means that behavior is a sign of spiritual accomplishment, as was the case with the Buddha. In the *Sāmaññaphala sutta*, for example, one is told that a Tathāgata arises in the world, an Arahant, fully enlightened Buddha, endowed with wisdom and conduct (*vijjācaraṇasampanno*).[39]

In chapter 2, while discussing the ethical aspect of *bodhicitta*, I gave a few examples of the spontaneous character of the behavior of the bodhisattva. I have also shown that commitment, at this level, had no role to play. As a matter of fact, such commitment, because it reinforces the distinction between subject and object, could even be counterproductive. This idea, however, is not meant to deny the importance of commitment in the context of spiritual progression; on the contrary, it is fully integrated in it. But, as the notion of threefold aspects of truth implies, it is to be seen not only as its cause but also as its description. The nature of this spiritual progression is the topic of the next section.

2. The cultivation of awareness

There is, I believe, a key passage in the *Bodhicaryāvatāra* that makes the cultivation of awareness quite explicit. This passage is closely connected to the one previously used to criticize *bodhicitta* as an object of concentration. I would therefore like to provide a fresh translation and to comment on it with the help of Prajñākaramati's Sanskrit commentary.

> Even if the world is known to be constituted of illusion, how could a tendency be destroyed, as the creator of an illusory woman who manages to fall in love with his [own creation]?
>
> [The reason is that] the impression disturbing [a clear perception of] reality of the creator has not been worn out. Consequently, in that moment of seeing her, his impression of emptiness is weak.
>
> By reinforcing the impression of emptiness, the impression [which causes the belief in] existence will be abandoned. And with the practice of [thinking] that nothing [existence as well as the idea of absence of existence] is, the impression of emptiness will afterwards also be worn out.

> When existence is not conceived of on account of imagining that it is not, then how can the idea of absence of existence, which is [now] without support, stand in front of the mind?
>
> If neither existence nor non-existence can stand in front of the mind, then [the mind], having no other alternative, will be without support and become pacified.[40]

This experience in which the impression of emptiness itself is dissolved and the mind pacified is called the emptiness of emptiness because all objects of imagination have been destroyed.[41]

At first, this passage identifies a problem related to the cause of one's attachment: if the world is an illusion, that is, without real existence, how can it defile the mind of the people? There is a problem because it is assumed that a thing, in order to leave a trace on a mind, must be truly existent. This idea has been used as an objection to the concept of emptiness itself. Indeed, in the *Vigrahavyāvartanī* of Nāgārjuna, the objector believes that it would not be appropriate to admit that things that are empty are capable of performing actions.[42] This objection is based on a misunderstanding of what it means when something is empty. As Nāgārjuna says, things are empty because they are dependently originated[43] and not because they are absent, so that objects like a cart, a pot, or a cloth, may perform specific functions such as carrying things and offering protection from cold.[44] Similarly, the example of the creator of an illusory woman who becomes infatuated in his creation is given as an argument in favor of the fact that things, although they are lacking intrinsic existence, can nevertheless cause the impregnation of mental habits such as desire. This example appears to be appropriate because one is told by the commentator Prajñākaramati that it is possible for certain magicians to create illusory objects by means of sacred formulas or drugs.[45] These objects were definitively unreal and yet, one, including their creator, could develop feelings of attachment toward them.

The reason why one is likely to develop such feelings of attachment is given in the second verse of this passage: it is because one's mind is permeated, so to speak, with the idea that things have an inherent existence;[46] and this prevents one from seeing things as they really are. *Samāropaḥ* usually means attribution or mental assumption. In the light of my explanation of the twofold awareness, I believe that it refers to the background that defines all objects of perception. This means that the idea that things are endowed with an inherent existence is not an object of perception, but rather, it is what defines all objects that are perceived. The word that is used to identify this phenomenon of impregnation is *vāsanā* (impression). The choice of this term is interesting by itself because it comes from the verbal root √*vās* that produces the verb *vāsayati*. According to Apte, it means (1) to scent, perfume, incense, fumigate, or make fragrant; (2) to steep or infuse; and (3) to spice or season.[47] More interesting is the process used to perfume, for example, cloths: one would put in a box one piece of cloth that has been soaked in perfume under a pile of unsoaked cloths; by the process of suffusion all the unsoaked cloths will be impregnated by the scent of the perfume. Similarly, the idea of inherent existence impregnates all objects of perception. Because of that, the impression that things lack inherent existence is weak if not totally absent.

This impression, according to Prajñākaramati, is caused by the successive repetition of acknowledging the wrong idea,[48] that things inherently exist, and it is comparable to an impregnation or a karma-formation that is planted like a seed in the mental continuum.[49] Given this process of impregnation, the antidote (*pratipakṣaḥ*) prescribed is to develop or to cultivate the impression that things lack inherent existence and also by the constant practice of thinking that nothing is actually existent.[50] This practice is not characterized by fixing one's mind on the idea that nothing exists, but rather, it is a kind of investigation involving every aspect of the cognitive faculty.

The term that is usually used to designate that investigation is *vicāra*. Indeed, a little bit further in chapter 9 of the *Bodhicaryāvatāra*, it is said,

> If, in the presence of an annihilating cause, there is no production of suffering, then it would mean that what is called "feeling" is the result of an attachment to a false idea.
>
> Therefore, this investigation is conceived as the antidote [of this unjustified feeling]. That is why, it is, for the yogis, the food—which consists of the content of any conceptual mind activity—of their meditative absorption.[51]

What is meant by this conceptual mind activity (*vikalpa*) is a passionless (*viviktaṃ kamaiḥ*) analysis (*vitarka*) of the idea that what is called feeling is the result of an attachment to a false idea.[52] What should be also noticed in this passage is the link between meditation (*dhyāna*) and *vicāra*; *vicāra* appears to bring about a deeper *dhyāna* and consequently, a greater peace of mind. Indeed, Prajñākaramati said that when one is investigating (*vicāryamāṇa*) the fact that in reality the "I" does not exist, one should not experience fear. Therefore, from investigation fear ceases.[53] A last point concerning this term is worth mentioning. In his commentary of the one hundred ninth verse of chapter 9 of the *Bodhicaryāvatāra*, Prajñākaramati cites *vimarśaḥ* as a gloss for *vicāraḥ*. This term means, according to Apte (1) deliberation, consideration, examination, or discussion; (2) reasoning; (3) conflicting judgment; (4) hesitation; (5) impression left on the mind by past good or bad actions; see *vāsanā*; and (6) knowledge.[54] This definition seems to encompass all major components of what is meant by *vicāra*. Firstly, it is a critical examination and reasoning on the basis of accepted truths, secondly, it is a hesitation in the sense that it challenges the assumptions of what is investigated, and finally, it is also the result of its activity, that is, it leaves a new impression on the mind of the investigator.

This investigation is what I called the cultivation of awareness. The content of awareness is the background that defines all objects of perception. In some Advaita Vedānta schools of thought, for example, it is said that the phenomenal world is a projection on a screen; this is true to the extent that the screen is not only a reality to be discovered but also something that has to be created or caused to be revealed. This cultivation is therefore characterized by building up an awareness of a background. In this regard, it might be interesting to draw a parallel with Christian iconography. According to the Slavic iconographers, the background of the icon is called light (*svet*). Its function is to specifically reveal the presence of the divine in the scene represented. In fact, every element of this scene is depicted in such a way that it is always the background that imposes itself. This is the effect that the iconographer has to reproduce in each of his or her icons whatever scene is represented. Similarly, the cultivation of awareness depicts the phenomenal world in such a way that the content of this awareness becomes more and more obvious. As such, the background is made to cover all aspects of existence or every and each moment of existence is caused to be viewed as a manifestation of it. I believe that when one looks at spiritual practice from this perspective, the differences between the various traditions of Buddhism such as Theravāda and Mahāyāna are only in terms of the content of awareness and not in terms of the spiritual approach. Let us look at two examples.

i. Examples of the cultivation of awareness

In the *Mahāsatipaṭṭhāna sutta* of the *Dīghā-nikāya*, a text of the Theravāda tradition, one finds the canonical explanation of the Noble Truth of Suffering: "And what, monks, is the Noble Truth of Suffering? Birth is suffering, ageing is suffering, death is suffering, sorrow, lamentation, pain, sadness and distress are suffering. Not obtaining what one wants is suffering. In short, the five aggregates of grasping are suffering."[55] It appears that, in this short explanation of the idea of suffering, one already finds two levels of investigation.

The first level is related to more conventional matters such as the loss of a loved one. It is a reflection on what our daily life has in store for us. It is meant to intensify our sense of dissatisfaction with the world. Historically speaking, it could be argued that this idea of suffering is above all a result of the conditions the early Buddhists found themselves in. Indeed, according to Ainslie T. Embree, it has been suggested that a great wave of pessimism marked the time of the Buddha; it "was due to the break-up of old tribes and their replacement by kingdoms wherein ethnic ties and the sense of security that they gave were lost or weakened, thus leading to a deep-seated psychological unease affecting all sections of the people."[56] Given this circumstance, many people commenting on the Buddhist tradition as a whole have been tempted to interpret the First Noble Truth of the Buddha as a reiteration of this mood of pessimism. Consequently, the reflection on the idea of suffering could be viewed as a means to awaken and to reinforce the desire to escape a dissatisfying world. This is probably one way of conceiving the significance of the First Noble Truth but I believe it is inappropriate: it fails to explain the philosophical developments that the Buddhists produced from investigating the various implications related to this idea of suffering.

I think that the First Noble Truth is not meant to serve as a kind of justification for spiritual involvement. On the contrary, the decision to find a way to change one's dissatisfying condition is always assumed in the teachings of the Buddha. Indeed, he always gives advice or refutes his challengers on questions concerning the way; there is no instance of proselytism on the part of the Buddha or of his disciples.[57] Instead, I am of the opinion that the investigation related to the idea of suffering is meant to deepen one's meditative absorption. One can easily imagine that the understanding of the painful nature of one's daily existence leads one to develop a sense of detachment from the things likely to cause pain. This attitude of renunciation is usually the first sign of spiritual progression. It is, however, possible that such understanding might not be sufficient: one may have doubts about the universality of the idea of suffering by arguing that despite the impression that life is suffering, it also has its good moments; one simply has to accept this alternation of ups and downs. In order to offset such a doubt, one's investigation has to reach a level beyond the psychological dimension.

It appears that there is a more subtle form of suffering that can only be perceived by the practice of what Vetter called the discriminative insight.[58] According to those who went beyond the ordinary sphere of perception, all existence is characterized by impermanence (*anicca),* by the absence of essence or hard core (*anatta*), and by its potential to lead to suffering or to the fact that it is unsatisfactory (*dukkha*). Each of these characteristics became the theme of many meditative practices as well as the source of the development of metaphysical theories concerning the nature of things. For instance, the meditation on the decaying body could be used to neutralize certain mental habits, as mentioned in chapter 3, but I would argue that its main purpose is to bring about an ever greater awareness of the idea of impermanence. As a matter of fact, those who pursued the investigation on the idea of impermanence, not satisfied to deal only with observable events, went as far as saying that existence consisted in a succession of very short moments (*kṣaṇa*) so that it lasts, according to certain schools of early Buddhism (the Sautrāntika in particular), a moment so brief that one is capable of perceiving only the trace of its occurrence.

The idea of absence of hard core, on the other hand, led to the formulation of the theory of the five constituents of being (*pañca-khandha*) and to the idea of no-self. According to this theory, a human being is made up of five aggregates or *khandhas*: form (*rūpa*), feeling (*vedanā*), perception (*saññā*), mental disposition (*saṅkhāra*), and consciousness (*viññāṇa*). Apart from these aggregates there is nothing more, hence no-self (*anatta*). This idea that a human being is made up of parts has been extrapolated to include all aspects of the perceivable world. Indeed, it was believed that the world consisted of imperceptible elements called *dharmas.* It might exceed the scope of the present research to investigate all the implications of this idea, but suffice it to say that this practice of discriminative insight, based on the idea that "all is suffering" has, judging from the fact that it has produced an important part of the conceptual structure of the majority of the Buddhists, covered a lot of ground in creating or revealing a context upon which all experiences of the phenomenal world find a new meaning. In other words, with all these Buddhist doctrines, it is difficult to argue that there is something that is not suffering.

The second example I would like to cite is taken from Nāgārjuna's *Mūlamadhyamakakārikā*. The philosophical goals of Nāgārjuna have been the subject of speculations among modern Buddhologists. Indeed, according to David Seyford Ruegg, "over the past half-century the doctrine of the Madhyamaka school, and in particular that of Nāgārjuna, has been variously described as nihilism, monism, irrationalism, misology, agnosticism, scepticism, criticism, dialectic, mysticism, acosmism, absolutism, relativism, nominalism, and linguistic analysis with therapeutic value."[59] All of these descriptions of what Nāgārjuna is or what he attempts to do in his *Mūlamadhyamakakārikā* assumes that the doctrine of dependent origination (*pratītya-samutpāda*), which is the central theme of his work, is only a means to an end. It would be much simpler to argue that the means is itself the end so that the idea of dependent origination is what appropriately describes one's only reality. In this circumstance, Nāgārjuna, if one wants to define him, is a dependent-originationist (*pratītyasamutpādavādin*). I think that it should be obvious that the whole enterprise of Nāgārjuna in the *Mūlamadhyamakakārikā* is to convince us, using even fallacious argumentation,[60] of the fact that everything, including our most established concepts such as cause and effect or movement, does not exist on its own. The purpose of all his reflection and investigation is to push to the background the idea of dependent origination, that is, to define all aspects of the phenomenal world in terms of it. In other words, what he is attempting to do is to "perfume" the phenomenal world with the idea of dependent origination. As with the cultivation of awareness of the idea that everything is suffering, the impressions left on the mind by the investigation of the implications related to the idea of dependent origination should bring about an attitude of detachment and thereby calm the anxious activity of the mind. So far, in my description of the cultivation of awareness, I have always assumed that the feeling of detachment was an immediate consequence of developing an ever greater awareness. In the next few paragraphs, I would like to show how such an awareness can create a feeling of detachment.

ii. The feeling of detachment

First, I would like to quote a passage that I believe confirms the fact that awareness of an idea that includes all aspects of the phenomenal world is interrelated with a feeling of detachment. This passage is taken from the *Mahāsaccakasutta* of the *Majjhima-nikāya* and appears to refer to a spiritual experience that the Buddha had before he left his family to search for immortality.

> This, Aggivessana, I thought, "I am fully aware as my father, the Sakyan, was ploughing, and I was sitting in the cool shade of a rose-apple tree, aloof from desires, aloof from unskilled states of mind, entering on the first meditation [*jhāna*], which is accompa-

> nied by thinking and discrimination, is born of aloofness, and is rapturous and joyful, and while abiding therein, I thought: 'Now could this be a way to awakening?' Then following on my mindfulness, Aggivessana, there was the consciousness: 'This is itself the Way to awakening.' "[61]

This entering of the first meditation is also called the experience of entering the Stream (*sotāpanna*) and is characterized, among other things, by giving up forever the belief in personality (*sakkāya-diṭṭhi*). This experience is also identified as the opening of the Dhamma-eye *(dhamma-cakkhu*) and, according to Buddhaghosa,[62] at this moment, one is said to have glimpsed *nibbāna*. Due to this experience, which is not devoid of cognitive content and even mental activity, the Buddha tells us that he entered a state of aloofness or detachment. At this point it may be worth noting some of the implications related to this state of mind.

In this passage, it is said the one becomes "aloof from the pleasures of the senses, aloof from unskilled states of mind." The term used to describe this state is derived from the Pāli verb *viviccati*. This verb means to separate oneself, to depart from, to be alone, and to separate.[63] It therefore seems that this state of detachment is characterized by the creation of a distance or a stepping back away from the stage of the phenomenal experiences such as passion and hatred. Consequently, this experience is not an annihilation of one's mental states, which is, as discussed in chapter 3, the main purpose of the practice of concentration on a single object, but rather, it is the establishment of a new relationship between these mental states and the one who experiences them. This means that spiritual practice, at some point, has nothing to do with chasing away bad habits or acquiring good ones. I believe that one passage of the *Mahāsatipaṭṭhāna sutta* of the *Dīgha-nikāya* confirms this.

> And how, monks, does a monk abide contemplating the various kinds of mind? Here, a monk knows a passionate mind as passionate, a mind free from passion as free from passion; a hating mind as hating, a mind free from hate as free from hate; a deluded mind as deluded, an undeluded mind as undeluded; a composed mind as composed, a distracted mind as distracted; a great mind as great, an undeveloped mind as undeveloped; a surpassed mind as surpassed, an unsurpassed mind as unsurpassed; a concentrated mind as concentrated, an unconcentrated mind as unconcentrated; a freed mind as freed, an unliberated mind as unliberated.[64]

Thus, the mind may take whatever form possible and this has no repercussion on the attitude of the individual. This is possible, not because of a sheer force of mind-control, but rather because of a redefinition of the meaning and the significance of these mental states, that is, the establishment of a new relationship between these mental states and the one who experiences them. This redefinition is the result of a transformation of what is viewed as their background. In order to make this point clearer, I would like to suggest an example taken from the field of dramaturgy.

The difference between a tragedy and a comedy is precisely based on this notion of distance. In a tragedy, for example, the tragic effect is created by eliminating the sense of distance that might exist between the spectator and the character. Everything is done so that the former fully identifies himself with the plight and the fate of the latter. In this context, the art of the dramaturge and that of the producer is to draw the spectator away from his or her usual reality and to absorb him or her into the plot of the play. At this point, the reality of the character becomes the reality of the spectator. In a comedy, it is exactly the reverse process that is going on.

Let us take, for example, the plays of Marivaux, a French author from the eighteenth century. The comical effect is achieved by creating a distance between the spectator and the reality of the characters. Most of his comedies are based on cases of mistaken identity. The spectator is aware of the mistaken identity while most of the characters are not. Thus, the spectator is aware of two levels of reality: the reality based on the mistaken identity and that based on the overall plot of the play. I said that most of the characters are unaware of the mistaken situation because, in most cases, there is one character who is not fooled. His function is very important in this process of creation of a distance between the spectator and the reality of the characters. He is the one who often addresses the spectator as a spectator, that is, as an observer. He makes sure by his repartees that the spectator understands what is going on at the level of the plot. This plot, and this is the most interesting part of the play, very often carries a distinct message. In the case of Marivaux's work, the message is that distinctions between social classes are, from the point of view of human nature, unjustified and unfounded. When looking more closely at the structure of such plays, one may notice that in fact three realities are involved: the first is related to the prejudices of the spectator before the play; the second is that of the characters acting under the assumptions of the mistaken situation. This second reality is the means for the realization of the third reality that has to be assimilated by the spectator. This structure incidentally corresponds to the three aspects of religious concepts: the plot evolving in accordance with the assumptions of the mistaken situation is the means as well as a manifestation of the new understanding that has to be assimilated, an understanding that is supposed to have a direct implication on the behavior of the spectator. In this way, one can see how theater could be used as a means of changing social awareness. In this regard, it might be appropriate to look at Bertolt Brecht's ideas concerning dramaturgy.

Brecht is a German dramaturge who lived in the early part of this century. He was very much concerned with the social role of the theater. He believed that much of the classics were reinforcing the social structure of his time that was based on inequality of social classes and injustice. This was made possible because spectators, as just mentioned in the case of a tragedy, were assimilating the reality of the plots with their own. Because of that, they were not capable of seeing and understanding what causes human tragedy. He thought that, if the theater ought to bring about a new awareness, that is, a knowledge of the root cause of human misery, spectators should be prevented from being absorbed into hopeless realities; they should become more detached from the situations they were confronted with. For that purpose, Brecht coined a new word: Entfremdungseffekt (the process of alienation).

One example of an application of this process was to let some actors, during the course of the play, walk through or in front of the stage with signs carrying slogans. The purpose was to distract the spectators from the plot as well as giving indications on how to understand the context in which this plot was articulated. At this point, it has to be said that Brecht was a Marxist and believed that the reality described by Marxist theory was scientific and objective. But nevertheless, because people were engrossed in their own social prejudices, they had to be instructed. Such was the role of one of his famous plays, *Mother Courage*. In this play, the spectator is asked to understand that greed has its price—Mother Courage makes a living on account of war but at the same time, loses her sons because of it—and that price is to be paid, not because of a certain fatality, but because of a lack of awareness of the causes of that tragic situation. It was believed by Brecht that, as soon as people would understand these causes, they would take action to eradicate them, that is, to overthrow the existing social and political system. This play showed in fact a greater maturity in applying the Entfremdungseffekt, because, instead of using external devices such as signs, the plot itself, by highlighting its inherent contradictions, created the effect of distance. In short, what Brecht did was to recycle tragedy, which was usually used for reinforcing existing prejudices, as a means of transforming social awareness, a role that appears to be reserved to comedy only. In a way, Brecht, most probably, without being aware of it, used the technique adopted by Nāgārjuna: to bring to the fore the inherent contradictions of the wrong way of looking at things. This brings me to explain what exactly this *vicāra* or "investigation" consists of.

iii. The breaking up of distinctions

Contradictions between things are based on the assumption that they stand in opposite relationship and as such, cannot be reconciled. Reconciliation will be, however, possible when the background defining them as opposites will be replaced by the awareness of another background harmonizing their differences. This latter statement comprises a pleonasm because as soon as one is aware of the new background, there are no differences to harmonize; like the fate of the barren woman's son, it is no longer a question to be addressed. It seems, therefore, that one way to force the realization of the all-encompassing background is to use one's analytic mind and imagination to break up the allegedly existing differences. This is done at all levels and in every circumstance. In chapter 6 of the *Bodhicaryāvatāra*, for example, one can read,

> There is no doubt about the fact that this entire world has been assumed by the Compassionate Ones. Therefore they should be seen as taking the forms of all beings. [In this circumstance] why should they [the beings] be treated with disrespect?
>
> This [understanding] pleases the Tathāgatas, fulfills one's ultimate purpose [Buddhahood] and dispels the suffering of the world. Therefore, this [the realization of this understanding] should be my vow.[65]

After telling us that one should not make any distinctions among beings, Śāntideva provides a simile that might help us assimilate this fact:

> For example, if a king's henchman is mishandling a citizen, then a far-sighted citizen will not be able to stand in the way [for fear of reprisal].
>
> Because the henchman is not alone, that his power is that of the king, similarly one should not show disregard for the weak whatsoever.
>
> Because his power is that of the Guardians of Hells and the Compassionate Ones, all beings should be highly respected in the same way that a servant would attend a demanding king.[66]

This practice of breaking up all distinctions is indeed applied to fit any case, "Saliva and faeces come from the same source, [that is, food and drink]. Why then faeces are repulsive whereas the drinking of saliva is something one likes?"[67] There are plenty of other examples in the *Bodhicaryāvatāra*, all variations of the idea that all distinctions are unjustified. This reflection is always done with the purpose of assimilating a view conducive to a behavior that is no longer dictated by making distinctions. In chapter 3, I referred to the practice of exchanging the selves; it is therefore in the context of the practice of breaking up distinctions that this spiritual technique ought to be understood. Instead of neutralizing mental activity, its main function is, as mentioned earlier, to bring about an awareness of the idea that all distinctions are not real.

Before looking in detail at the various components of the practice of cultivation of awareness, I would like to end the present chapter by showing that, as alluded to while discussing the significance of the *Bodhicaryāvatāra*, the practice of devotion could be considered as an autonomous spiritual practice instead of being some kind of prerequisite for another practice.

3. The practice of devotion

At the very end of the *Sutta-nipāta* there is a remarkable description of the spiritual experience of a disciple of the Buddha called Piṅgiya. After having praised the qualities of the Buddha, Piṅgiya is asked by his interlocutor, the Brahmin Bāvari, why he does not spend all his time, every moment, with Gotama the Buddha? To this Piṅgiya answers, "I do not spend one moment away from him. With constant and careful vigilance it is possible for me to see him with my mind as clearly as with my eyes, in night as well as day. And since I spend my nights revering him, there is not, to my mind, a single moment spent away from him."[68] Then Piṅgiya said that he had a vision of the Saṃbuddha upon which the Buddha commented, "Piṅgiya, other people have freed themselves by the power of faith. Vakkali, Bhadrāvudha and Āḷavi-Gotama have all done this. You too should let that faith release you; you too will go beyond the realm of death."[69] According to Paul Williams, Piṅgiya's description of his spiritual experience is perhaps difficult to interpret because it does not classify as fully fledged devotionalism.[70] It appears instead to be connected with the practice of *buddhānusmṛti*, a practice in which the meditator recollects the features of the Buddha systematically and in detail.[71] In this practice, according to Buddhaghosa, the meditator "attains the fullness of faith, mindfulness, understanding and merit. . . . He conquers fear and dread. . . . He comes to feel as if he were living in the Master's presence."[72] I believe that my understanding of the practice of the cultivation of awareness may give us some clues about what is going on. The recollection of the features of the Buddha are not to be considered as objects of concentration or of visualization but rather as means to make obvious the constant presence of the Buddha. In this way, the Buddha, or what it represents, becomes the background from which all things find their meaning. And Buddhaghosa says rightly that such a projection translates itself into a feeling of the Master's presence that is, it is assumed, a very pacifying emotion.

In chapter 2 of the *Bodhicaryāvatāra,* one can witness one of the first fully fledged confessions of sins of Buddhist history. It has been argued that this confession was a way to purify one's mind, that is, a preparatory practice. I believe that it need not be so. A confession of sins always involves a confessor, in the case of Śāntideva's confession, it is the Buddhas and the great Bodhisattvas, and as such, it could be viewed as a way to cultivate an ever-increasing awareness of their presence; the more one has sins to confess, the more one becomes aware of the presence of one's confessors and of what they represent. In a moment of total awareness, sins are always present but, precisely because of this awareness, they have lost their grips. In fact, at this moment, sins have never become so obvious and present: they are what fuels one's awareness of what is seen as the only reality. Similarly, one may say that Jesus has never been so close to his Father the moment he uttered before dying on the cross: *Elôi, Elôi, lema sabachthani.*[73] For this reason I believe that what is described in chapter 2 of the *Bodhicaryāvatāra* is more than just a preliminary practice. On the contrary, it could be considered a spiritual means that is as powerful as the meditation on the concept of emptiness. Given this understanding, one may also reevaluate briefly the significance of *saddhā/ śraddhā* (faith or confidence).

i. *Saddhā/śraddhā*

As can be seen from the Buddha's response to Piṅgiya's account of his spiritual experience and of Buddhaghosa's explanation of the practice of *buddhānusmṛti,* faith appears to play an essential role in the devotional approach to enlightenment. But what exactly this role is, scholars of Buddhism have different opinions. One of the most common beliefs is probably that expounded by Jayatilleke, "Thus *belief* (saddhā) is regarded only as a first step towards knowledge, with which it is replaced. It is not valuable in itself and bears no comparison with the final knowledge, which results from the personal verification of the truth."[74] What this means is that faith is a prerequisite to an experience of knowledge. Similar to the performance of an experiment, what it is meant to prove is accepted first on the basis of faith, then, after the experiment, it is on the basis of personal experience. This view also assumes that faith is somewhat inferior to the experience of knowledge. For Sangharakshita, however, faith has a more affective connotation and as such, seems to play a more significant role despite the fact that it is still perceived as a preliminary step. Indeed, faith is "the capacity for being emotionally moved and stirred by something that transcends the senses and even the rational mind—at least for the time being. [Faith is also] the act (expressed by 'taking refuge') or state (condition of being established in the refuge) of acknowledging unquestioningly that the man Gautama, or what appears as the man Gautama, is in possession of Full Enlightenment."[75] In short, given the soteriological context propounded by Sangharakshita, faith is the very act of commitment to a spiritual practice culminating in the experience of Wisdom. It seems to me that there might be another way of interpreting the relationship between faith and the experience of knowledge.

According to Gethin, "*saddhā* is the instigator of a process which culminates in *paññā* which in turn reinforces *saddhā*."[76] In support of his affirmation, he quotes J. R. Carter: "*Saddhā* and *paññā* when taken together do not fit into "faith and reason." Rather, they express a dynamic process where *saddhā* is active in one wanting to know, coming to know in part and *paññā* becomes more pervasive in one coming to know and knowing fully, in truth."[77] This understanding of *saddhā* is, I believe, very close to what I described as the cultivation of awareness. Indeed, faith is comparable to the exercise of investigation (*vicāra*) and knowledge appears to correspond to the background revealed or created by this exercise. As such, faith is hardly to be distinguished from knowledge. In this regard, it might be interesting to quote a passage from the *Ratnalka-dhāraṇi.*

> Faith is the guide, the mother, the producer, the protector and that which increases of all virtues, expels desires, brings across the flood of passions; faith shows the city of bliss, it is the calm of the undefiled thought, firmly rooted in honor and devoid of pride. Faith is the wealth of the treasury, the best feet to walk on, it is a hand that keeps a hold on welfare. . . . Faith is not attached to the happiness that attaches, it is freed from all unfavorable states: it is the best and unique happy

state. Faith goes beyond the path of Māra, it shows the path of supreme deliverance. As a cause, faith has the undecaying seed of virtues, it causes the tree of wisdom to grow, increases the happiness of perfect knowledge.[78]

This passage bears a striking resemblance to what has been said about the significance of *bodhicitta* and *saddharma* earlier. For this reason, I believe that it is not appropriate to assimilate faith to a kind of preliminary spiritual exercise, however valuable it may appear.

There is another word, often used with *śraddhā* in connection with the practice of cultivating awareness, which might confirm what has been just said concerning the significance of faith. This word is *chanda* as in *hīne śrāvaka-pratyekabuddha-yāne adhimuktiḥ śraddhā chandaḥ vā* (trust, faith, or *chanda* in the inferior paths of the *śravakas* and the *pratyekabuddhas*)[79] or as in *saṃbodhau chandam śraddhām prāthanām praṇidhim* (desire, longing, faith, or *chanda* in enlightenment).[80] According to Apte, this term means (1) wish, desire, fancy, liking, or will; (2) free or willful conduct; (3) subjection or control; and (4) meaning, intention, or purport.[81] These translations, however, appear too general and do not seem to render the full implication of the use of *chanda* in the phrases just mentioned. In this regard, Louis de la Vallée Poussin noted that "le voeu de Bodhi (*chanda-samādhi*) est comparé à la poule qui couve son oeuf." (The vow of Bodhi is compared to a hen sitting on her eggs.)[82] The idea behind this image is that one day, the Bodhisattva, like a chick, will see the light or break through his shell.[83] What this means is that *chanda* is somehow related to a process of incubation, something similar to the activity of watching and guarding. Indeed, according to the *Patisaṃbhidāmagga*, "the meaning of chanda is to be known as root; it is to be known as basis; it is to be known as exertion; it is to be as success; it is to be known as commitment; it is to be known as taking hold; it is to be known as standing near; it is to be known as nondistraction; it is to be known as seeing."[84] As in the case of *śraddhā*, *chanda* seems to describe one aspect of the cultivation of awareness. If *śraddhā* is to be more related to the idea of confidence, as cultivated in the context of devotion, *chanda* may very well imply the notion of an ever-increasing commitment to enlightenment. In this regard, the *Vibhaṅga*, according to Gethin, describes the *chanda-samādhi* "as a concentration or one-pointedness of mind gained by making the desire to act the 'overlord' or 'dominant.' "[85] Again, this commitment ought not to be viewed as an act of will but rather as a description of what it means to tread the path of enlightenment.

4. Conclusion

Given this discussion concerning the practice of cultivation of awareness, how then is *bodhicitta* to be interpreted? *Bodhicitta*, as the desire for enlightenment for the sake of all sentient beings, is a description of one's true reality. This description is then valid for all aspects of existence, that is, there is no moment when one does not act for the benefit of all beings. The spiritual path that one has to follow is therefore simply to develop an awareness of this fact. The cultivation of such awareness, because it is an attempt to redefine the true nature of all one's actions, the bad ones as well as the good ones, brings about a feeling a detachment. From this feeling of detachment, a sense of peace of mind begins to establish itself on account of, among other things, being relieved from the responsibility of being involved in the course of one's actions. Then, if this awareness is maintained long enough, it will result in the full realization of the idea that one's actions are always performed for the sake of all sentient beings. What remains to be said at this point is how this practice of the cultivation of awareness is to be understood.

In many instances in the Mahāyāna literature, including the *Bodhicaryāvatāra*, one finds the following passage, "O great king, constantly remember, draw to your attention and contemplate the earnest aspiration, the faith, the longing and the desire for illumination, even when you are walking, standing still, sitting, sleeping, awake, eating and drinking."[86] This passage constitutes the essence of the cultivation of awareness. Indeed, three expressions or, to be more exact, injunctions should be noticed. These are remember (*anusmara*), draw to attention (*manasikuru*), and contemplate (*bhāvaya*). These injunctions are what I identified as the three aspects of the cultivation of awareness, that is, renunciation, conversion, and contemplation.

Earlier, I said that it was important to maintain an awareness of whatever the background reality might be in order to bring about its full realization. In the Scriptures, it seems that this is like a state of contemplation. In Sanskrit the words used are *dhyāna* or *samādhi*. This state is characterized by a deep calmness of the mind but it is not yet the final experience. In other words, it seems that it is not permanent and, as discussed later, one can slip away from it. This happens mainly because one pays attention again to the world most probably on account of desire, anger, or hatred.

At this moment, one has to remember what should be the true "object" of one's awareness. This is the aspect of renunciation. The basic idea underlying the aspect of renunciation is an acknowledgment of the fact that one is going in the wrong direction by paying attention, for example, to the objects of one's desires. To express that idea, the injunction *remember* seems appropriate because it always presupposes a giving up, a relinquishment, or a renunciation of what is preoccupying the mind at a given moment.

After renouncing what is preoccupying the mind, one has to redirect attention toward the true "object" of awareness. This is the aspect of conversion. *Conversion* should not be understood in the sense of "changing religion" but simply as of "redirecting attention." In order to redirect attention, it appears that one of the favored strategies of the *Bodhicaryāvatāra* is to provoke a sense of crisis or urgency. The fear to be reborn in hells, for example, is often used. This is, in brief, the cultivation of awareness that I would like to discuss in the remaining chapters.

(105)

5

The aspect of renunciation

The three aspects of the cultivation of awareness are *renunciation*, *conversion*, and *contemplation*. These expressions have been chosen because they describe three different types of activities. First, there is the idea of stepping back away from a detrimental or unskillful awareness. To use a simile, it is like pressing the clutch to release the drive shaft from the engine. *Renunciation* should therefore be understood in the sense of disengaging one's mind from whatever keeps it busy. Secondly, to use the same simile, one has to put into gear in order to move forward. Similarly, after disengaging the mind from an unskillful awareness, one has to engage it toward the beneficial or skillful awareness. Consequently, *conversion* seems to be quite appropriate in expressing this idea of engaging the mind. Finally, after having engaged the clutch, one could give gas to increase speed, and as such, *contemplation* describes everything that could be done to become more and more established in the skillful awareness. This simile is not devoid of interest because it also tells us that the more one increases speed, the harder it is to shift to a lower gear. Similarly, the more one is established in one's contemplation of the skillful awareness, the harder it is for the unskillful awareness to affect one's mind.

In addition to these types of activity, this threefold division could be justified by the fact that there also seems to be in Buddhist literature three types of discourse related to the instructions of the aspirant to enlightenment. First, there are the discourses on the causes of one's distraction from the skillful things, that is, basically that which has to be renounced in order to progress spiritually. In these discourses one is often reminded of the evil consequences of following one's unskillful or unwholesome tendencies. As a matter of fact, one finds in this context examples of literary creativity and imagination whose purpose seems to literally try to scare one off from being "possessed" by them. In the second type of discourse, one is showed the way to follow. This is most probably the role of taking vows. In this context, one is told of the benefits of converging one's mind toward making the right choice. Finally, once one has made the right choice, one is given instruction on how to hold it and, consequently, brings to fruition the promised benefits. Discourses fostering faith (*śraddhā*), in the sense discussed earlier, or intensifying investigation (*vicāra*), are given to keep the aspirant to enlightenment on the right track. What I intend to do in the following chapters is to analyze these types of discourses and their spiritual and philosophical implications. Before that, however, there is one point I would like to clarify concerning this division of the cultivation of awareness. This point has to do with the nature of the relationship between these aspects.

The fact that I argue that there are three aspects to the cultivation of awareness, does not mean that they have an independent existence. When one aspect is considered, the other two are also present, like the ideas of child and father are when one refers to a person as a mother. Take, for example, the aspect of renunciation that is expressed by the injunction remember (*anusmara*). This verb, being transitive, always refers to an object so that one can say that this injunction comprises both the activity of disengaging and engaging the mind. In other words, the injunction remember always triggers a shift of attention from one object of the mind to another. More convincingly perhaps, the activity of contemplation (*bhāvaya*) could be viewed as a more intense activity of paying attention (*manasikuru*) as well as being a form of renunciation by warding off or keeping at bay what may disturb it. These three aspects could in fact be assimilated to only one action, namely, the decision to engage or convert one's mind in a way similar to an act of faith. Let us take, for example, the decision to acknowledge that one is enlightened: this decision would be the only thing that is to be done in order to become enlightened. This may appear odd, but taking into consideration the structure of the practice of cultivation of awareness, it cannot be otherwise. Indeed, if one doubts that one is enlightened, then attention has already been distracted from the fact that one is enlightened and consequently one cannot be absorbed and transformed by it. At this point, one has to relinquish the causes of one's doubts and to redirect attention to the fact that one is enlightened, that is, to acknowledge the fact again that one is enlightened. In other words, the reason why one is not enlightened is because of one's doubts. Therefore, clearing away the doubts (renunciation) allows one to acknowledge one's reality of enlightened being (conversion) and to be absorbed by it (contemplation). In fact, not only the three aspects of this cultivation exist in dependence of each other, but also the cultivation itself is dependent on conditions for its existence or appearance. I would now like to present a simple simile to demonstrate how it can be so.

Let us take, for example, the temperature of a room regulated by a thermostat. When the room temperature is the same as the one set by the thermostat, then nothing happens. But when the temperature varies, then the thermostat reacts by sending a signal to a machine that warms or cools the room. This means that the mechanism for regulating the room temperature enters into function only when there is a discrepancy between it and the temperature set by the thermostat. Similarly, the cultivation of awareness enters into function when one becomes aware of a discrepancy between two realities at the same time. Let's provide another example: the sense of equilibrium. The function of our sense of equilibrium is to reestablish equilibrium; once this is done, it is no longer felt. In a way, this sense of equilibrium as well as the set temperature of the thermostat have the same role as that of a religious truth. Both are a means to bring about a change of state as well as its description. Similarly, a religious truth becomes a means, something that can be distinguished and appropriated, the moment when what it describes is no longer seen as the only reality. Again, let's give another simile: Let's imagine that red is the true color of reality. Certain objects are seen as red, that is, as examples of this reality; others are not. The red objects are thus pointers to this reality. This reality can, let's say for the sake of the simile, be experienced by putting on glasses with red lenses. Such glasses allow one to see everything in red. Once they are put on, what happens to the red objects? They simply disappear. They will reappear only when one takes the red glasses off. In the context of the cultivation of awareness, it is real or it makes sense only for those who are dissatisfied with their own condition. This is incidentally true for any soteriological context: it is a creation of the seekers of "salvation"; take away the seeker, that is, the one who has a desire to be saved, then there is no notion of salvation and therefore no path leading to it.

Despite the fact that the three aspects of the cultivation of awareness cannot be seen as independent entity, it is, from a practical point of view, appropriate to start our discussion with the aspect of renunciation. Indeed, it seems that for many aspirants to enlightenment the path begins with an experience of enlightenment itself. This experience that happens without previous preparation or anticipation does not usually last. In this regard, it might be interesting to relate the experience of Sri Ramana Maharshi, an Indian saint who lived in the beginning of this century. In the language of Indian philosophy, he is said to have "realized the Self"; that is to say, that he had recognized that the "Self" is the only true reality, as I would say, the background from which everything finds its meaning. It is usually said that such realization is the fruit of a long and arduous spiritual practice but in the case of Sri Ramana, it happened spontaneously, without prior effort or desire. Indeed, according to his biography, when Sri Ramana, was sixteen years old he "was suddenly gripped by an intense fear of death. In the following few minutes he went through a simulated death experience during which he became consciously aware for the first time that his real nature was imperishable and that it was unrelated to the body, the mind, or the personality."[1]

In the case of Sri Ramana, this experience was permanent, but for many others, who had a similar experience, it was a temporary one. For them, however, this experience set a new standard in terms of quality of being, to use this simile, it set the temperature of the thermostat to a new level, and, consequently, triggered an urge or desire to get rid of everything incompatible with it. This is, I believe, the real beginning of the path for the aspirant to enlightenment, that is, the search for the lost paradise accompanied by an acute sense of what is irrelevant to one's own true happiness. Again, one can see that the desire for enlightenment is not quite an act of will; it is the tension resulting from an awareness of two realities, one that is beneficial and one that is not. In this circumstance, the desire intensified, not on account of forceful motivation, but rather on account of a clearer awareness of one's acknowledged reality. I believe that this understanding of the idea of desire allows us to see the full significance of the practice of ritual.

In the previous chapters, it was said that the arising of *bodhicitta* (*bodhicitta-utpāda*) is the beginning of the spiritual career of the Bodhisattva and that, within the Mahāyāna tradition, it has been institutionalized into a rite of initiation. In this regard, one remembers that Sangharakshita argued that this rite of initiation became, in the course of time, a social event without much spiritual significance. Because of that, still following Sangharakshita's thoughts, it has to be rediscovered or replaced with something that will bring about the original attitude of the aspirant to enlightenment that is defined as the basic act of commitment to the ideals of Buddhism. This may seem plausible but again I believe that this view fails to see the full significance of the event of the arising of *bodhicitta* by assimilating it to an act of will.

The arising of *bodhicitta*, given the context of the cultivation of awareness, is the moment when one becomes aware of the fact that one's true reality is to desire the welfare of all sentient beings, that one is already a Bodhisattva. One possible way of triggering this moment of awareness is simply by being told about it. A ritual of initiation is also a way to trigger this by being an actualization of one's reality as a Bodhisattva. Consequently, a ritual hardly degenerates, as Sangharakshita seems to imply in his discussion of *bodhicitta*: what happens instead is that the aspirant fails to recognize it as a description of his true reality. In other words, it is up to each individual to make this ritual of initiation a transforming experience; it is his or her degree of participation—not his or her initial commitment—that will allow the ritual to operate a transformation. The desire to save all sentient beings becomes then a description of the state of mind of the one who has undergone this transformative experience. In fact, a ritual is like a picture, an icon of a spiritual reality that is quite stable in its material manifestations. If there is a degeneration, it is not the ritual but rather one's understanding of its significance: one forgets its transformative power, one no longer uses it as a way to acknowledge one's true reality. Therefore, rituals do not need to be changed; they simply need to be rediscovered.

The fact that one aspect of the cultivation of awareness has been called renunciation may lead one to interpret the path to enlightenment in terms of the mirror metaphor. According to this metaphor, the mind is like a mirror covered by dust, namely, the mental tendencies (*kleśas*). This view of the spiritual path, which seems to have been fully articulated in the context of the Chinese philosophical traditions including Buddhism, presupposes the existence of a pure nature in each sentient being that has to be uncovered. In this context, the notion of purification is quite appropriate and can almost be taken literally. Spiritual practices consist therefore in getting rid of these mental tendencies by whatever means possible. In the context of the cultivation of awareness and more particularly of the aspect of renunciation, the mental tendencies (*kleśas*) are not what is causing a problem to spiritual progression. In fact, mental tendencies are never a problem because the very fact that one is aware of their existence is already a sign that one is engaged in the cultivation of awareness. In other words, the *kleśas* are a means for this cultivation. In fact, they are not only a means, but also a product of the cultivation of awareness itself and as such, they have no independent existence apart from it. This is what I would like to clarify next.

i. The *kleśas* (mental afflictions) and the cultivation of awareness

While discussing Sri Ramana's spiritual experience, I mentioned that, for most of us, such an experience is temporary, that is, there is always the possibility to slip back into our afflicting states of mind, to loose awareness of the beneficial reality. It is said that the mental afflictions (*kleśa*) are the cause of this spiritual regression. Indeed:

> These powerful *kleśa*-enemies push me instantly into [the hell-fires] into which even the mount Meru does not leave ashes.
>
> Not even all my enemies have such a very long [almost] endless life-span as that of my *kleśa*-enemies.
>
> All [the other enemies] can accomplish some good if properly served. These *kleśas* are, however, causing enormous suffering if served.[2]

These *kleśa*-enemies are mainly craving and hatred (*tṛṣṇādveśādi-śatravaḥ*)[3] and are compared to the hooks of fishermen: "This hook thrown by the fishermen is like the *kleśas*; it is terrible when one is caught by it. For the guardians of hells, after bringing you to the Kumbhi-hells, will cook you there."[4] Having identified the cause of our state of misery, Śāntideva invites us to undertake a militarylike expedition against them. "I shall become an hostile fighter, a leader [in the war against all the *kleśas*]; except [against] those kinds of *kleśas* which are fighting the *kleśas*."[5] What Śāntideva is telling us in this last verse is that hatred against hatred is acceptable and legitimate. This may appear paradoxical but it is not if one takes into consideration the type of weapon that is required to fight the *kleśas*: "Where will these [*kleśas*] go, they which dwell in my mind, after having been banished from it? Where will they stand [being ousted of the place] in which they destroy me? These wretched *kleśas* are to be conquered by the sight of Wisdom. I, whose mind is slack, do not do any efforts."[6] The efforts that are required are precisely to acquire a wisdom that consists in understanding that "*kleśas* do not dwell [are not to be perceived] in objects, not in the sense-organs and not even between these two. They do not exist anywhere else. What then are these [*kleśas*], they which churn the entire world? They are illusion [*māyā*]. Therefore give up the fear in your heart and be enthusiastic for acquiring Wisdom! Why torture yourself in hells for no reason?"[7] In other words, as Prajñākaramati commented, these wretched *kleśas* have to be investigated from the point of view or with the help of the ultimate truth.[8]

I have already discussed in chapter 4 how this investigation (*vicāra*) is to be understood. I described it as the way to cultivate the awareness that what is seen (the phenomenal world) is to be perceived in terms of an idea such as that of the emptiness of all things. In other words, it is the effort to transform an idea that can be "grasped" by the mind into a "vision" of a background defining everything that can be apprehended by the mind. I also argued that this cultivation does not eliminate the *kleśas*, but rather it renders them groundless and consequently inoffensive. Now, if one begins to see the *kleśas* as groundless or as illusory, this presupposes that one is already aware of another background defining them as such. This means that the *kleśas* may be considered as the worst enemies of spiritual achievement, but the discourse on the *kleśas* itself is a good ally in one's endeavor of cultivating an auspicious awareness. In fact, the more one is aware of the *kleśas* and sees the spiritual damage they can incur, the more one becomes established in the understanding of the fact that they are groundless and consequently, the less dangerous they become. In fact, the very idea of *kleśa* is made up by the mind engaged in this awareness and, to some extent, one can say that the more *kleśa* one is aware of, the better it is. A simile may be appropriate to understand why it is so. A fallen tree in a forest is just a fallen tree. The same fallen tree on a road is a fallen tree but also an obstacle for those who travel on that road. Then, where does the notion of obstacle come from? It simply comes from an awareness of the road. It is therefore in this sense that *kleśa* is a product of the practice of cultivation of awareness. The discourses whose theme are related to the danger of the *kleśas* are to be considered as part of the aspect of renunciation because the auspicious awareness is experienced through what is to be renounced. According to the Mahāyāna tradition, it seems that it is the Perfection of patience (*kṣānti-pāramitā*) that best incorporates that aspect of renunciation as a means of cultivating awareness.

ii. *Kṣāntipāramitā* (the Perfection of patience)

Pāramitā is usually translated as "perfection," "supremacy," and "mastery."[9] In this regard, Har Dayal has discussed the possible etymology of this expression. One such etymology, which has been propounded by Burnouf in particular, states that it is derived from *pāram+ita* (gone to the other shore). This view is denied, based on a passage of the *Bodhisattvabhūmi*, on the ground that it comes from the adjective *parama* (the highest) and the suffix *tā*, a suffix used in Sanskrit to transform nouns and adjectives into abstract substantives.[10] Taking into consideration the significance of the image of reaching the other shore in Buddhist writings as well as the uncertainty of Indian etymology, I believe that these two interpretations can easily be justified. At this point, I am not as much interested in determining the exact etymology of this term as to evaluate its significance for the aspirant to enlightenment. As will be seen shortly, I am of the opinion that a *pāramitā* is to be understood in the same way as a religious truth, that is, as a means and a description of a goal to be attained. In the case of the *kṣānti-pāramitā*, it is a state of mind where there is absence of wrath[11] and anger.[12] In the case of *kṣānti* the metaphysical aspect may be less obvious than the ethical one, but, as just discussed, it would not be a Perfection if a clear understanding of the things as they are was absent. In this regard, the *Āryaśatasāhasrā prajñāpāramitā sūtra* says, "Kauśika, just as for hundreds or thousands of persons born blind who are without a guide to enter in the right road, how can they reach the city [it leads to]? Similarly, Kauśika, the five Perfections would be eyeless like persons born blind without being led by the Perfection of Wisdom; without it, not being able to enter into the right path to realization [*bodhi*], how could they reach the city called omniscience?"[13] As the text further argues, it is only when the *pāramitās* include the Perfection of Wisdom that they are fit to be called Perfections.[14] Let us see how this can be understood in the context of the Perfection of patience.

According to Vaman Shivaran Apte, *kṣānti* means (1) patience, forbearance, or forgiveness; and (2) the state of saintly abstraction.[15] In Prajñākaramati's commentary, this term is often confounded with *kṣamaḥ* or *kṣamā* (patience, forbearance, or forgiveness)[16] as in *evaṃ kṣamo bhajet* (having thus entertained forbearance),[17] and sometimes glossed as *titikṣā* (endurance, patience, resignation, or forbearance)[18] as in *yataḥ kṣāntyā titikṣayā* (therefore with patience [glossed as] *titikṣayā*).[19] Thus, the primary and fundamental connotation of *kṣānti* is to endure and consequently, not to be carried away by the *kleśas* which, in the present case, are mostly anger and hatred. In other words, *kṣānti* is a kind of remedy[20] against the disease of anger and hatred as well as repugnance (*pratigha*) and malice (*vyāpāda*).[21] According to Prajñākaramati, *kṣānti* is to be divided into three categories: (1) *kṣānti*, or endurance in the face of suffering (*duḥkha-adhivāsanā-kṣānti*), (2) *kṣānti*, or the ability to avoid responding to other people's provocation (*parāpakāra-marṣaṇakṣānti*), and (3) *kṣānti*, or endurance in one's resolve to abide to the *dharma* (*dharma-nidhyāna-kṣānti*).[22] These categories do not refer to three different attitudes but rather to three different contexts in which one's patience can be exercised.

Given this description of *kṣānti*, one may be led to view it as a cultivation of a kind of force, like that of the ascetics who are able to endure painful conditions. Indeed, this may appear as a legitimate way to interpret Śāntideva's following verses:

> There is nothing which is difficult to practice. Therefore, by practicing of little sufferings one is able to endure great sufferings.
> One should not be delicate in the face of cold, heat, rain, wind, travel, disease, capture and beating, otherwise suffering will increase.[23]

This interpretation would be true if it were not for Prajñākaramati's explanation. Indeed, according to the *Pitāputrasamāgama sūtra*, such endurance is possible not because the Bodhisattva does not feel the agony of suffering but rather because he experiences the joy (sukha) of suffering.[24] This *sukha*, as mentioned in chapter 2, is a characteristic of the state of mind of the Bodhisattva who is ready to give up even his own body for the sake of all beings. This means that, because the emotion of joy, even for unenlightened beings, is never forced, one may understand the force to endure suffering, not as something resulting from willpower, but rather as a spontaneous reaction resulting from having achieved a certain state of mind. In this circumstance, these verses from the *Bodhicaryāvatāra* are to be seen not as a pep talk to endure pain, but rather as a way to level out distinctions between phenomena. In other words, the equanimity that is to be developed by the cultivation of the Perfection of patience is not physical but mental. This explanation is, however, not without a problem: if *kṣānti* is above all a state of mind where, as just mentioned, there is an absence of anger, how then is it possible to bring about this state of mind? Does it require motivation? This is what I would like to discuss next by looking at how the mind functions according to the various clues given by the *Bodhicaryāvatāra*.

iii. The workings of the mind

In chapter 2, I discussed the idea that one's behavior is the result of one's state of mind. The passage from one state of mind to another, let us say from a mind whose main characteristic is hatred (*dveṣa-citta*) to one that is friendly (*maitra-citta*), appears to be described by expressions composed of the prefix *ut* and the verbal root √*pad*. As another example of this one finds, "Thus, I should not abandon or reject a friendly mind (*maitracittam*) towards all beings; not even a mind of repugnance or hatred (*pratighacittam*) should be produced (*utpādayitavyam*) towards the burning stick [which is used to torment me]).[25] In this regard, one may also notice the use of the derivatives of the verbal root √*cyu* that means (1) to fall or drop down; and (2) to come out of, flow, or issue from; drop; trickle; or stream forth from.[26] The verb *cavati*, for example, in Sanskrit as well as in Pāli, is especially employed to denote the passage from one state of existence to another and, as such, it is contrasted or equated to the verb *utpadati*, as in *te ca sattā sandhāvanti, saṃsaranti, cavanti upapajjanti* (and these beings run around, transmigrate, pass away, or arise).[27] Given this understanding, how is it then possible to move or be moved from one state of mind to another?

Also in chapter 2, while analyzing the various semantic applications of *citta*, I argued that this word ought to be understood in terms of the blending of the passive and the active. With this model the desire for enlightenment, for example, was explained as a state of mind whose main characteristic is to desire enlightenment. Given the implications of the Buddhist doctrine of dependent origination (*pratītyasamutpāda*), I also compared this state of mind to a living being that has to be fed to be kept alive or destroyed by starving it. I believe that this image is very appropriate to describe how the passage from one state of mind to another is brought about.

Within the context of the cultivation of awareness, this blending of the passive and the active appears to dissolve itself so that the active aspect becomes clearly distinct from the passive one. This can best be seen in what I called the dialogue between the *I* and the *me*. The *I* is the active aspect, the captain of the ship, to use a previous simile, whereas the *me*, as an object perceived by the *I*, is the state of mind that has to be changed, that is, the passive aspect that undergoes transformation. In the *Bodhicaryāvatāra* one finds a few examples of this dialogue, "I, whose mind is slack, do not do any efforts."[28] There are other examples of it that are more explicit, for instance, "If other people are happy after praising someone who has acquired merits, why, Oh mind, don't you also rejoice after praising him?"[29] Prajñākaramati paraphrases this verse thus, "Oh mind, why don't you experience the pleasure of joy?"[30]

Like the three aspects of the cultivation of awareness and the cultivation of awareness itself, the *I* and the *me* are not to be viewed as independently existing entities: the *me* only exists from the point of view of the *I* whereas the latter is only a product of the *me*; they both produce each other like the ideas of father and son. Let us just imagine a man standing in the sun who can only see his shadow. The perception of his own shadow produces a consciousness of himself. Let us further assume that his standing in the sun is a cause of suffering; then, seeing himself, that is, the shadow, will always be a sign of being in a state of suffering. Talking to his shadow, the way the *I* addresses the mind as in the previous example (or the *me*), is like talking to that which creates it. If the talking results in making that which creates the shadow move under a tree (something that is incidentally making another shadow, only this time it covers the whole ground), then the shadow disappears, and by the same token, the perception and the consciousness of it. For the one who suffers from the sun, his release is then brought about the moment his shadow becomes that which defines his whole world, namely, the shadow of the tree. In a way, it is his own shadow that guided him to the tree by not disappearing when making wrong moves, and confirmed his release by disappearing when he placed himself under the shadow of the tree. Similarly, at this point, the *I* and the *me* become without distinctions again, that is, when the cultivation of awareness (not the awareness) has ceased. In the meantime, the only meaningful action the *I* can do, after having acknowledged his new reality, as defined by *bodhicitta*, for example, is to bring the *me* to the same realization of this new reality. At first, the *I* sees that the *me* does not see the reality as he does. The way the *me* reacts is for the *I* the sign that the *me (or mind)* is behaving according to another set of assumptions. The task of the *I* becomes then to challenge the validity (or the reality) of these assumptions because they are the food that feeds the state of mind (the *me*) and that keeps it alive. If one destroys these assumptions, then one annihilates by the same token the state of mind that has been feeding on them. This idea of food is in fact given by the *Bodhicaryāvatāra* itself and I am sure that it is not exclusive.

> The food of mental affliction is entertaining what is not desired and destroying what it is; having obtained [this kind of food] hatred is seen and destoys me.
>
> That is why I shall destroy this food of my enemy because it has no other function than to kill me.[31]

In this regard, it may be appropriate to quote a passage from the *Saṃyutta-nikāya*. "Just as, *bhikkhus*, this body needs food, depends on food to exist, and without food does not exist, just so, *bhikkhus*, the five *nīvaraṇas* [hindrances] need food, depends on food to exist, and without food do not exist."[32] And again, how is this food to be destroyed? According to Prajñākaramati, it is by simply understanding that what causes it to be is not real,[33] that is to say, by investigating (*vicāra*) their true nature; such investigation is in effect to redefine them as being not real. The real cause of one's mental afflictions is therefore the absence of such investigation.[34]

So far, I have discussed the role of *vicāra* without really analyzing the implications it may have for the content of this investigation. In one of these passages, one noticed the use of the expression *paramārthataḥ* in connection with *vicāra* (n. 8). This expression usually means "according to the ultimate truth." Are we to understand that there is really an ultimate truth? I may very well begin to answer this question by giving R. M. L. Gethin's opinion on this matter:

> In the present context the discussion of the particular foods for the *nīvaraṇas* and *bojjhaṅgas* [factors of awakening] tends to dissolve

> any distinction between speculative philosophy and meditation practice. For to abandon the *nīvaraṇas* and develop the *bojjhaṅgas* is to see and understand how certain things feed the *bojjhaṅgas* and the *nīvaraṇas*. This is to know how one thing arises conditioned by another, which is, of course, to know *paṭicca-samuppāda*. [35]

What this exactly means is that whatever the content of one's investigation is, it is true, in the context of the cultivation of awareness, in so far as it produces a deepening of one's awareness of whatever one tries to be aware of. Consequently, there is no difference, in the context of such investigation, between what one may consider as true knowledge (*paramārtha*), and beliefs (not *sraddhā*) such as the doctrine of karma or the existence of the various types of hells. More specifically, in the context of this awareness from the point of view of the aspect of renunciation, knowledge and beliefs are used primarily, as mentioned earlier, to destroy the assumption that the objects of one's perception are truly existent and consequently, that their distinctions are real. Here is one example of a *paramārthataḥ* statement, "Who does hate whom? Truly (*paramārthataḥ*), the hatred which is intended, of whom is it, on account of which fault is it?[36] In this context, *paramārthataḥ* refers to the idea that everything is dependent on something else (*paravaśaṃ sarvam*).[37] Consequently, on the basis of this "fact," hatred is no longer justified.

As for the use of beliefs, the purpose is identical. In fact, it is very difficult, if not impossible to make a distinction between a belief and a "fact." A distinction can perhaps be made on the basis of the style of the discourse: when one is dealing with beliefs, one's reflection is like a fantasy that involves a lot of creativity. For example, we have seen in chapter 3 the idea that the body of one's beloved is not different from the decaying bodies in the cemetery. Another interesting example is probably the transformation of the meaning of *kalyāṇamitra*.

A *kalyāṇamitra*, within the Buddhist tradition, is a spiritual friend whose task is to help the aspirant in his progression toward enlightenment. Usually it is a master or a *guru* who is the most important *kalyāṇamitra* for the aspirant to enlightenment. The *kalyāṇamitra* is generally considered a superior being on account of his spiritual achievement and on account of his ability to help. In this regard, Śāntideva says, "One should never abandon a spiritual friend even at the cost of one's life. He is one who is preserving the vows of the Bodhisattva and who is proficient in the knowledge of the Mahāyāna."[38] These are the two qualities that qualify anyone to be a *kalyāṇamitra*. One's spiritual friend could be to a lesser extent one's colleague in the search for enlightenment; in this case, he might not be as good as the master but at least he is well-intentioned. Or, in a less obvious way, it can also be one of the Great Bodhisattvas such as Mañjuśri or Avalokiteśvara. These Great Bodhisattvas can be venerated in order to progress spiritually.[39] Therefore, if one had to classify all sentient beings in terms of their ability to help the spiritual seekers, then the *kalyāṇamitra* would be at the very top. In the *Bodhicaryāvātara*, however, this classification does not hold: even those beings, who harbor an intention to harm others, are *kalyāṇamitra*. Indeed, "those who are conspiring against me by destroying my reputation, etc., are in fact protecting me from falling into lower states of being."[40] These people are, as Prajñākaramati says, one's *kalyāṇamitra* and not one's injurer.[41] For this reason, there is no reason to hate them.[42] Similar to the *paramārthataḥ* statements, fantasy is therefore used as a way of destroying the idea that, in the case of the *kṣāntipāramitā*, someone is our enemy and even the idea that his actions are harming us. The ideas, which are in fact the manifestation of a specific way of viewing the world, are the food of the hating mind (*dveṣa-citta*). They have to be destroyed, more specifically, the view that produces them, in order to annihilate the hating mind. It would be nonsensical to achieve this result by eliminating all enemies. In this regard, Śāntideva gives an interesting simile, "Where shall I find enough leather to cover the entire earth? Just by wearing leather-shoes, the earth will be covered."[43] These leather shoes are, in the context of the cultivation of the awareness of the idea that the world is devoid of independent existence, the realization that the world is indeed devoid of independent existence. Having identified the role of the *paramārthataḥ* statements, what is then the significance of *paramārthataḥ*?

While discussing the metaphysical aspect of religious language in chapter 4, I argued that the ultimate truth (*paramārtha*) is beyond conceptualization not in the sense that words cannot say anything about the ultimate reality, but rather that, whatever it says about it is true of it but always in a partial manner. The limitations of language are therefore seen not in terms of its inability to express the ultimate reality but rather in its inability to express everything about it. Like describing a running horse, it is impossible to report everything it does at every moment, but it is possible to describe it in such a way that one distinguishes it from a running dog or a standing horse. Therefore, what is characterized as *paramārthataḥ* is something that can be viewed as a partial description of the truth that has been acknowledged or implied. Consequently, because there can be a multitude of descriptions of the truth that serves as the basis of the cultivation of awareness, there can be as well an unlimited number of *paramārthataḥ* statements. In this sense, referring back to the doctrine of skillful means (*upāya*), there can be a great diversity of truth-statements, but nevertheless these statements remain within the framework or context of what they are referring to. In a way, the great constructions of speculative philosophy are only articulations of simple ideas, like the binary system of 1s and 0s that is the basis of all the complex operations performed by my computer. These truth-statements are also comparable to the shapes a building can assume: they are unlimited from the point of view of human imagination but limited from the point of view of the properties of the material it is made of. Given the notion of the three aspects of religious truths, I would also argue that the behavior of the Bodhisattva is to be understood along the same lines: it is consistent but unpredictable or, it is limited but it is impossible to know what its limitations are.

I would like to now end the discussion of the aspect of renunciation of the cultivation of awareness. Our understanding of how the mind works, that is, how the *I* and the *me* interact is, however, not complete yet. So far, we have seen how the mind can be disengaged from the claws of the world or, to use my previous simile, to press the clutch in order to release the drive shaft from the engine. I also argued that the Perfection of patience (*kṣāntipāramitā*), as a means and a description of what it means to be in a state of disengagement, was the best embodiment of this aspect of renunciation. It remains to be seen how the mind can be engaged again into gears. This is the function of the aspect of conversion, and this is the subject of the next chapter.

6

The aspect of conversion

In the preceding chapter, I began a discussion of the idea of food whose function is to maintain a state of mind that is "alive." I showed, for example, that a hating mind (*dveṣa-citta*) could be annihilated by simply starving it. To starve a mind did not mean, however, to abstain from the food that nourishes it, but rather to come to understand, through the exercise of investigation (*vicāra*), that this food has, so to speak, no nutritive quality. Given this understanding of what it means to starve a mind, I consequently argued that the more food one views as lacking nutritive quality, the more one's awareness of the notion of nutritive quality becomes stronger. If, in the context of the aspect of renunciation, this awareness is to be developed through one's analysis of the deficient food (e.g., the *kleśas*), then, in the context of the aspect of conversion, it is now to be strengthened by looking at food that has such nutritive quality. This will be effected by paying attention to whatever is beneficial for the cultivation of awareness. What is beneficial, as in the case of the aspect of renunciation, are especially the *paramārthataḥ* statements. In other words, the aspect of conversion calls for a more intense awareness by looking directly at what reinforces one's cultivation of awareness. In the context of the aspect of conversion, the discourse is no longer about what has to be avoided, but rather, it talks about what is good for one's spiritual progression, that is, about that which ought to be one's refuge. Indeed, "so long as I have not attained perfect enlightenment, I shall seek refuge in the Buddha, the *dharma*, and the community of Bodhisattvas (the *saṅgha*)."[1]

In the context of the cultivation of awareness, to take refuge in the Buddha would be, as argued in chapter 4, to develop an awareness of his constant presence or of his spiritual virtues; to take refuge in the *dharma* is to acknowledge, among other things, the truth of emptiness and of its manifold articulations (*pratītyasamutpāda*, *sarvaṃ duḥkham*, *anatta*, etc.); and to take refuge in the community of Bodhisattvas is, I would argue, to cultivate an awareness of the fact that one is such a Bodhisattva. To some extent, the cultivation of awareness based on *bodhicitta* corresponds to the taking of refuge in the *saṅgha*. In this regard, it would be interesting to compare what Sangharakshita has to say about *bodhicitta* and its connection to the *saṅgha*: "*Bodhicitta* is more likely to arise in the case of a number of people working hard together, and stimulating and sparking one another off, rather than in the solitary individual, in whose case it may tend to be like an individual experience in the narrower sense."[2] I do not deny the importance of one's colleagues in the search for enlightenment—as mentioned in the preceding chapter, these colleagues are to some extent one's *kalyāṇamitra*—but I believe that this interpretation diminishes the spiritual significance of the *saṅgha* as one of the three Refuges. Indeed, it seems that the *saṅgha*, as the community of Bodhisattvas, is, like any other Buddhist truth, a way to describe a reality that gives meaning to everything as well as being a means to the realization of that reality. In other words, the *saṅgha* is more than just a group of people helping one another on the spiritual path, like someone would help a friend to do a particular job, but rather, as I argued while discussing the significance of rituals, it is, by becoming part of it, an actualization of what one is to become. The taking of Refuge in the *saṅgha* creates the conditions for the cultivation of awareness and as such, there is nothing more to do than to become fully aware of the reality described by what it means to be part of it. Thus, the taking of Refuge in the *saṅgha* is not only the beginning of the spiritual career of a Bodhisattva, but it is also its fulfillment.

The expressions used to bring about a conversion are usually, in Buddhist Sanskrit literature, derivatives of *manas* and √*kṛ* as, for example, *idam duḥkham mahārtha-sādhakatvāt soḍhum ucitam iti manasi kartavyam* (One ought to remember that this suffering is to be borne because it is the means to achieve the great goal),[3] or more simply, *paribhuñjatā ca evaṃ manasikāra utpādayitavyaḥ* (he who consumes [food] should remember the following [that there are eighty thousand types of worms in the body that rely on this energy for their happiness]).[4] One is also told by Prajñākaramati that "*Manasikāra* is that mind which is "fixed" on perfect enlightenment or Buddhahood [which is defined] as the intent to reach it by means of the desire to rescue all sentient beings."[5] According to Apte, *manasikāra* means perfect perception, full consciousness, mental concentration, or resolution.[6] According to the Buddhist Hybrid Sanskrit Dictionary, it means fixing in mind, mental concentration, intense attention, thought, or notice.[7] It appears then that the activity described by *manasikāra*, or any other derivative of *manas* and √*kṛ*, may show various degrees of intensity. For example, to a lesser degree, one may think about the fact that everything lacks intrinsic existence to justify that one ought not to be involved in them—at this point, it is just a simple idea, a kind of working hypothesis—and to a greater degree, one may be fully aware—here, the obviousness of this idea is beyond doubt, it is an experiential knowledge—of all the implications of the fact that everything lacks intrinsic existence. In both cases, one can say that the idea that everything lacks intrinsic existence is present in the mind.

This notion of intensity is quite crucial to understand the process of the cultivation of awareness: it explains the idea that the means is also the goal, or, to acknowledge, for example, that one's true nature is to help all sentient beings is itself the experience of the arising of *bodhicitta*. If one views this experience as a flash of light, as a kind of spiritual knockout, then it is difficult to accept the idea that deciding that one is a Bodhisattva is to become one at once. In fact, if the arising of *bodhicitta* is a change of state of mind, this change need not be a "cataclysm in one's mental organization," to use Suzuki's expression. Let us imagine that one has serious money problems. On account of this, one is consumed by anxiety. Then one learns that one is about to inherit a huge sum of money so that all debts may be paid off. Even if one does not yet have the money, one feels quite released and can even incur more debts. The very idea that one is going to inherit a lot of money is sufficient to change one's outlook on life and above all, the way one feels about a "bad" financial situation. In the same way, the decision to acknowledge certain ideas, to simply put in one's mind (*manasikṛ*) certain thoughts, already brings its results.

Although the aspect of conversion may be reduced to a simple decision or acknowledgment, as suggested by the expressions issued from *manas* and √*kṛ*, it is not devoid of difficulties. The main obstacle encountered is certainly to maintain one's attention to that which is considered beneficial spiritually. Indeed,

> The thief which is the absence of alertness, following the lack of mindfulness, will take away the accumulated merits and those who have been deprived of them will finish in one of the evil states of being.
>
> The group of thieves which are the *kleśas* are waiting to enter [in one's awareness, i.e., to disrupt the cultivation of awareness]. Once they have entered, they steal it and kill the means or conditions for the attainment of a happy state of existence.[8]

This activity (or struggle), which consists of maintaining one's attention steady, appears to be best described by *smṛti-samprajanya*, a concept that is closely related to the Perfection of discipline (*śīla-pāramitā*). In this regard, Prajñākaramati says, "Whatever practices are performed for the sake of *samādhi*, they are in harmony with or included in *śīla*. For that reason, those who wish to obtain *samādhi* ought to practice *śīla* which consists of *smṛti-samprajanya*."[9]

It appears that *smṛti* and *saṃprajanya* are descriptions of the dynamics of *manasikṛ*. Indeed, *smṛti* seems to correspond to its object: "That is why *smṛti* should never be allowed to leave the mind which is like a door. If it is gone, it has to be reestablished by means of thinking of the sufferings of the lower realms."[10] This means that a mind that is cultivating an awareness of a beneficial thought is like the door to the full realization of what it describes. If the thought leaves the mind, then the mind itself is no longer such a door and one may be doomed because of this change of mind. The reason why *smṛti* is allowed to slip away is because the container is not tight enough. Indeed, "A person who lacks alertness cannot retain what has been heard, thought about or contemplated just as a jar with a hole that leaks water."[11] Consequently, to stop any possible leak, a person must be alert and keep a constant watch on his or her mind.[12] The purpose of the discourse related to the notion of *saṃprajanya*, which is mainly found in chapter 5 of the *Bodhicaryāvatāra* (Guarding alertness), is then to constantly bring back the mind on the right track, to redirect it again and again in the appropriate direction. Indeed, "Remembering again and again the fact that I have obtained after a long time this wonderful moment, I hold this mind which is unshakable like Mount Sumeru."[13]

It seems to me that the function of the discussion related to *smṛti* and *saṃprajanya*, within the context of the *Bodhicaryāvatāra*, is to give some kind of perspective to the notion of *manasikṛ*, that is, to show its various degrees of intensity. With the idea of *saṃprajanya* one may distinguish between that which, at first sight, allows no difference between thinking about an idea and being fully absorbed by it. It appears, however, that *saṃprajanya*, which corresponds to the activity of preventing the mind from slipping away from a beneficial thought (*smṛti*), is just the beginning of this increase in intensity. There is in the *Bodhicaryāvatāra* another discourse that appears to contribute to a greater intensification of the cultivation of awareness. This discourse is mainly found in the context of the discussion of the Perfection of endeavor or strength (*vīryapāramitā*). Indeed, similar to the parallel between the aspect of renunciation and the Perfection of patience (*kṣānti-pāramitā*), the aspect of conversion seems to be best exemplified by the Perfection of endeavor. I therefore intend to show next how this Perfection contributes to the cultivation of awareness.

i. *Vīryapāramitā* (the Perfection of endeavor)

According to Apte, *vīryam* means among other things (1) heroism, prowess, or valor; (2) vigor or strength; (3) virility; (4) energy, firmness, or courage; and (5) power or potency.[14] In this regard, Franklin Edgerton, in his Buddhist Hybrid Sanskrit Dictionary, seems to combine both the idea of heroism and that of energy by translating it as heroic energy.[15] I believe that, as will be shown in the context of the *Bodhycaryāvatāra*, both connotations are justified. Indeed, courage, endeavor, heroism, energy, and strength are usually the qualities needed in the face of danger or in the face of a difficult task to perform. As such, *vīrya* could be understood as effort and perseverance. Given the multitude of rebirths a Bodhisattva has to go through before reaching enlightenment, effort and perseverance are of the utmost necessity. Referring back to D. T. Suzuki's description of the *Satori* experience, *vīrya* appears to be the only true spiritual quality that brings this experience about so that *bodhicitta*, according to him, is to be assimilated almost exclusively to effort and perseverance. In the context of the cultivation of awareness, however, I do not believe that this kind of effort, based on the distinction between a path to follow and a goal to reach, is appropriate. In this context, *vīrya*, and more particularly *vīryapāramitā*, is not to be seen as a valorization of effort or perseverance, but rather, as a means to maintain one face-to-face with whatever idea that serves as the basis of the cultivation of awareness. In other words, it is the act of facing that counts and not the annihilation of what may impede it. Similar to the *kleśas* in the context of the aspect of renunciation, awareness of what causes lack of vigor and heroism is already to have vigor and heroism. Given this understanding of *vīrya*, effort and motivation, the way they are normally understood, are consequently just skillful means to maintain a conversion of the mind toward or literally facing what is beneficial to this awareness. Indeed, doing efforts assumes an awareness of a goal or an objective; this awareness is what really brings about the transformation and not the actual efforts. This is what I intend to clarify next.

To some extent the connotations associated with the injunction remember (*manasikuru*) are very similar to that related to the idea of waking up. Indeed, in the *Bodhicaryāvatāra*, *vīrya* is seen as the remedy against lethargy or laziness (*ālasyaṃ*): "What is *vīrya*? It is an inclination towards what is beneficial. And what are its opposing factors? It is lethargy, attachment to what is contemptible, despondency and self-contempt." The causes of this lethargy are "enjoying illusory pleasure, a craving for sleep and absence of reaction when confronted to the suffering of *saṃsāra*."[16] The last cause does refer to the feeling of dissatisfaction as the real beginning of a spiritual path and consequently, as the cause of the appearance of the cultivation of awareness. Its absence is then perhaps the greatest calamity, spiritually speaking.

After having identified the various causes of lethargy, Śāntideva tries to awaken one's consciousness of the situation one finds oneself in:

> Being caught by the hunter which is the *kleśas*, you have entered into the net of rebirth. Why don't you know today that you have come to the mouth of death?
>
> Don't you see that people of your kind are systematically being killed? You are as asleep as a buffalo in the presence of a butcher.
>
> You are constantly under the surveillance of the Lord of death, without any escape. How is it that you relish enjoyments, sleep and pleasure?[17]

What Śāntideva is trying to achieve with this type of discourse is, I believe, to create a sense of crisis or urgency. Indeed,

> As you collect the prerequisites [for wholesome practice] death is to come soon. Having abandoned lethargy at that inopportune time what will you do?
>
> Thinking: "I have not achieved this," "What I have started remains half-done," you exclaim: "Oh, I am dead" when death suddenly has come.[18]

This sense of crisis is not better expressed than by the attempt to arouse fear from what is not beneficial to spiritual progression: "Your fear that you are like a live fish [about to be eaten] is appropriate. And why? Because of the intense suffering in hell for one who has done evil."[19] The reason for the creation of this sense of crisis or urgency is, on the one hand, to destroy any illusions concerning the eventual benefits offered by being attached to the phenomenal world, namely, viewing it as independently existent—this is the aspect of renunciation—and on the other hand, to leave one avenue of escape for the mind. This avenue is what is really beneficial for the spiritual progression; this is the aspect of conversion. In a way, it is like building a wall around oneself and leaving one door open in order to go out.

The more one feels cooped up by the walls, the more one is likely to have the desire to escape. It is in this sense that I previously said that awareness of what is causing a "lack" of *vīrya* is to some extent already a manifestation of it. Indeed, what causes the desire to escape as well as the knowledge of the way to escape? It is the wall; without it, there is not even a door. This is incidentally a variation of my argument concerning the role of confession that is not to be seen as a kind of preliminary practice but rather as a means of cultivating the awareness of the presence of the Buddhas and Bodhisattvas, an awareness that is as liberating as the realization of emptiness. In this regard, I would like to quote Polanyi again:

> Precatory prayers are perhaps, of all parts of religious worship, the most empty of ordinary-action significance. It might be considered remotely meaningful to feel gratitude that God is good—even though we think he could not be otherwise. But how can one presume either to advise or to plead with him to do something good for someone? Such entreaties should logically mean that we do not trust that he will know or will do what is best without our intercession. However, such prayer, in its most sincere form, is obviously a supreme act of trust.[20]

In other words, the act of mistrust that is the precatory prayer is actually one of trust. Similarly, the discourse describing one's state of lethargy and despondency, like the discourse related to the fact that one is entangled in the *klésas*, renders one immune from this kind of state as well as pointing at the way to escape permanently from them. As a matter of fact, in the present context, to be immune and escaping are two descriptions of the same thing, viewed from two different points of view, that is, the aspect of renunciation and that of conversion. Indeed: "[*Vīrya*] is self-control by means of lack of despondency, strength and cleverness. It is also the practice of exchanging or transforming of one's self with other's."[21] As mentioned before, this practice of exchanging one's self with another's is a way of cultivating an awareness of the fact that there is no difference between oneself and the others, in other words, the realization of emptiness that is the highest goal of the aspirant to enlightenment.

The sense of crisis therefore gives the right direction one should turn one's mind to. Taking into consideration the idea of intensity just discussed, it seems, however, that it is just the beginning of what one might called *vīrya*. Indeed, the first reaction from turning one's mind toward what is beneficial seems to be fear: "I am afraid at the prospect of giving up my hands and feet. The distinction between heavy and light made by me is due to my lack of investigation."[22] Again, giving one's limbs up, or more specifically, the readiness of giving them up is what it means to be a Bodhisattva and this state of being, as confirmed by the second part of the last verse, is intimately related to an understanding of how things really are, that is, as defined by the idea of emptiness. Consequently, the idea of emptiness itself can be the cause of fear. Although fear must be eventually overcome, it is not devoid of interest in the context of the cultivation of awareness. Fear has the quality, if one may say so, to make real what is not. A person who suffers from a particular phobia, for example, sees as real what is the product of his or her imagination. In other words, fear could be used as some kind of factor of intensification. The only problem with the feeling of fear is that it has a limited effect: if it is not subdued, one may run away from what causes it and then everything has to start from the beginning, namely, to bring back one's attention toward the beneficial thought (emptiness, *bodhicitta*, etc.). It is here, therefore, that *vīrya* becomes significant. Its task is to maintain a sufficient level of "strength," by investigating (*vicāra*)—not by means of willpower—that beneficial thought, that is, its various articulations and applications. To use a simile, this activity is like trying to join two magnets at their respective positive poles not by forced pressure but rather by causing a change of polarization in one of the magnets. Within the context of the aspect of conversion, this appears to be the specific function of *māna*. According to the *Bodhicaryāvatāra*, *māna* is used to help the Bodhisattva to face adversities. Indeed, "*māna* should be applied in three things: karma, minor or secondary tendencies and strength. 'This can be done only by me alone'—this is called being proud of actions."[23] In this context, *māna* somewhat means "perseverance on account of self-confidence." *Māna* can also be considered a synonym of *sthāma*, or "perseverance in what has been undertaken."[24]

Māna, however, is not without ambiguity.[25] According to Apte, it has the following meanings: (1) respect, honor, or regard, respectful consideration; (2) pride (in a good sense), self-reliance, or self-respect; (3) haughtiness, pride, conceit, self-confidence, or vanity; (4) wounded sense of honor; (5) jealous anger; and (6) opinion or conception.[26] In the spiritual context, it is often equated to one's ego and as such, it is a major hurdle to spiritual progression.

> How is it that someone is doing a work that is incumbent upon me to do. If because of my ego or egoistic attitude (*māna*) I do not do that work, it is better that my ego be destroyed.

> Led into the lower states of existence by the ego, their joy being destroyed even in human existence. They are like slaves eating from others' hands, they are emaciated fools ugly to see.[27]

In this regard, Matics also argues that pride (*māna*) has

> a double meaning with which translators find it difficult to cope. It is pride in the sense of lively spirit, respect, regard, honor, consideration of oneself and others; it is what Poussin has called "*la fierté*," "*héroïsme robuste*," and it is closely associated with *sthāman*—"station, seat, place; strength, power," a word widely used in Buddhist Sanskrit texts in its second meaning as strength or power. . . . At the same time, *māna* has the simple meaning of arrogance, of pride in the wrong and bad sense of the word, which makes others unhappy and which holds one back from progress along the Bodhisattva path. As such, it is listed in the *Dharmasaṃgraha* as one of the six evil feelings (*ṣaṭkleśāḥ*), viz., "passion, hostility, arrogance, confusion, error, and doubt." *Māna* is also included in a comparable list called "the hosts of Māra" or "the ten fetters."[28]

As can be seen from the previous passage, Śāntideva is indeed aware of the two connotations of *māna* and even makes a sort of philosophical pun with it: "Those beings who are overcome by their ego (*mānavijitāḥ*) are contemptible, not those who are self-confident (*māninaḥ*). The one who is self-confident (*manī*) is not controlled by the enemies whereas others are by the enemies such as the ego (*mānaśatruvaśāḥ*).[29] According to Matics, "no comparable use of pride exists in the religions of the world"[30] and as such, that is, in the sense of self-confidence, it "is a pervasive attribute, and when one becomes aware of it, it may be noticed as an underlying theme in many utterance of the Bodhisattva as he undertakes the great task of the emancipation of all beings."[31] In other words, *māna* is contributory to the tranquillity of the mind and as such, "it is another form of Mindfulness, of being ever-alert that the passions may not pervade the Citta, and its special stress is only that one must be quick to take remedial action whenever danger threatens."[32]

I agree with Matics that *māna* is another theme for developing mindfulness, but, as argued so far, I do not believe that it is possible that distinctions, from the point of view of the cultivation of awareness, can be made between *māna* as one's ego and *māna* as self-confidence. An awareness of both connotations is a means of cultivating awareness of the reality they are referring to. However, if one insists that there is a difference between the two kinds of *māna*, I would say that the negative *māna* is the theme of a cultivation of awareness in the context of the aspect of renunciation whereas the good *māna* is considered a means to strengthen self-confidence, that is, to face adversities, in the context of the aspect of conversion.

Given this understanding of *māna*, one can say that it is not much different from *vicāra* or to some extent, from *śraddhā*. In fact, I believe that the difference in meaning between these terms lies, not in the nature of the activity they call for, but rather in the description of their fruits or even, it is the same fruit seen from different perspectives. Indeed, one can say that, *māna* being the power to maintain an awareness of what is beneficial spiritually—like fear, desire renders real its object—*śraddhā*, the confidence issued from maintaining such awareness and *vicāra*, the discrimination resulting from it, all three are the fruits as well as the causes of an ever greater awareness of what is beneficial. In other words, the cultivation of an awareness of the idea of emptiness, for example, produces an understanding of the fact that everything is empty and this understanding could be expressed in terms of *vīrya* (or *māna*), *śraddhā*, and *vicāra*, that is, on account of this understanding one has more endeavor, confidence, and wisdom. As a matter of fact, not only those three, but also all the *pāramitās* such as *kṣānti*, *dhyāna*, *dāna*, and *śīla* could be interpreted thus. This is another way of saying that the *pāramitās* are both the means and the goal to reach and as such, they are only different ways of expressing what it means to reach it. At this point, I believe it may be appropriate to finish a discussion, begun while analyzing the significance of the Eightfold path, concerning the tendency to view the various *pāramitās* as successive stages of spiritual achievements.

In chapter 4 I argued, with the help of Tong Ba Mai and H. Saddhatissa, that the members of the Eightfold path are not to be seen as progressive steps but rather as primary as well as interdependent. Each of these members must be perfected simultaneously and as such, they are supporting each other. In this regard, Gethin seems to go a little further by suggesting that "by developing just one of the thirty-seven *dhammas* (any aspect of the four *satipaṭṭhānas*) to its full one comes to the conclusion of the path to awakening."[33] In support of his affirmation, Gethin looked at the concept of *ekâyana* discussed in the *Mahāsatipaṭṭhāna sutta* of the *Dīgha-nikāya*. In the *sutta*, one can find the following formula: "*Ekâyana, bhikkhus*, is the path for the purification of beings, for overcoming sorrow and distress, for the disappearance of pain and discontent, for the attainment of the right path, for the realization of *nibbāna*, that is, the four *satipaṭṭhānas*."[34] The interpretation of this *ekâyana* formula has been the subject of various speculations among Buddhist scholars. For one, it has been translated as "the narrow path" or the "sole, exclusive path." Gethin rejects these interpretations as inappropriate and argues that according to this formula the path is "unified, clear, well defined and single."[35] In other words, a path that is devoid of doubt. Therefore, still according to Gethin, "the four *satipaṭṭhānas* embrace a conception of the essentials of Buddhist practice that is clear and direct. In this sense, more than any other remaining sets, the four *satipaṭṭhānas* provide a description of the path right from basics direct to the final goal and are, it seems, deserving of the epithet *ekâyano maggo.*"[36] This is exactly what I meant when I said that *māna* is not much different from *vicāra* and *śraddhā*. With regard to the *pāramitās*, this idea of one for all is also confirmed in the *Bodhicaryāvatāra*. In his commentary of the first verse of chapter 9, Prajñākaramati tells us that all the *pāramitās* are considered means if Wisdom is predominant in them.[37] For the Perfection of giving (*dānapāramitā*), for example, this means to give with the knowledge that there is no distinction between a giver, a thing given, and a receiver.[38] In other words, the activity of giving is a way of cultivating an awareness of the idea that there is no intrinsic difference between a giver, a thing given, and a receiver. As such, the *dānapāramitā* is like any other *pāramitā*, even the *prajñāpāramitā*, if one understands them as means as well as description of the goal.

When one looks at other passages in the Buddhist Sanskrit literature, however, one might get another impression concerning the relationship between the various *pāramitās*. Indeed, in the *Āryaśatasāruya-prajñāpāramitā*, one is told, "Thus, O Kauśika, the Perfection of Wisdom predominates over the Perfection of giving of the Great Beings, the Bodhisattvas; it predominates over the Perfection of discipline, of patience, of endeavor and of contemplation."[39] In other words, the Perfection of Wisdom, whose nature is to investigate *dharma*, prevails over the other Perfections.[40] With regard to the relationship between the other *pāramitās*, the idea of hierarchy or steps appears then to be justified:

> Thus, the Perfection of giving is the first step or cause for attaining enlightenment because it accumulates merits as a prerequisite [is included in the prerequisite of merits]. Similarly, the Perfection of discipline serves as accompaniment during the progression towards higher states of existence. It is also the cause of the acquisition of higher knowledge and joy. The Perfection of patience, on account of being a remedy against hatred which is itself an obstacle to patience,

> also proceeds for the attainment of Buddhahood when it has accumulated the prerequisites which are the Perfections of giving and discipline. And this auspicious triad of giving, discipline and patience, which is recognized as the prerequisites of merits, cannot be without the Perfection of endeavor, which arises for the sake of destroying all obstacles on account of being the cause of the two types of prerequisites [merits and knowledge]. The Perfection of contemplation is also possible when the knowledge of the reality as such arises in the mind of him who is endowed with the Perfections [just mentioned].[41]

This idea of hierarchy or spiritual stages also seems to be confirmed by the introductory verses of each chapter of the *Bodhicaryāvatāra* dealing with the *pāramitās:*

> Having thus practiced patience, one should [work on] endeavor because enlightenment lies in vigor. There is no merit without vigor as there is no movement without wind.[42]

> Having thus developed endeavor, one should fix one's mind on contemplation because a man whose mind is unstable is like a person stuck within the fangs of *kleśas.*[43]

How is it then possible to reconcile the fact that each *pāramitā* may serve as a means to the final goal and to the idea that there appears to be some sort of progression between them where each is a prerequisite to the next up to the Perfection of Wisdom?

I believe that one may reconcile both ideas by referring again to the notion of intensity. This would mean that the practice of giving, as an exercise in contemplation of awareness, is less intense, that is, it could be practiced without being fully established in it. This is how I interpret the following verse of the *Bodhicaryāvatāra*: "With regard to [the experience of] fear [of burning from fire, etc.] and [at the time] of the ceremony [of the taking of refuge in the three jewels], if one is incapable [of maintaining a steady mind], one may relax just as [relaxation] is possible in the practice of discipline while practicing the Perfection of giving."[44] In this passage, the Perfection of giving is not really a prerequisite for the practice of the Perfection of discipline, because both are practiced at the same time, but rather, it appears as something easier to practice or to relate to as a means of cultivating awareness. As just mentioned, it is also on the basis of the notion of intensity that I distinguished between the three aspects of the cultivation of awareness. While *kṣānti* corresponds to the aspect of renunciation and *vīrya*, to the aspect of conversion, *dhyāna*, the Perfection of contemplation, is what best described the aspect of contemplation with the assumption that this aspect contributes to a more intense cultivation of awareness. Before discussing this last aspect, however, there is one point I would like to clarify with regard to this idea of intensity.

The notion of *puṇya* and *pāpa* usually refers to the idea of accumulation of merits and demerits. Within the context of the cultivation of awareness, however, this idea of accumulation is still appropriate but it has to be complemented with that of direction. We have already seen that the mind can either be turned toward what is beneficial spiritually or away from it. When one's mind is turned toward it, it can be said that one is accumulating *puṇya*, away from it, *pāpa*. This means that *puṇya* and *pāpa* are not really two different things, but rather, they are the same thing viewed from two different directions. Indeed, accumulation of *puṇya* is elimination of *pāpa*, and elimination of *puṇya* is accumulation of *pāpa*. To give an idea of the exact interaction between the ideas of accumulation and direction, I would like to give a simile. Let us imagine that one is traveling on a road joining two countries. When one arrives at the border, one can see a sign on which one may read: Welcome to X and Thank You for Visiting Y. Once the border is crossed, one can see on the back of the same sign the following: Welcome to Y and Thank You For Visiting X. Such is the line between *puṇya* and *pāpa*. This simile may be further exploited. Once one has crossed the border and gone deeper into country X, one is likely to undergo some transformations: learning new habits, a new language, and possibly losing the old one. The deeper one goes into country X, that is, losing more and more contact with country Y, the more one assimilates what is characteristic of country X, the more intense and thorough is one's experience of this country. Similarly, an accumulation of merits can be understood as a kind of intensification of one's experience of cultivation of awareness. It is in this sense that I believe that the metaphor of *puṇya* and *pāpa* has to be viewed: in terms of both the ideas of accumulation and direction.

With the aspect of conversion, we have seen what it means for a mind to engage itself again. It is basically by turning it toward what is beneficial for it. This action of turning is a simple one; the difficulty comes when one tries to maintain it in the right direction. The efforts required for maintaining it are, however, not a product of motivational strength or willpower but rather the result of cultivating an awareness of an idea that gives it no reasons to turn away and all the reasons to stay put. This idea and its fruits are the beneficial food of the mind. In a way, the food of the mind and the mind itself are the same thing: similar to the distinction between the *I* and the *me*, the distinction is made on account of the feeling of hunger, namely, the sense of dissatisfaction and consequently, it is an illusion from the point of view of a state of perfect satisfaction.

7

The aspect of contemplation

What has been said thus far about the workings of the mind suggests a model very close to that of cybernetics. Basically, this model explains how a system maintains its structure by means of controlling its feedback. The thermostat used as a simile in chapter 5 is such a system that tries to maintain its structure, that is, to maintain a room temperature at a constant level. Similarly, the mind that is in contact with the phenomenal world reacts to it. What defines the nature of its reactions is the way in which it perceives this phenomenal world. If it is perceived as something truly existent, specific reactions will be triggered that in turn are likely to reinforce the idea that the world is truly existent. This is the positive feedback with regard to a mind centered on the idea based on a perception of the phenomenal world as truly existent. This same mind, however, may accept a new constant, like fixing a new temperature for the thermostat, defined in terms of the idea that the phenomenal world lacks intrinsic existence or that it is interdependent. At first, the acceptance of this new constant is likely to create a situation of tension with the already accepted assumption. Both constants are in fact mutually exclusive and what is positive for one is negative for the other and vice versa. In other words, the reactions issued from the idea that the world is interdependent is a negative feedback for the assumption that it is truly existent. These reactions are therefore the food of the mind discussed previously. The cultivation of awareness is consequently to maintain an awareness of a new constant and the practice will intensify on account of the positive feedback reinforcing it.

Given this understanding of the workings of the mind, one can see what causes this awareness to occur: it is precisely the tension that results from an awareness of the two constants that creates it and brings it into function. At this point, it has to be clear that one is not really dealing with two different awarenesses. Indeed, when one is acting, for example, in conformity with the idea that the phenomenal world is truly existent, one is not really aware of this idea. But when one has an awareness of it, one is also aware of what negates it or at least, of the possibility that it can be negated. That is why an awareness of the two constants is already a sign that the cultivation of awareness has started. Conversely, when one is not engaged in it, then no awareness is present in the mind. That also explains why the *kleśas*—the very fact that one uses the term is a sign of awareness—are a means to this cultivation. As a matter of fact, it cannot be otherwise because, as already mentioned, the *kleśas* are themselves a creation of the mind engaged in this awareness.

It might be interesting to open a parenthesis with regard to the implications of the parallel between the workings of the mind and the model of cybernetics. It has been fashionable to draw such parallels between the ideas of modern science and religious truths. Fritjof Capra, in his book *The Tao of Physics*, has, for example, compared the discoveries of quantum physics with some of the insights of Hinduism and Buddhism. The assumptions behind such parallels were that the spiritual traditions of Eastern mysticism, with their particular means of investigation, reveal the same truths or laws discovered by modern science. In other words, the parallels were made from the point of view of the presuppositions of science, namely that there are laws that are truly existent and that can be discovered. If one draws the same parallel, this time from the perspective of the presuppositions of religious thinking, then one has to say that our scientific knowledge is a creation of the mind. The reason why we know something is because we feel that something has to change. The desire for change creates or reveals a knowledge that would eventually result in bringing about the desired change and maintaining the newly created situation changeless. Therefore, contrary to Capra who argues that religions are doing science, I would say that science is religion. In other words, the distinction between discovery and creation is not as sharp as one may usually assume.

It seems that the cultivation of awareness also functions like an exponential equation, that is, its rate of intensification is not constant but it increases every time new positive feedback reinforce the awareness. Similar to population growth, every time people are born, the rate of growth increases. The idea that awareness increases exponentially is what characterized the aspect of contemplation. More specifically, it explains what happens at this point and the explanation itself is a feedback that intensifies the cultivation of awareness. This is what I will consider next. Before that, however, I would like to show how one can view this awareness from the perspective of the aspect of contemplation.

To come back to previous discussions, what is of concern here is what it means to watch and guard, or what exactly is being watched and guarded. We have seen that the aspect of renunciation is whatever it takes not to be disturbed from this activity and that the aspect of conversion corresponds to turning one's mind toward what is to be watched and guarded. This activity, even from the point of view of the aspect of conversion, is not to be conceived of as fixing one's mind onto an object. In this regard, it might be interesting to quote Herbert V. Guenther who wrote on the subject of the mind in the context of Buddhist psychology:

> Nowadays, some people who take the Buddha's words out of context and make a display of meditation, meditate by concentrating on what appears before their visual perception, but Asanga has stated very clearly that concentration does not take place in sensory perception but in categorical perception, and the objective reference is not the visible object that is present in sensory perception, but its precept.[1]

Furthermore, he added that the "specific function of intense concentration is said to provide a basis for an awareness in which one has a state of mind settled in itself, (a mind) taking every individual aspect of the perceptual situation as it is and never occurring in a vacuum, even though attention may shift within this perception (from one aspect to another)."[2] These comments confirm, I believe, what I argued in chapter 4 concerning the nature of the content of one's awareness in the context of this awareness. What one is watching and guarding, to use Polanyi's words, is a focus awareness, the tacit knowledge from which every object of one's perception finds its meaning. In fact, this point should not be too hard to figure out. If one sees somebody as a father or a mother, for example, what is characterized by the word *as* is the focus awareness and it does not change regardless of the situation or the transformations, like aging and even dying, of the person characterized as the father or the mother. To fix one's mind onto or to hold to the idea of emptiness therefore is to "see" the world as empty and in practice it means to constantly "pay attention" to, or be aware of, the implications, assumptions, and so forth of what is characterized by the word *as*, that is, emptiness. With reference to the practice of devotion or to what is identified as such within the various spiritual traditions, one can understand this idea of focus awareness by looking at the implications related to the use of the preposition *with* as in "X is with Y." The truthfulness of this statement does not depend on some kind of objective observation like the position or the distance between the persons designated as X and Y, but rather, on X's subjective understanding of what it means to be with Y. Even when, for example, Y dies, X can still argue that "Y is with me." In fact, the permanent absence of Y may be for X the occasion to cultivate a more intense feeling of Y's presence, a presence that is, however, felt in a different way. In this circumstance, one can easily see how certain objects or events, which are insignificant for the majority of people, reinforce this impression of the presence of the other without being the other. It goes without saying that this impression of the presence of the other has a direct consequence on how the person who entertains such impression feels and behaves. This is again the reason why I do not really see a substantial difference between what is called devotion and meditation. Again, it does not also make sense, at least from the point of view of this awareness, to consider devotional practices for instance, as a prerequisite to the meditation of emptiness.

The model of the workings of the mind would not be completed if we were not to add another important element. Taking again the simile of the thermostat maintaining a constant temperature, let us imagine that at this very temperature certain things occur. For example, a plant may find the optimal condition of its growth or there may be a chemical reaction such as fermentation. These reactions happen because the temperature is maintained at the right level. With regard to the cultivation of awareness, this means that its spiritual fruits such as absence of fear and compassion occur, so to speak, by themselves. The idea of seed, which is dear to the ancient Buddhist philosophers, is in this context very appropriate. In this regard, I would like to quote Gethin's concluding remarks concerning his study of the *bodhi-pakkhiyā dhammā*, in the context of the *Nikāya* and *Abhidhamma*:

> . . . . the ordinary mind is not to be understood as uniform in character. In fact the ordinary mind is very complex and very subtle; it is of many different kinds; it has many different and contradictory tendencies. Some of these kinds of mind and some of these tendencies are more useful than others in trying to wake up the mind. Some kinds of ordinary mind actively perpetuate the sleep of the defilements, while some kinds of ordinary mind actually approximate rather closely to the waking mind itself. In other words, some states of mind, some tendencies are to be cultivated, other are to be curbed. The task, then, is to maximize these *kusala* or "skilful" tendencies, to use the technical terminology of the texts. How does one go about this? The

> problem is that in ordinary everyday states of mind, while these skilful tendencies may often arise, they are always in danger of being crowded out. . . . we must attempt to still the mind—we must practise calm (*samatha*) and concentration (*samādhi*). . . . in calm, still states of mind the natural "skilful" tendencies of the mind tend to come into their own—they naturally grow and strengthen, and the mind becomes clearer.[3]

The last sentence means that the idea that serves as the basis of the cultivation of awareness becomes a more obvious description of what is perceived by the mind. It is for this reason that it is possible to argue that the world is a creation or a product of the mind only. Indeed, according to Candrakīrti's *Madhyamakāvatāra sūtra*, "the world of beings and the world of objects are made by the mind alone. It is said that the whole universe is born out of acting (karma) and without the mind, karma is not."[4] In other words, the mind creates itself the conditions of its survival and of its growth. A hating mind, not only imagines a world that justifies its hatred but reorganizes it as real, on account of its actions or reactions, so that it may prosper. Once such a mind is engaged in this dynamics, there is no limit to what it can do. If this dynamics does not lead the hating mind to the destruction of what supports it, that is, the physical body, it may stop spreading death the moment it sees, by a kind of sudden insight, as it was the case in Aśoka's conversion, that this dynamics or vicious circle is leading to self-destruction. At this moment, the description of hells one can find in the *Bodhicaryāvatāra* is small potatoes. This is for many the beginning of psychological and spiritual recovery.

I believe that, given Gethin's explanation of the *bodhi-pakkhiyā dhammā*, it might be appropriate at this point to finish my discussion of the meaning of the title of Śāntideva's work, that is, *Bodhicaryāvatāra*. In chapter 1, I discussed the meanings of *bodhi* and *avatāra*. With regard to *bodhi*, it refers to the goal of the Mahāyāna aspirant. It could be translated as "enlightenment" or "awakening." At this point it is not important to determine which translation is the most appropriate; suffice it to say, however, that *bodhi* as the goal of the Bodhisattva, taking into consideration what has been argued so far concerning the nature of religious language, is also a description of what it means for a Bodhisattva to realize it. In other words, *Bodhisattva* refers both to a being in search of *bodhi* as well as a being who has realized *bodhi*. Consequently, *bodhi* may refer to all the spiritual qualities or *pāramitās* of the accomplished Bodhisattva. Indeed, Bodhisattvas are described as those beings whose minds are centered on arranging the happiness of all beings.[5] This is, as often mentioned, the means and the goal of the spiritual approach of the Bodhisattva.

Concerning *avātara*, I argued that it may refer to a kind of passage from one mental state to another. It is like stepping into a stream or setting foot on the path leading to *bodhi*. If this word can be translated as "introduction," then it has to be understood in its more literal sense, namely, the act of putting in or the state of being into something. Given Gethin's understanding of the *bodhi-pakkhiyā dhammā*, I believe that this interpretation of *avatāra* is still appropriate. *Caryā*, then, remains to be analyzed.

I think that it should be quite obvious at this point that *caryā* is the path or the stream to *bodhi*. It is not a path where spiritual progression depends on one's efforts or motivation. It is rather a state of being or a mental state in which, as Gethin just said, "the natural 'skilful' tendencies of the mind tend to come into their own," in which "they naturally grow and strengthen." If efforts are required, it is to maintain that skillful state of mind. In other words, *caryā* does not refer to a spiritual path in the usual sense of the term, that is, having rules to follow, spiritual exercises to practice, stages to aim at, and so forth, but rather to a place to reside on account of which enlightenment is assured. It would certainly exceed the scope of the present work, but I believe that it might be interesting to compare the notion of *caryā*, in the sense just mentioned, with that of *buddhakṣetra* (Buddha-fields) or that of Pure lands. Indeed, the *buddhakṣetra* is considered a place where the path to enlightenment can be best practiced and where enlightenment itself is even assured.

There are a few passages in the *Bodhicaryāvatāra* itself that confirm the understanding of *caryā* as just suggested. In the chapter on *kṣānti*, it is said: "Thus if I retaliate towards [those who are tormenting me], this will not protect or help them. Such conduct will undermine my own *caryā*; that is why they, the unfortunate ones, are destroyed."[6] The meaning of this verse is that people who are tormenting the Bodhisattva are in fact helping him in his practice of the Perfection of patience. Conversely, however, retaliation, that is, to return evil for evil, will not help them at all. On the contrary, this course of action will destroy them. The point I want to make here is that *caryā*, as the practice of the Perfection of patience, is another word for the cultivation of awareness. *Caryā*, as the course of conduct of the Bodhisattvas,[7] is sometimes translated as *ācāra* (conduct, behavior, or observance).[8] Consequently, one may note the following verse: "The various *pāramitās* like *dāna*, etc., are graded as one being superior to the preceding ones. The lower *pāramitā* should not be abandoned for the sake of the superior one because [all *pāramitās*] are comparable to a dam (*ācārasetutaḥ*)."[9]

What Śāntideva means by this simile is that *ācāra*, which is the practice or observance of the Perfections (*śikṣāsaṃvaralakṣaṇaḥ*), is a dam that holds the skillful tendencies that are here characterized by water.[10] As can be seen from this last example, *śikṣā* also designates the behavior of the Bodhisattva or his practice and, similar to *ācāra*, it has to be protected: "on account of attending to *bodhicitta* and of protecting or guarding the rules of conduct or the practice [of the Bodhisattva], I should increase the skillful tendencies."[11] At this point, it could be argued that *śikṣā-saṃvara-rakṣaṇa* simply means to follow a set of rules of conduct the same way one would do to accomplish a task, in other words, an activity involving motivation and guidelines to follow. This would be true if it were not for the fact that the resolve to follow the Bodhisattva's rules of conduct is preceded by the grasping of *bodhicitta*.[12] The fact that the arising of *bodhicitta* is a prerequisite to the practice of the Bodhisattva's rules of conduct leaves no doubt as to the nature of this practice. In other words, because *śikṣā* is preceded by *bodhicitta-utpāda*—the latter being the beginning of one's engagement into the cultivation of awareness—it is, as well as *caryā* and *ācāra*, to be considered as a fruit of this cultivation of awareness, as the sum of all the skillful tendencies. Consequently, *śikṣā-saṃvara-rakṣaṇa* is the cultivation of awareness. Thus:

> Just as the Buddhas of ancient times have got hold of *bodhicitta* and just as they remained afterwards well-established in the practice of the Bodhisattvas, likewise I will be the one who will cause *bodhicitta* to arise for the sake of the universe, likewise also, I will practice or follow the practice of the Bodhisattva properly or in proper order.[13]

In other words, to maintain an awareness of *bodhicitta* is the same as cultivating it because it allows the skillful tendencies to do their work. At this point, I believe that it might be appropriate to say a word about what these skillful tendencies are.

These tendencies are also called the roots of happiness (*kuśalamūla*) as in "Then it is said, O king, that you, who have a lot to do, will raise among the gods on account of ripening the root of happiness which consist of and are leading to perfect enlightenment."[14] This passage, which, according to Kamalaśīla's *Bhāvanākrama*, comes from the *Āryarājāvavādakasūtra*, is the continuation of the one I quoted in chapter 4 in support of the idea of having three aspects to the cultivation of awareness. This latter passage is preceded by the following: "Because you, O king, who are busy and have a lot to do and unable to practice the Perfections of giving up to that of

Wisdom, [constantly remember, draw to your attention and contemplate. . . .]"[15] How is it then that the king is advised to abandon the practice of the *pāramitās* for the sake of cultivating an awareness of the desire of enlightenment? I have just said that the practice of the *pāramitās*, which is the cultivation of awareness, are what allows the roots of happiness or the skillful tendencies to develop; there is therefore a contradiction. In other words, if the skillful tendencies are the spiritual qualities described by the *pāramitās*, that is, readiness to give, discipline, patience, endeavor, calmness of mind, Wisdom, and so forth, why should the king forsake the practice of what leads to the development of these spiritual qualities to acquire these same qualities? The only explanation I can give is that the intention of this passage is not to incite someone to abstain from the practice of the *pāramitās*, but rather to challenge a misunderstanding of what it means to practice them. And what is the nature of this misunderstanding? It is to assume that the practice of the *pāramitās* precedes the arising of *bodhicitta*. Given this view, the practice of the Perfections is not the *caryā* that was just discussed in which one ought to enter or step into. It can only be a practice that reinforces a dualistic notion of the spiritual path, that is, the idea that there is a doer and something to be done. Indeed, this passage is used by Prajñākaramati to discuss the significance and the implications of the two types of *bodhicitta*: "There are great merits in *saṃsāra* for him who has an aspiring mind; they are not, however, as uninterrupted as the flow of merits produced by him who has an engaging mind."[16] In other words, one has to convert one's mind (*praṇidhi*) toward *bodhicitta* so that the skillful tendencies produce their effect (*prasthāna*) and not the other way round. Moreover, the difference between *bodhipraṇidhicitta* and *prasthānacitta* is again a question of intensity. Indeed, *bodhipraṇidhicitta* can be the fact of taking the decision to acknowledge the reality described by *bodhicitta*, whereas *prasthānacitta* is to maintain the awareness of what has been acknowledged. They are therefore not meant to distinguish two different types of practice. Consequently, I believe that if a distinction is made, as done in this passage, between the practice of the *pāramitās* and the cultivation of an awareness of the desire for enlightenment, it is for the sake of challenging the idea that the practice of the *pāramitās* may precede the arising of *bodhicitta* and, by the same token, the assumption that this practice depends on one's efforts and motivation.

While discussing those skillful tendencies, we should not assume that they have an independent existence; on the contrary, similar to the idea of the *kleśas*, they are a creation of the mind engaged in the cultivation of awareness. This means that the awareness of these tendencies is a description of such mind as well as a means to its existence. In other words, one cannot speak about these tendencies if one is not experiencing them, and speaking about them is a means to cultivate one's awareness of them and consequently of the underlying idea giving them their signification. In this circumstance, it might be "more objective" to describe what they do instead of what they are.

As mentioned before, one of the key ideas to understand the cultivation of awareness is that of intensity. As already explained, it accounts for the hierarchy among the *pāramitās* as well as the nature of one's spiritual endeavor. In the context of the *Bodhicaryāvatāra*, this idea is not explicitly mentioned. Instead, one finds the notion of purification. Thus,

> Having taken this impure form, it [*bodhicitta*] transforms it into the priceless form of a *Jina* [an accomplished Bodhisattva]; it is like a gold-making elixir. So, hold fast to what is called *bodhicitta*.
>
> Like the fire at the time of the great dissolution, [*bodhicitta*] burns away the great sins in one moment. Its immeasurable praise was made by the wise Lord Maitreya to Sudhana.[17]

What is implied in these two sentences is that *bodhicitta*, or the cultivation of an awareness of what *bodhicitta* means, has the power to purify sins or what is the cause of one's suffering. Moreover, this purification is not gradual but instantaneous (*kṣaṇena*). How can it be so? This awareness, at its very first beginning, is comparable to turning on a light on a new reality where *kleśas* or sins become visible at once. That is why I argued before that it is not possible to see the *kleśas* without the spotlight of this awareness. I also said that the fact that one sees them, one is immune from their influence. Being caught by the *kleśas* always presupposes losing sight of them. Even the idea of being caught is not appropriate because the moment one is aware of being caught by them, one is no longer caught; and when one is really caught, then one is not in a position to say: "I am caught." That is why it is possible to say that purification is instantaneous: the transition between awareness of *kleśas* and lack of it does not admit degrees. This is another way of saying that the cause of enlightenment is the decision to acknowledge that one is enlightened. If purification is sudden, how can it be equated to the idea of intensification, as just mentioned?

What is intensified is not the purification but the ability to remain in the state of purification. Purification is perhaps instantaneous but the state of mind that allows it may be reversible. In other words, this awareness, even at a very deep stage of contemplation, is never secured before one reaches the moment when one is no longer aware that one is aware, that is, as long as one knows to be engaged in the cultivation of awareness. Before that moment, however, it still remains a nice place to be, happy with one's sins, where one experiences peace of mind and joy in the midst of the big storm produced by the *kleśas.* In other words, this place to be is like a shelter, a refuge, an island, and so forth. Indeed, "Having committed the most abominable sins one escapes instantaneously on account of taking refuge [in *bodhicitta*], as someone finds shelter by a strong man in the face of great dangers. Why is it not, then, resorted to by ignorant beings?"[18] The idea of purification therefore does not refer to a process, but rather to a state of mind or a state of being whose characteristic is peacefulness and joy on account of an awareness of one's sins and *kleśas.* This means that purification of the mind, as referring to a gradual process eliminating the causes of suffering, is not to be taken literally but as a skillful means (*upāya*). Indeed, if one bows a hundred thousand times in front of the Buddha, it is not the bowing that is likely to purify but rather the awareness of the Buddha one is bowing to. Similarly, the desire for enlightenment based on one's efforts and motivation can be beneficial if it allows one to maintain an awareness of what it means to reach the desired goal; but it is not, if one is only aware of one's efforts or the necessity to do them. This distinction is perhaps very subtle but it makes all the difference.

At this point, it might be difficult to say more about the aspect of contemplation of the cultivation of awareness. In this process, being comparable to that of incubation, there is not much to see for an external observer. We are like one sitting in front of an egg waiting to see it hatch. Because we assume that it will hatch, we also presuppose that something is happening in the egg from the moment it was laid by the hen. This assumption is also the basis of my idea of intensity to explain this awareness. Thus, I wonder if this explanation of this process and consequently, of the path to enlightenment, namely, what I believe to be the appropriate soteriological context, could not be recycled into a means of cultivation of awareness. Once again, the line between creation and discovery, subjectivity and objectivity, is very thin. Also thin is the demarcation between the descriptive and the performative nature of language. The view concerning the nature of religious language I suggested in chapter 4 was therefore an attempt to show how it is still possible to maintain a hope for efficacy despite the fact that the basis of what gives us a certain degree of confidence in our actions has been challenged. In other words, even if our understanding of reality is a creation of the mind, it nevertheless remains real as long as one feels that there is a problem to solve. Therefore, there is no problem without solution, or knowledge of a problem is not possible without some degree of awareness of its solution. The Wright brothers asked why instead of how birds fly, modern aviation was born. The most sophisticated airplanes of today are still based on the solution given to this simple question. In other words, the moment the question was asked, some degree of awareness of the principles of aerodynamics evolved. In fact, the question did not reveal the new awareness; it is rather the new awareness that produced the question. That is why it appears that religion, as well as science, are more concerned with understanding problems and their implications than elaborating solutions. Consequently, subjectivity refers to the fact that there is no problem without a subject and objectivity emerges the moment more than one subject share a problem. At this point the efforts done by the subjects to understand the very problem they share is likely to result in the creation of what we identify as scientific or religious knowledge.

Before ending this chapter, there is one last point I would like to discuss. Referring back again to the previous passage taken from the *Āryarājāvavādaka sūtra*, after the king has been introduced to the cultivation of awareness, his interlocutor adds,

> [constantly remember, draw to your attention and contemplate. . . .] Do rejoice, after having accumulated and maintained [or supported] the roots of happiness, of past, present and future times, belonging to you and to all Buddhas, Bodhisattvas, Aharants, solitary Buddhas and non-Buddhist people. After having rejoiced with the best of joy, offer acts of worship to all Buddhas, Bodhisattvas, solitary Buddhas and Aharants and having offered acts of worship, practice equanimity towards all beings. Then, in order that all beings may obtain omniscience which is the fulfillment of the *dharma* of all Buddhas, mature in unsurpassed perfect awakening everyday at all three times of the day [that is, always].[19]

The first part of this passage quite obviously refers to the experience of entering the first *bhūmi* called *pramuditā*. Indeed, after having told us that *bodhicitta* has somehow arisen in him, Śāntideva says, "Today the universe is invited by me to this joy [or happiness experienced] by the Buddhas in the presence of all the Protectors. May all gods and demons (*asūras*) rejoice."[20] This experience is elsewhere described in a more colorful way,

> The Bodhisattvas become the sons of the Buddhas and appear before them with [or on account of] all their skillful tendencies. As

> such, they are standing in the spacious, fragrant and cool lotus [a place where Wisdom, compassion, happiness, etc. are the characteristics of the mind], their splendor nourished by the sweet speech of the conquerors and with their true body issued from the lotus of enlightenment created by the Sages.[21]

The experience of joy, being one of the main characteristics of the first spiritual stage of the Bodhisattva, the injunction *anumodayasva* (do rejoice!) is to be considered more as a description of this spiritual experience than as an invitation to do specific actions. Similarly, the second part of this passage ought to be understood as being a description of what happens when a Bodhisattva-aspirant becomes a Bodhisattva-son of the Buddha and not as a prescription to perform acts of worship (*pūja*). These acts are indeed expressions of gratitude, a kind of thanksgiving rather than ordinary acts of offering. I believe that if such acts of offering were intended in this passage, it would not make sense to mention them following the experience of joy just described. The same reasoning applies to the third part of the passage where one is enjoined to mature in unsurpassed perfect enlightenment. The term translated by mature is *pariṇāmaya*. According to Edgerton, this verb means to ripen, mature, develop, change into,[22] or in its substantive form (*pariṇāmanā*): change, alteration, ripening, or development.[23] This word is one of the six forms of *pūja* performed by the Buddhists and as such, it has been interpreted as "transfer of merits."[24] According to Sangharakshita, that "would be the climax of the preliminary devotional practices."[25] In the present context, however, this interpretation would not be appropriate for the reasons just mentioned. It is also used as the title of the last chapter of the *Bodhicaryāvatāra*, thus giving the impression of some kind of finale. This means that the transfer of merits is more than just a form of devotional practice; it is also a description of the behavior of the accomplished Bodhisattva. Given this understanding, it appears that the injunction *pariṇāmaya* refers not to a process but rather to its result. In other words, the intention of the passage is to say: be like a mature fruit, that is, available to all for their benefits. This is the consummation of the cultivation of awareness. At this point, even awareness of the cultivation of awareness vanishes. Indeed, does a Bodhisattva know that he is one who provides some benefits to others? It seems that he is not; it is his nature to be so, "Monks, for one whose body is calmed, there is no need to think, 'I feel happiness.' This, monks, is in conformity to the nature of things (*dhammatā esā*) that one whose body is calmed feels happiness."[26]

As it is probably for the nature of all things:

So also the element water does not think as follows: I provide sufficient moisture to the seed. The element fire also does not think as follows: I ripen the seed. The element air also does not think as follows: I scatter the seed away. The element space also does not think as follows: I do the work of protecting the growing the seed from any hindrances. And the element season does not think as follows: I do the work of maturation of the seed.[27]

Conclusion

There is one story, taken from the *Lieh Tzu*, a Taoist text compiling the thoughts of Lieh Tzu, the alleged teacher of Chuang Tzu, which, I believe, gives a good idea of the definition of the cultivation of awareness. The story goes as follows: a man lost his ax. He suspected his neighbor's son and began to observe him. He believed that, judging from his appearance, he was an ax thief; his facial expression was that of an ax thief; his way of talking was exactly that of an ax thief. All his movements, all his being was distinctively expressing the fact that he was an ax thief. Some time afterward, this man, digging in his garden, found his ax. When he saw his neighbor's son again, all his movements, all his being had nothing more of an ax thief.

When one looks at the phenomenal world, one's reality always comprises objects and a background that defines them. In the case of our man in this anecdote, the background is the conviction that his neighbor's son is an ax thief. His observations are only reinforcing his conviction. This conviction has, however, been destroyed instantaneously when he found the "stolen" ax in his garden. At this moment, has he really found the "stolen" ax, or is it the "lost" ax? Would our man ever search for a "stolen" ax? In our story, the man was lucky to find it by chance. But let us imagine that another neighbor had convincingly established the fact that his neighbor's son cannot possibly have stolen the ax, that it is even impossible that his ax could have been stolen so that it must be lost or misplaced. The moment our man accepts this eventuality as a true fact, he starts looking for the "lost" ax. His conviction will then determine his behavior and attitude. Now, let's assume that our man's ax is really lost. With regard to his conviction, one can say that the reality of the "founded" ax is also present in his mind. This reality does not tell him where to find it nor when it will be found: it only sets into motion an appropriate behavior that will eventually lead him to find his ax. In this regard, the path to enlightenment is often compared to following the directions of a map. I believe this analogy is inappropriate because the way one takes to reach the goal is unpredictable. Again, a conviction, or the acceptance of a reality as true, only brings about the favorable conditions for the expected result to occur; these conditions, however, could be anything. Their function is to lead to the expected result, but in what way? Simply by being a true description of the initial conviction. In other words, whatever way one takes, it always reinforces one's "conviction of reality." If it does not, then there is not even a path and a goal to reach. It is to this kind of radicalism that the process of cultivation of awareness introduces us: the beginning of the path is the end and one can never stand in between because the distinction between the beginning and the end presupposes another conviction incompatible with the one to reinforce. One can never dwell in two incompatible convictions at the same time. In fact, to talk of two convictions reveals that one is already established or aware of the liberating conviction whereas the one who acts on the assumptions of a conviction leading to suffering does not see any alternative at all. This awareness is therefore very much comparable to a mirror maze: before entering it, one does not see oneself, while being in it, one's own reflection can be seen, and when coming out, it disappears. In the context of the *Bodhicaryāvatāra*, this phenomenon corresponds to what I described as the dialogue or perhaps more appropriately, the monologue between the *I* and the *me*.

To understand the dynamics of this awareness, I quote a short passage taken from the *Āryarājāvavādaka sūtra*. Again, this passage goes as follows, "O great king, constantly remember, draw to your attention and contemplate the earnest aspiration, the faith, the longing and the desire for illumination, even when you are walking, standing still, sitting, sleeping, awake, eating and drinking."[1] I said that the three injunctions *remember*, *draw to attention*, and *contemplate* described in a nutshell the three aspects of this awareness: renunciation, conversion, and contemplation. These aspects were distinguished due to the degree of intensity in one's awareness to be cultivated. What is then the significance of "even when you are walking, standing still, sitting, sleeping, awake, eating and drinking."

If this awareness sees the phenomenal world in terms of an idea such as emptiness, it is impossible to develop such awareness if one is cut out from the phenomenal world. To see a person as a friend, what is referred to by the word *as* cannot be experienced without seeing or experiencing that which is as. . . . In other words, the phenomenal world, even understood, or perhaps because understood as illusory, is the support of one's awareness to be cultivated. Let us come back to the simile of the mirror maze. While being in it, one sees one's reflections in the mirrors knowing perfectly well that these are only reflections. By seeing them, however, one indirectly perceives a distance or a space between them and oneself. This distance can only be perceived by looking at the reflections of oneself. By looking closely at the various reflections, one perceives that some come from a closer mirror, some from other mirrors that are farther. Slowly one begins to develop a more acute sense of the distance or space between the reflections and oneself. It is this sense of space that reveals the way to follow in order to come out of the maze. At some point, one's sense of distance may be so developed that one would walk through the maze as though the mirrors were plain walls. And when one eventually comes out of the maze, the reflection disappears but the sense of distance or space remains. Only this time, the experience is overwhelming. When one looks at a person who went through the maze and a person who did not, what exactly has been added in the experience of the former? Certainly not space because, even for the latter, actions or movements would be impossible without it. What has been added is just an awareness of what always is. The sojourn in the maze did not bring about the creation of something new, but rather it forced the awareness of what already is.

As a final point, I would like to come back to where I started. Given the soteriological context suggested in the present research, what would be an appropriate translation for *bodhicitta*? I would say that *bodhicitta* means a mind fully pervaded—a mind can only be fully pervaded—of a thought (which functions like the name of a category) whose content is the desire for enlightenment for the sake of all beings. In a shorter form, the thought of the desire for enlightenment. However accurate this translation may be, there is something missing. We have seen in chapter 1 that *bodhicitta* referred to metaphysical realities or concepts such as the Cosmic Body of the Buddha (*Dharmakāya*) or Reality as such (*Bhūtatathātā*). Why is it that most Buddhist Mahāyāna traditions came to assimilate *bodhicitta* to such realities? In this research, I have demonstrated that a lot of ideas, for example, the notion of emptiness of all things or the immanent presence of the Buddha, could be used as a basis for the cultivation of awareness. For this reason, I argued that the *Bodhicaryāvatāra* can be divided into three autonomous parts, each having its own theme for this awareness. Why then did *bodhicitta* and not the other themes or ideas become so prominent? It appears to me that one can compare the development of the concept of *bodhicitta* to that of a trademark such as Coca-Cola®. This word is not only the name given to a brownish sticky liquid but also of a wide range of ideas and impressions often identified as "the American way of life." As such, the word *Coca-Cola*® is untranslatable. Similarly, *bodhicitta* came to be assimilated to a specific spiritual approach and especially the fruits it produces, and consequently it referred to more than what a word-to-word translation of it could express. The best translation I can therefore imagine for *bodhicitta* is *bodhicitta*™.

Notes

Introduction

1. See, for example, Michael Pye, *Skilful Means: A Concept in Mahāyāna Buddhism*. London: Duckworth. 1978.

2. Id., p. 5.

3. Id., p. 101.

4. Id.

5. khīṇā jāti vusitaṃ brahmacariyaṃ kataṃ karaṇīyaṃ nāparaṃ itthattāyati pajānāti (D, I-84).

Chapter 1

1. SED, p. 1169.

2. According to Richard Hayes, a Buddhist scholar from McGill University, the term *enlightenment* has been borrowed from a European movement that tried to appropriate Asian ideas. He therefore favored the term *awakening* because, in his opinion, the imagery of light is not appropriate to describe the ultimate experience of Buddhism. This view was criticized by Dan Lusthaus on the ground that indeed the Mahāyāna literature considerably uses the metaphor of light in situations connected to spiritual achievement (Communication on an electronic discussion forum [Buddha-L], July 1994).

3. SED, p. 707.

4. Dayal (1932), p. 59.

5. Hopkins (1984), p. 171.

6. Suzuki (1950), p. 171.

7. Sangharakshita, in Subhuti (1994), p. 89.

8. Joshi (1971), p. 70.

9. Crosby and Skilton (1996).

10. Hayes (Communication on an electronic discussion forum (Buddha-L), July 1994).

11. Lusthaus (Communication on an electronic discussion forum (Buddha-L), July 1994).

12. The story goes as follows: A rich man had many children. They were playing in his house while it caught fire. The father tried to warn them of the danger, but the children did not respond; they were too busy playing. Then the father thought, "If I and my children do not get out at once, we shall certainly be burned. Let me now, by some skillful means (*upāya*), cause my children to escape this disaster." Knowing that to which each of his children was predisposed, the father told them, "Here are rare and precious things for your amusement, if you do not come and get them, you will be sorry for it afterward. So many carts are now outside the gate to play with." Thereupon, the children, hearing their father, rushed out of the burning house. The father, seeing that his children had safely escaped, sat down in the open with a mind at ease and ecstatic joy. At this point each of his children asks him to give them the carts that were promised. Then the father gave to his children, instead of ordinary carts, equally each a great cart adorned with all the precious things, a cart they never had before and never expected to have.

13. Pye (1978), p. 5.

14. In French, the expression *upāya* has been translated by *artifice salvifique* (L. de la Vallée Poussin), thus assuming a more obvious deceptive connotation.

15. See Peter N. Gregory, *Sudden and Gradual: Approaches to Enlightenment in Chinese Thought.*

16. Yu (1974), p. 421.

17. Hayes (1988), p. 33.

18. According to Williams (1989), p. 58: ca. 695–743; according to Nakamura (1989), p. 287: ca. 650–750.

19. Nakamura (1989), p. 288.

20. Williams (1989), p. 58.

21. Id., p. 198.

22. Ruegg (1981), p. 83.

23. sāṃpratam bodhicittagrahaṇāya tatrābhilāṣam utpādayitum anuśaṃsām avatārayan āha (BCA, p. 8).

24. teṣāṃ saṃvarāvatāraṃ . . . tasya avataraṇam. avatīryate tasmin vā anena iti avatāro mārgaḥ, yena bodhisattvapadaprāptau sugatatvam avāpyate (BCA, pp. 4–5).

25. La Vallée Poussin (1907), p. 143.

26. This date has been questioned by de Jong (1975), p. 161.

27. Pezzali (1968), p. 48.

28. Ruegg (1981), p. 82, note 267.

29. Dayal (1932), p. 56.

30. Gyatso (1989), p. 5.

31. In *Bouddhisme: études et matériaux*, Louis de La Vallée Poussin has edited only chapter 9 on the basis of which he has provided a description of the Bodhisattva's path.

32. Williams (1989), p. 203.

33. Ruegg (1981), p. 84.

34. de Jong (1975), p. 177.

35. Id., p. 168.

36. This argument was put forward by H. Śāstri in an article entitled "Śāntideva" published in *Indian Antiquary*. 42, Bombay, 1913, pp. 50-51. The name "Bhusuku" was given to Śāntideva because he was perfect in the Bhusuku meditation.

37. Pezzali (1968), p. 45, note 80.

38. Ruegg (1981), p. 85.

39. Sharma (1990), p. xii.

40. In many instances, Prajñākaramati indicates to his reader alternative readings of a verse he is commenting on.

41. Suzuki (1950), p. 168.

42. Id., p. 169.

43. According to Nakamura (1989), the term *aññācitta* seems to be the predecessor of *bodhicitta*. *Aññācitta* is a Pali term translated as "the thought of gnosis" or "the intention of gaining Arahantship." (T.W. Rhys Davids. *Pali-English Dict.* p. 14).

44. Suzuki (1970), p. 40.

45. Id.

46. Id., p. 61.

47. Id., p. 72.

48. Suzuki (1950), p. 173.

49. This text is usually attributed to Nāgārjuna. This is, however, contested by Nakamura (1989), p. 243 because it refers to the concept of *ālayavijñāna* (store-consciousness), a concept that became prominent after Nāgārjuna's time.

50. Suzuki (1970), p. 297.

51. Id., p. 298.

52. Joshi (1971), p. 75.

53. Id.

54. *Guhyasamājatantra*, chapter 18, verse 37 (Quoted in Nakamura [1989], p. 333).

55. nityaṃ prabhāsvaraṃ śuddhaṃ bodhicittaṃ jinālayam, sarvadharmayaṃ divyaṃ nikhilāspadakāraṇam (Pra.vi.si, 2-29).

56. saṃbuddhā bodhisattvāḥ ca tvattaḥ pāramitāguṇāḥ, saṃbhavanti sadā nātha bodhicitta namo 'stu te (Pra.vi.si, 3-11).

57. Suzuki (1950), p. 175.

58. Id., p. 173.

59. Id., p. 174.

60. "A survey of the conception of bodhicitta," in *The journal of Religious Studies*. Dept. of Religious Studies, Punjabi University, Patiala, Vol. 3, No. 1. pp. 70–79.

61. Joshi (1971), p. 77 (Diacritical marks missing in quote).

62. Subhuti (1994), p. 84.

63. Id., p. 98.

64. Id., p. 88.

65. Id.

66. Id., p. 95.

67. Id.

68. Id., p. 93.

69. Id.

70. Id., p. 94.

71. Id., p. 100.

72. Id., p. 102.

73. Matics (1970), p. 34.

74. Subhuti (1994), p. 103.

75. Borne (1984), p. 1673.

76. Subhuti (1994), p. 96.

77. bhavacārakabandhano varākaḥ sugatānāṃ suta ucyate kṣaṇena, sa narāmaralokavandanīyo bhavati sma udita eva bodhicitte (BCA, I-9).

Chapter 2

1. PED, p. 491.

2. Joshi (1971), p. 72.

3. sarvasattvottāraṇapraṇidhānaṃ mama. mayā sarvasattvāḥ parimocayitavyāḥ. mayā sarvajagatsamuttārayitavyam. jātikāntārājjarākāntārād vyādhikāntārāt cyutyupapattikāntārāt sarvāpattikāntārāt sarvāpāyakāntārāt sarvasaṃsārakāntārāt sarvadṛṣṭigahanakāntārāt kuśaladharmapraṇāśakāntārād ajñānasamutthitakāntārāt tad ete mayā sarvasattvāḥ sarvakāntārebhyaḥ parimocayitavyāḥ (quoted in Śs, B280).

4. Williams (1989), p. 197.

5. Joshi (1971), p. 72.

6. Id., p. 71.

7. bodhisattvaḥ sarvasattvānāṃ vartamānānāgatasarvaduḥkhadaurmanasyopaśamāya vartamānānāgatasukhasaumanasyotpādāya ca niḥśāṭhyataḥ kāyavāṅmanaḥparākramaiḥ prayatnaṃ karoti (Śs, B15).

8. kṛtvādau eva yatnena vyavasāyāśayau dṛḍhau, karuṇāṃ ca puraskṛtya yateta śubhavṛddhaye (Śs, B276).

9. Joshi (1971), p. 74.

10. bahukalpakoṭībhiḥ kadācit buddhaḥ utpadyate lokahitaḥ maharṣī, labdho 'dhunā saḥ pravaraḥ kṣaṇo 'dya tyajati pramādaṃ yadi moktukāmaḥ (quoted in Śs, B203).

11. udyajya yathā ghaṭata nityaṃ pāramitāsu bhūmiṣu baleṣu, mā jātu sraṃsaya vīryaṃ yāvat na budhyathā pravarabodhim (quoted in Śs, B203).

12. Śs, B280.

13. Śs, B203.

14. Śs, B323.

15. Śs, B4.

16. Śs, B11.

17. It is a *karmadhāraya* compound in which a word expressive of the standard of comparison is compounded with another denoting the common quality or ground of comparison (A Higher Sanskrit Grammar, p. 133).

18. SED, p. 707.

19. Tucci (1980), p. 193.

20. SED, p. 708.

21. Ross Reat (1990), p. 107.

22. Id., p. 142.

23. Radhakrishnan (1957), p. 453.

24. Lambert Schmithausen (from unpublished lecture notes).

25. yogaḥ cittavṛttinirodhaḥ (Y.S, I. 2)

26. This doctrine is also called codependent origination. Western translators of Buddhist scriptures have used both translations without much consideration for their implications in Western philosophy.

27. Nanayakkhara (1961), p. 172.

28. Walshe (1987), p. 540 (n. 55).

29. *Webster's New Collegiate Dictionary* (1977), p. 528.

30. līnacittaṃ bodhisattvānāṃ na saṃvidyate (quoted in Śs, B20).

31. na pratighacittam utpādayati (quoted in Śs, B135).

32. bodhisattvacaryābhilaṣitacitta (Śs, B24).

33. sarvayācanakābhilaṣitacitta (Śs, B24).

34. svaśarīrānapekṣacitta (Śs, B24).

35. tyāgacittavegāt utsṛṣṭasarvaparigrahaḥ (Śs, B34).

36. Ross Reat (1990), p. 320.

37. PED, p. 664.

38. na cittasya vaśī parityāgāya (Śs, B20).

39. *Saddharmapuṇḍarīka*, edited by Kern and Nanjo, p. 414 (Suzuki [1950], p. 171).

40. Suzuki (1950), p. 171.

41. Id.

42. Id., p. 172.

43. Id., p. 173.

44. BHD, p. 229.

45. Id.

46. PED, p. 268.

47. Dargyay (1981), p. 103.

48. See Dargyay (1981), p. 104, for complete reference concerning this passage and for Tsong-kha-pa's argumentation.

49. Śs, B19.

50. Śs, B90.

51. Śs, B18.

52. durlabhāḥ kulaputra te sattvāḥ sattvaloke ye anuttarasyāṃ samyaksambodhau praṇidadhati, atas te durlabhatarāḥ sattvāḥ ye 'nuttarāṃ samyaksaṃbodhim abhisaṃprasthitāḥ (G.Vy, S492). Prajñākaramati quotes this passage in his commentary of verse I-15 in the BCA with a few differences: durlabhāḥ kulaputra te sattvāḥ sattvaloke ye anuttarasyāṃ samyaksambodhau cittaṃ praṇidadhati, tato 'pi durlabhatamāste sattvāḥ ye anuttarāṃ samyaksaṃbodhim anuprasthitāḥ iti.

53. tad bodhicittaṃ dvividhaṃ vijñātavyaṃ samāsataḥ, bodhipraṇidhicittaṃ ca bodhiprasthānam eva ca (BCA, I-15).

54. gantukāmasya gantuḥ ca yathā bhedaḥ pratīyate, tathā bhedo 'nayoḥ jñeyaḥ yāthāsaṃkhyena paṇḍitaiḥ (BCA, I-16).

55. Sharma (1990), p. 15.

56. tadyāpi nāma kulaputra bhittam api vajraratnaṃ sarvapraviśiṣṭaṃ suvarṇālaṃkāram abhibhavati, vajraratnanāma ca na vijahāti, sarvadāridryaṃ vinivartayati, evam eva kulaputra, āśayapratipattibhinnam api sarvajñatācittotpādavajraratnaṃ sarvaśravakapratyekabuddhaguṇasuvarṇālaṃkāram abhibhavati, bodhicittanāma ca na vijahāti, sarvasaṃsāradāridryaṃ vinivartayati iti (quoted in Śs, B9).

57. vināpi caryayā bodhicittam upakārakam iti jñātavyam (Śs, B9).

58. Sharma (1990), p. 15.

59. Suzuki (1950), p. 172.

60. cinteya sadā vicakṣaṇaḥ bhaveya buddhaḥ ahaṃ ime ca sattvāḥ. etat ca me sarvasukhopadhānam (quoted in Śs, B354).

61. evaṃ tān anusmarati. evaṃ ca tān anusmṛtya tadguṇapariniṣpattyarthaṃ smṛtim upasthāpayati. tad ucyate buddhānusmṛti iti (quoted in Śs, B322).

62. Williams (1989), p. 202.

63. sarvasattvottāraṇapraṇidhānaṃ mama (Śs, B280).

64. yaccittaṃ praṇidhānād utpannaṃ bhavati tat praṇidhicittam (BCA, p. 24).

65. niṣparidāha ya osari raśmi tāya duśīlaya codita sattvā, śīlaviśuddhipratiṣṭhita bhūtvā cinta janenti bhaveya svayaṃbhūḥ. karmapathe kuśale pariśuddhe śīla samādayi yadbahusattvān, bodhayi cittasamādapanena raśmi nivṛtta sa niṣparidāhaḥ (Śs, B336).

66. One could, for example, argue that, because one is preoccupied by material considerations, he or she can never express such a desire.

67. dānādipravṛttivikalaṃ (BCA p. 16).

68. rātrau yathā meghaghanāṃdhakāre vidyutkṣaṇaṃ darśayati prakāśam, buddhanubhāvena tathā kadācit lokasya puṇyeṣu matiḥ kṣaṇaṃ syāt (BCA, I-5).

69. SED, p. 1120.

70. Id.

71. Id.

72. Walshe (1987), p. 335.

73. Gethin (1992), p. 29.

74. SED, p. 467.

75. Gethin (1992), pp. 71-2.

76. Joshi (1971), p. 71.

77. Gethin (1992), p. 31.

78. Dayal (1932), p. 85.

79. See Gethin (1992), p. 31, for the details of the argumentation. Basically, according to both Childers and Geiger, the Middle Indo-Aryan *satipaṭṭhāna* does indeed represent a sandhi of *sati* and *upaṭṭhāna.*

80. catunnaṃ bhikkhave satipaṭṭhānānaṃ sanudayañ ca atthagamañ ca desissāmi. taṃ suṇātha sādhukaṃ manasikarotha . . . pe . . . ko ca bhikkhave kāyassa samudayo. āhārasamudayā kāyassa samudayo ti ādīsu hi satigocaro satipaṭṭhānan ti vuccati.

tathā kāyo upaṭṭhānam no sati, sati upaṭṭhānañ ceva sati cā ti ādīsu. tass'attho patiṭṭhāti asmin ti paṭṭhānaṃ. kā patiṭṭhāti. sati. satiyā paṭṭhānaṃ satipaṭṭhānaṃ padhanam ṭhānam ti vā paṭṭhānaṃ. satiyā paṭṭhānaṃ satipaṭṭhānaṃ hatthi-ṭṭhāna-assa-ṭṭhānâdīni viya (Vibh-a, 214).

81. cattāro satipaṭṭhānā bhāvitā bahulīkatā satta bojjhaṅge paripūrenti ti ādīsu pana sati yeva satipaṭṭhānan ti vuccati. tass'attho patiṭṭhātī ti paṭṭhānaṃ; upaṭṭhāti; okkantitvā pakkhanditvā pavattatī ti attho. sati yeva paṭṭhānaṭṭhena sato paṭṭhānaṃ. atha vā saraṇaṭṭhena sati upaṭṭhānaṭṭhena paṭṭhānaṃ. iti sati ca sā paṭṭhānañ ca ti pi satipaṭṭhānaṃ (Vibh-a, 214-5).

82. Gethin (1992), p. 33.

83. bodhicittaṃ hi kulaputra bījabhūtaṃ sarvabuddhadharmānām. kṣetrabhūtaṃ sarvajagatśukladharmavirohaṇatayā, dharaṇibhūtaṃ sarvalokapratiśaraṇatayā (G.Vy, S494).

84. anāthānāṃ ahaṃ nāthaḥ sārthavāhaḥ ca yāyinām, pārepsūnāṃ ca naubhūtaḥ setuḥ saṃkrama eva ca. dīpārthinām ahaṃ dīpaḥ śayyā śayyārthinām ahaṃ, dāsārthinām dāso bhaveyaṃ sarvadehinām. cintāmaṇiḥ bhadraghaṭaḥ siddhavidyā mahauṣadhiḥ, bhaveyaṃ kalpavṛkṣaḥ ca kāmadhenuḥ ca dehinām (BCA, III-17–19).

85. ayam eva mayā kāyaḥ sarvasattvānāṃ kiṃkaraṇīyeṣu kṣapayitavyaḥ tadyathāpi nāma imāni bāhyāni catvāri mahābhūtāni pṛthivīdhātuḥ abdhātuḥ tejodhātuḥ vāyudhātuḥ ca nānāsukhaiḥ nānāparyaiḥ nānārambaṇaiḥ nānopakaraṇaiḥ nānāparibhogaiḥ sattvānāṃ nānopabhogaṃ gacchanti, evam eva ahaṃ imaṃ kāyaṃ caturmahābhūtasamucchrayaṃ nānā[sukhaiḥ] nānāparyaiḥ nānārambaṇaiḥ nānopakaraṇaiḥ nānāparibhogaiḥ vistareṇa sarvasattvānām upabhogyaṃ kariṣyāmi iti (quoted in Śs, B21-22).

86. iti hi bodhisattva ātmānaṃ sarvasattveṣu niryātayan sarvakuśalamūlopa-kāritvena sarvasattvānām kuśalamūlaiḥ sa[manvā]haran pradīpasamamātmānaṃ sarvasattveṣu upanayan. . . . (quoted in Śs, B22).

87. na tadvastūpādātavyaṃ yasmin vastuni nāsya tyāgacittam upadyate. na tyāgabuddhiḥ krameta. na sa parigrahītavyo yasmin parigrahe na utsarjanacittam utpādayeta, na sa parivāra upādātavyo yasmin yācakaiḥ yācyamānasya parigra-habuddhiḥ utpadyate. na tadrājyam upādātavyam, na te bhogāḥ, na tadratnam upādātavyam, yāvat na tatkiṃcid vastūpādātavyam, yasmin vastuni bodhisattvasya aparityāgabuddhiḥ utpadyate (quoted in Śs, B21).

88. hastaṃ hastārthikebhyo dāsyāmi, pādaṃ pādārthikebhyo netraṃ netrārthikebhyo dāsyāmi, māṃsaṃ māṃsārthikebhyaḥ, śoṇitaṃ śoṇitārthikebhyo majjānaṃ majjārthikebhyo 'ṅgapratyaṅgānyaṅgapratyaṅgārthikebhyaḥ, śiraḥ śirorthikebhyaḥ parityakṣyāmi (quoted in Śs, B21).

89. api tu khalu punar yasya yasya yena yena yadyadkāryaṃ bhaviṣyati, tasmai tasmai sattvāya tattat deyam (Śs, B21).

90. yeṣāṃ yeṣāṃ sattvānāṃ yena yena arthaḥ, tattadeva me harantu, hastaṃ hastārthinaḥ, pādaṃ pādārthinaḥ iti (Śs, B21).

91. lābhī ca satkṛtaḥ ca aham icchanti bahavaḥ ca mām, iti martyasya saṃprāptāt maraṇāt jāyate bhayam. yatra yatra ratiṃ yāti manaḥ sukhavimohitam, tattat sahasraguṇitaṃ dukhaṃ bhūtvā upatiṣṭhati. tasmāt prājño na tām icchet icchāto jāyate bhayam, svayam eva ca yāti etad dhairyaṃ kṛtvā pratīkṣatām (BCA, VIII-17–19).

92. aparitrasyanābhimukhena akhedacittotpādena bodhisattvaḥ svahṛdayaṃ parityajan yācakebhyaḥ (Śs, B25).

93. atītya yuṣmadvacanaṃ sāṃprataṃ bhayadarśanāt, śaraṇaṃ yāmi vo bhīto bhayaṃ nāśayata drutam (BCA, II-54).

94. bhayaṃ kena me dattaṃ niḥsariṣyāmi vā katham, avaśyaṃ na bhaviṣyāmi kasmāt me susthitaṃ manaḥ (BCA, II-60).

95. Sharma (1990), p. 64.

96. Matics (1970), p. 152.

97. Driessens (1993), p. 34.

98. bodhisattvaḥ svaśarīram ākṣipya rudhiram anuprayacchan yācakebhyaḥ praharṣitabodhicitto bodhisattvacaryābhilaṣitacitto 'paryāttaveditacittaḥ sarvayācanakābhilaṣitacittaḥ sarvapratigrāhakāvidviṣṭacittaḥ sarvabodhisattvatyāgapratipatpratipanno 'nivartyayā prītiprasrabdhyā svaśarīrānapekṣacittaḥ svaśarīrādrudhiram anuprayacchan jñānāyatanamahāyānaprasṛtacetā mahāyānāviniṣṭamanā iṣṭamanāstuṣṭamanāḥ prītamanā muditamanā maitryamanāḥ sukhamanāḥ prasannamanāḥ pramuditaprītisaumanasyajāto majjāmāṃsaṃ svaśarīrāt parityajan yācanakebhyaḥ (Śs, B24).

99. tadyathā kulaputra cintāmaṇirājamukuṭānām mahānāgarājñāṃ nāsti paropakramabhayam, evam eva bodhicittamahākaruṇācintātramaṇirājamukuṭāvabaddhānāṃ bodhisattvānāṃ nāsti durgatyapāyaparopakramabhayam iti (Śs, B178).

Chapter 3

1. I believe that the failure to appreciate this blending of passivity and activity may lead one to a wrong interpretation of Eastern religious concepts. The idea of karma, for example, viewed exclusively from its passive attributes, is assimilated to the notion of predestination and consequently, it is a negation of free will. This would be a wrong interpretation of the concept since free will, or its correlative, the principle of responsibility, has always been acknowledged in Eastern thought. A

better interpretation would then be to say that karma implies that one is subjected to exercising free will.

2. Griffiths (1986), p. xv.

3. Id., p. 13.

4. Id.

5. Y.S, I-33, in Radhakrishnan (1957), p. 459. See p. 74, 229.

6. anirodham anutpādam anucchedam aśāvataṃ, anekārtham anānārtham anāgamam anirgamaṃ, yaḥ pratītyasamutpādaṃ prapañcopaśamaṃ śivaṃ, deśayām āsa saṃbuddhaḥ taṃ vande vandatāṃ varam MKV, ed. L. de la Vallée Poussin, p. 11, in Kalupahana (1986), p. 101.

7. prahrutaṃ batedaṃ kulaputra cittaṃ viṣayeṣu. tasya yā nivāraṇā parirakṣā ekāgrībhāvo damaḥ śama upaśamo vinayaḥ, ayam ucyate saddharmaparigrahaḥ (quoted in Śs, B42).

8. yānyapīmāni bhagavan gaṅgānadīvālikasamāni bodhisattvapraṇidhānāni, tāni ekasmin mahāpraṇidhāne upanikṣiptāni antargatāni anupratiṣṭhāni yaduta saddharmaparigrahe. evaṃ mahāviṣayo bhagavan saddharmaparigraha iti (quoted in Śs, B42).

9. syādyathāpi nāma devi mahābalavato 'pi puruṣasyālpo 'pi marmaṇi prahāro vedhanīyo bhavati bādhākaraḥ ca, evam eva devi mārasya pāpīyasaḥ parītto 'pi saddharmapa[rigraho] vedhanīyo bhavati, śokāvahaḥ paridevakaraḥ ca bhavati. na ahaṃ devi anyam ekam api dharmaṃ kuśalaṃ samanupaśyāmi mārasya pāpīyasa evaṃ vedhanyaṃ śokāvahaṃ paridevakaraṃ ca yathā ayam alpo 'pi [saddha]rma-parigraha iti (quoted in Śs, B42).

10. syādyathāpi nāma devi sumeruḥ parvatarājaḥ sarvān kulaparvatān abhi-bhavannabhirocate ca samabhirocate coccatvena vipulatvena ca, evam eva devi mahāyānikasya kāyajīvitanirapekṣasya ne cāgṛhītacittasya saddharmaparigraho navayānasaṃprasthitānām api kāyajīvitasāpekṣāṇāṃ mahāyānikānāṃ sarvān kuśalān dharmānabhibhavati iti ādi (quoted in Śs, B43).

11. aśucipratimām imāṃ gṛhītvā jinaratnapratimāṃ karoti anarghām, rasajātam atīva vedhanīyaṃ sudṛḍhaṃ gṛhṇata bodhicittasaṃjñam. suparīkṣitam aprameya-dhībhiḥ bahumūlyaṃ jagad ekasārthavāhaiḥ, gatipattanavipravāsaśīlāḥ sudṛḍhaṃ gṛhṇata bodhicittaratnam (BCA, I-10-11).

12. SED, p. 678.

13. Id., p. 973.

14. tatrātmabhāve kā rakṣā yad anarthavivarjanam (Śs, B44).

15. idaṃ ca anarthavivarjanam āryagaganañjasūtre saddharmadhāraṇoyataiḥ bodhisattvaiḥ bhāṣitam (Śs, B44).

16. tasmin kāle vayaṃ kaṣṭe tyaktvā kāyaṃ sajīvitam, saddharmaṃ dhārayiṣyāma sattvānāṃ hitakāraṇāt (Śs, B47).

17. SED, p. 866.

18. Id.

19. Id., p. 860.

20. Id.

21. sudṛḍhaṃ gṛhṇata: yathā gṛhītaṃ punar na calati. gṛhṇīta iti prāpte gṛhṇata iti yathāgamapāṭhāt (BCA, p. 12).

22. Gyatso (1989), p. 23.

23. Desjardins (1969), p. 24.

24. nāmedhyamayamanyasya kāyaṃ vetsītyanadbhutam, svāmedhyamayam eva tvaṃ taṃ nāvaiṣīti vismayaḥ (BCA, VIII-56).

25. ayam eva hi kāyo me evaṃ pūtirbhaviṣyati, śṛgālā api yadgandhānnopasarpeyurantikaṃ (BCA, VIII-31).

26. ātmānaṃ ca parāṃśca eva yaḥ śīghraṃ trātum icchati, sa caret paramaṃ guhyaṃ parātmaparivartanam (BCA, VIII-120).

27. na nāma sādhyam buddhatvaṃ saṃsāre api kutaḥ sukham, svasukhasya anyaduḥkhena parivartam akurvataḥ (BCA, VIII-131).

28. tasmāt svaduḥkhaśāntyarthaṃ paraduḥkhaśamāya ca, dadāmi anyebhyaḥ ātmānaṃ parān gṛhnāmi ca ātmavat (BCA, VIII-136).

29. Matics (1970), p. 99.

30. Id., pp. 99-100.

31. Id., p. 99.

32. pralambamuktāmaṇihāraśobhānāścarān diṅmukhamaṇḍanāṃstān, vimānameghān stutigītaramyān maitrīmayebhyo 'pi nivedayāmi (BCA, II-18).

33. suvarṇadaṇḍaiḥ kamanīyarūpaiḥ saṃsaktamuktāni samucchritāni, pradhārayāmyeṣa mahāmunīnāṃ ratnātapatrāṇyatiśobhanāni (BCA, II-19).

34. ādāya buddhayā munipuṅgavebhyo niryātayāmi eṣa saputrakebhyaḥ (BCA, II-6).

35. kadalīva phalaṃ vihāya yāti kṣayam anyat kuśalaṃ hi sarvam eva, satataṃ phalati kṣayaṃ na yāti prasavati eva tu bodhicittavṛkṣaḥ (BCA, I-12).

36. See chap. 1, note 12.

37. Pye (1990), p. 40.

38. śāsanaṃ bhikṣutāmūlaṃ bhikṣutā eva ca duḥsthitā, sāvalambanacittānāṃ nirvāṇam api duḥsthitam. kleśaprahāṇāt muktiḥ cet tad anantaram astu sā, dṛṣṭaṃ ca teṣu sāmarthyaṃ niṣkleśasya api karmaṇaḥ. tṛṣṇā tāvat upādānaṃ na asti cet saṃpradhāryate, kim akliṣṭā api tṛṣṇā eṣāṃ na asti saṃmohavat satī. vedanāpratyayā tṛṣṇā vedanā eṣāṃ ca vidyate, sālambanena cittena sthātavyaṃ yatra tatra vā. vinā śūnyatayā cittaṃ baddham utpadyate punaḥ, yathā asaṃjñisamāpattau bhāvayet tena śūnyatām (BCA, IX-45-49).

39. śāsanaṃ buddhatvopāyābhyāsaḥ (BCA, p. 53).

40. duḥsthitā śūnyatādarśanam antareṇa asamañjasā kevalasatyadarśanato na yujyate (BCA, p. 316).

41. tasmāt satyadarśanato mukti iti na vaktavyam (BCA, p. 316).

42. LaVallée Poussin, AbhidhK, v.1 note 4 (Quoted in BHS, p. 198).

43. tasmāt sarvadharmaśūnyatā eva avidyāpratipakṣatvāt saṃsārasantativicchittihetuḥ avasīyate na kevalaṃ satyadarśanam (BCA, p. 317).

44. Sharma (1990), p. 406.

45. Schmithausen (1987), p. 19.

46. Griffiths (1986), p. 63.

47. Reps (1957), p. 21.

48. ataḥ teṣām upalambhadṛṣṭīnāṃ duḥsthitā na nirālambanacittānām (BCA, p. 317).

49. bhagavān āha. tasmāt tarhi, subhute, bodhisattvena mahāsattvena evam apratiṣṭhitaṃ cittam utpādayitavyam, na kvacit pratiṣṭhitaṃ cittam utpādayitavyam, na rūpapratiṣṭhitaṃ cittam utpādayitavyam, na śabdagandharasaspraṣṭavyapratiṣṭhitaṃ cittam utpādayitavyam iti. tasmāt śūnyatā eva bodhimārgaḥ iti sthitam (BCA, p. 321).

50. Polanyi (1962), p. 55.

51. Polanyi (1975), p. 34.

Chapter 4

1. chos ni shes bya lam dang ni, mya ngan 'das dang yid kyi yul, bsod nams tshe dang gsung rab dang, 'byung 'kyur nges dang chos lugs la'o (quoted in Hodge [1990], p. 156).

2. Pye (1990), pp. 38–39.

3. Dve'me Tathāgataṃ abbhācikkhanti. Katame dve? Yo ca neyyatthaṃ suttantaṃ nītattho suttanto ti dīpeti; yo ca nītatthaṃ suttantaṃ neyyattho suttanto ti dīpeti (A, I-60).

4. Jayatilleke (1963), p. 362.

5. Id., pp. 361–62.

6. Kōgen (1982), chap. 8.

7. Pye (1990), p. 39.

8. Id.

9. saṃvṛttiḥ paramārthaḥ ca satyadvayam idaṃ matam, buddheḥ agocaraḥ tattvaṃ buddhiḥ saṃvṛtiḥ ucyate (BCA, IX-2).

10. Pye (1990), p. 38.

11. vyavahāram anāśritya paramārthaḥ na deśyate (MMK, XXIV-10).

12. Gethin (1992), p. 215.

13. Subhuti (1994), p. 133.

14. Id.

15. Lamotte (1958), p. 45.

16. Walshe (1987), p. 25.

17. Gethin (1992), p. 211.

18. ariyena nu kho ayye aṭṭhaṅgikena maggena tayo khandhā saṃgahītā, udāhu tīhi khandhehi ariyo aṭṭhaṅgiko maggo saṃgahīto ti. na kho āvuso Visākha ariyena aṭṭhaṅgikena maggena tayo khandhā saṃgahīta, tīhi ca kho āvuso Visākha khandhehi ariyo aṭṭhaṅgiko maggo saṃgahīto (M, I 301).

19. ettha yasmā maggo sappadeso tayo khandhā nippadesā, tasmā ayaṃ sappadesattā nagaraṃ viya rajjena nippadesehi tīhi khandhehi saṃgahīto (Vism, XVI 95, see Gethin [1992], p. 211, n. 94, for the meanings of *sappadesa* and *nippadesa*).

20. Gethin (1992), p. 211.

21. Id., p. 212.

22. Id., p. 209.

23. seyyathâpi bho Gotama hatthena vā hatthaṃ dhopeyya, padena vā padaṃ dhopeya. evaṃ eva kho bho Gotama sīlaparidhotā paññā; paññāparidhotaṃ sīlaṃ, yattha sīlaṃ tattha paññā, yattha paññā tattha sīlaṃ, sīlavato paññā paññāvato sīlaṃ, sīlapaññānañ ca pana lokasmiṃ aggaṃ akkhāyatī ti (D, I-124).

24. sīlaparibhāvito samādhi mahapphalo hoti mahânisaṃso, samādhiparibhāvitā paññā mahapphalā hoti mahānisaṃsā (D, II-81).

25. Gethin (1992), p. 209.

26. Id.

27. Mai (1994), pp. 83–84.

28. passaddhakāyassa, bhikkhave, na cetanāya karaṇīyaṃ sukhaṃ vediyāmī ti. dhammatā esā, bhikkhave, yaṃ passaddhakāyo sukhaṃ vediyati. sukhino, bhikkhave, na cetanāya karaṇīyaṃ cittaṃ me samādhiyatū ti. dhammatā esā, bhikkhave, yaṃ sukhino cittaṃ samādhiyati. samāhitassa, bhikkhave, na cetanāya karaṇīyaṃ yathābhūtaṃ jānāmi passāmī ti. dhammatā esā, bhikkhave, yaṃ samāhito yathābhūtaṃ jānāti passati. yathābhūtaṃ, bhikkhave, jānato passato na cetanāya karaṇīyaṃ nibbandāmi virajjāmī ti. dhammatā esā bhikkhave, yaṃ yathābhūtaṃ jānaṃ passaṃ nibbandati virajjati (A, X-1, ii).

29. Saddhatissa (1971), p. 46.

30. Gethin (1992), p. 212.

31. Id.

32. Id., p. 207.

33. alaṃ Subhadda. tiṭṭhat'etaṃ sabbe te sakāya paṭiññāya abbhaññaṃsu, sabbe vā na abbhaññaṃsu udāyu ekacce abbhaññaṃsu ekacce na abbhaññaṃsū ti. dhammaṃ te Subhadda desessāmi. taṃ suṇāhi sādhukaṃ manasikarohi bhāsissāmī ti . . . yasmiṃ kho Subhadda dhammavinaye ariyo aṭṭhaṅgiko maggo na upalabbhati, samaṇo pi tattha na upalabbhati dutiyo . . . tatiyo . . . catuttho pi tattha samaṇo na upalabbhati. yasmiñ ca kho Subhadda dhammavinaye ariyo aṭṭhaṅgiko maggo upalabbhati, samaṇo pi tattha upalabbhati dutiyo . . . tatiyo . . . catuttho pi tattha samaṇo upalabbhati (D, II-151).

34. Gethin (1992), p. 205.

35. Id.

36. Id., pp. 205–6.

37. soto soto ti ha Sāriputta vuccati. katamo nu kho Sāriputta soto ti. ayaṃ eva hi bhante ariyo aṭṭhaṅgiko maggo soto, seyyathīdaṃ sammādiṭṭhi. pe. sammāsamādhī ti. sādhu sādhu Sāriputta . . . sotâpanno sotâpanno ti hidaṃ Sāriputta vuccati. katamo no kho Sāriputta sotâpanno ti. yo hi bhante iminā ariyena aṭṭhaṅgikena maggena samannāgato. ayaṃ vuccati sotâpanno. . . . (S, V-347).

38. seyyathâpi bhikkave puriso arañña pavane caramāno passeyya purāṇaṃ maggaṃ purāṇañjasaṃ pubbakehi manussehi anuyātaṃ so taṃ anugaccheyya taṃ anugacchanto passeyya purāṇaṃ nagaraṃ purāṇaṃ rājadhānim pubbakehi manussehi ajjhāvutthaṃ ārāmasampannaṃ vanasampannaṃ pokkaraṇīsampannaṃ uddāpav-

antaṃ ramaṇīyaṃ atha kho so bhikkhave puriso rañño vā rājamahāmattassa vā āroceyya. yagghe bhante jāneyyāsi. ahaṃ addasaṃ araññe pavane caramāno purāṇaṃ maggaṃ . . . purāṇaṃ nagaraṃ . . . ramaṇīyaṃ. taṃ bhante nagaraṃ māpehī ti (S, II-105–6).

39. D, I-62.

40. jñāte māyopamatve 'pi kathaṃ kleśo nivartate, yadā māyāstriyāṃ rāgastatkartuḥ api jāyate. aprahīṇā hi tatkartuḥ jñeyasaṃkleśavāsanā, tad dṛṣṭikāle tasyāto durbalā śūnyavāsanā. śūnyatāvāsanādhānāt hīyate bhāvavāsanā, kiñcit nāsti iti ca abhyāsāt sā api paścāt prahīyate. yadā na labhyate bhāvo yo na asti iti prakalpyate, tadā nirāśrayo 'bhāvaḥ kathaṃ tiṣṭhet mateḥ puraḥ. yadā na bhāvo na abhāvaḥ mateḥ santiṣṭhate puraḥ. tadā anyagatyabhāvena nirālambā praśāmyati (BCA, IX-31–35).

41. sarvasaṅkalpahānāya śūnyatāmṛtadeśanā (BCA, p. 304). This is taken from the *Catuḥstava*, a text allegedly attributed to Nāgārjuna (Nakamura (1980), p. 242).

42. na ca etat iṣṭam—śūnyā api sarvabhāvāḥ kāryakriyāsamarthā bhaveyuḥ (Bhattacharya [1978], p. 97).

43. pratītyasamutpannatvāt (Bhattacharya [1978], p. 108).

44. yathā ca pratītyasamutpannatvāt svabhāvaśūnyā api rathapaṭaghaṭādayaḥ sveṣu sveṣu kāryeṣu kāṣṭhatṛṇamṛttikāharaṇe madhūdakapayasāṃ dhāraṇe śītavātātapaparitrāṇaprabhṛtiṣu vartante (Vv, verse 22).

45. mantrauṣadhisārthyavinirmita (BCA, p. 302).

46. vastusvabhāvatāsamāropāt (BCA, p. 302).

47. SED, p. 1419.

48. paramparābhyastamithyāvikalpa (BCA, p. 302).

49. bījabhūtacittasantatisaṃskārādhānam (BCA, p. 302).

50. kiñcit na asti iti abhyāsāt (BCA, IX-33).

51. viruddhapratyayotpattau duḥkhasya anudayo yadi, kalpanābhiniveśo hi vedanā iti āgataṃ nanu. ataḥ eva vicāraḥ ayam pratipakṣaḥ asya bhāvyate. vikalpakṣetrasaṃbhūtadhyānāhārāḥ hi yoginaḥ (BCA, IX-92–93).

52. kalpanābhiniveśo vedanā iti (BCA, p. 364).

53. aham eva na kiñcit vastuvat . . . ito 'pi vicārāt trāso nivartate (BCA, p. 325).

54. SED, p. 1459.

55. katamañ ca bhikkhave dukkhaṃ ariyasaccaṃ? Jāti pi dukkhā, jarā pi dukkhā [vyādhi pi dukkhā], maraṇaṃ pi dukkhaṃ, sokaparidevadukkhadomanassupāyāsā pi

dukkhā, yam p' iccham̩ na labhati tam pi dukkham̩, sam̩khittena pañcupādānakkhandhā dukkhā (D, II-305).

56. Embree (1988), p. 45.

57. One possible exception to this is the case of the disciple who made a display of supernatural powers in order to attract people to the practice of the Buddhist path. We are told that he was reprimanded by the Buddha thus settling the question on the use of such "spiritual pyrotechnic" as a means to convert people.

58. Vetter (1988).

59. Ruegg (1981), p. 2.

60. In this regard, see Hayes (1994).

61. Tassa mayham̩ Aggivessana etad ahosi: Abhijānāmi kho panâham̩ pitu Sakkassa kammante sītāya jambucchāyāya nisinno vivicc' eva kāmehi vivicca akusalehi dhammehi savitakkam̩ savicāram̩ vivekajam̩ pītisukham̩ pathamam̩ jhānam̩ upasampajja viharitā, siyā nu kho eso maggo bodhāyâti. Tassa mayham̩ Aggivessana satānusāri viññāṇam ahosi: eso va maggo bodhāyâti (M, vol I, p. 246–47).

62. cf. Visuddhimagga, 22.126.

63. PED, p. 638.

64. kathañ ca bhikkhave citte cittânupassī viharati? Idha bhikkhave bhikkhu sarāgam̩ vā cittam̩ 'sarāgam̩ cittan ti' pajānāti, vītarāgam̩ vā cittam̩ 'vītarāgam̩ cittan ti' pajānāti, sadosam̩ vā cittam̩ 'sadosam̩ cittan ti' pajānāti, vītadosam̩ vā cittam̩ 'vītadosam̩ cittan ti' pajānāti, samoham̩ vā cittam̩ 'samoham̩ cittan ti' pajānāti, vītamoham̩ vā cittam̩ 'vītamoham̩ cittan ti' pajānāti, sam̩khittam̩ vā cittam̩ 'sam̩khittam̩ cittan ti' pajānāti, vikkhittam̩ vā cittam̩ 'vikkhittam̩ cittan ti' pajānāti, mahaggatam̩ vā cittam̩ 'mahaggatam̩ cittan ti' pajānāti, amahaggatam̩ vā cittam̩ 'amahaggatam̩ cittan ti' pajānāti, sauttaram̩ vā cittam̩ 'sauttaram̩ cittan ti' pajānāti, anuttaram̩ vā cittam̩ 'anuttaram̩ cittan ti' pajānāti, samāhitam̩ vā cittam̩ 'samāhitam̩ cittan ti' pajānāti, asamāhitam̩ vā cittam̩ 'asamāhitam̩ cittan ti' pajānāti, vimuttam̩ vā cittam̩ 'vimuttam̩ cittan ti' pajānāti, avimuttam̩ vā cittam̩ 'avimuttam̩ cittan ti' pajānāti (D, II-299).

65. ātmīkṛtam̩ sarvam idam̩ jagat taiḥ kṛpātmabhiḥ na eva hi sam̩śayaḥ asti, dṛśyanta ete nanu sattvarūpāḥ ta eva nāthāḥ kim anādaraḥ atra. tathāgatārādhanam etad eva svārthasya sam̩sādhanam etad eva, lokasya duḥkhāpaham etad eva tasmāt mama astu vratam etad eva (BCA, VI-126–27).

66. yathā ekaḥ rājapuruṣaḥ pramathnāti mahājanam, vikartum̩ na eva śaknoti dīrghadarśī mahājanaḥ. yasmāt eva sa ekākī tasya rājabalam̩ balam̩, tathā na durbalam̩ kiṁcit aparāddham vimānayet. yasmāt narakapālāḥ ca kṛpāvantaḥ ca tadbalam, tasmāt ārādhayet sattvān bhṛtyaḥ caṇḍanṛpam̩ yathā (BCA, VI-128–30).

67. ekasmāt aśanāt eṣāṃ lālāmedhyaṃ ca jāyate, tatrāmedhyam aniṣṭaṃ te lālāpānaṃ kathaṃ priyaṃ (BCA, VIII-49).

68. nāhaṃ tamhā vippavasāmi muhuttam api brāhmaṇa, gotamā bhūripaññāṇā gotamā bhūrimedhasā. yo me dhammamadesosi sandiṭṭhikamakālikaṃ, taṇhakkhaya-manītikaṃ yasya natthi upamācchaci. passāmi taṃ manasā cakkhunā 'va, rattiṃ divaṃ brāhmaṇa appamatto, namassamāno vivasemi rattiṃ, teneva maññāmi avippavāsaṃ (Sn, 1140–42).

69. yathā ahū vakkali muttasaddho, bhadravudho āḷavigotamo ca. evam eva tvaṃ 'pi pamuñcassu saddhaṃ, gamissasi tvaṃ piṅgiya maccudheyyapāraṃ (Sn, v. 1146).

70. Williams (1989), p. 218.

71. Id.

72. Id.

73. Mc 15. 34 (Lord, lord, why have you forsaken me).

74. Jayatilleke (1963), pp. 397–98.

75. Subhuti (1994), p. 212.

76. Gethin (1992), p. 111.

77. J. R. Carter, *Dhamma: Western Academic and Sinhalese Buddhist Interpretations: A Study of a Religious Concept.* Tokyo. 1978 p. 104 (Quoted in Gethin [1992], p. 111).

78. śraddha purogata mātṛjanetrī pālika vardhika sarvaguṇānām, kāṅkṣavinodati oghapratārāṇi śraddhanidarśani kṣamapurasya. śraddha anāvikalacittaprasādo mānavivarjitagauravamūlā, śraddha nidhānadhanaṃ caraṇāgraṃ pāṇi yathā śubhasaṃgrahamūlam. śraddha asaṃgata saṅgasukheṣu akṣaṇavarjita ekakṣaṇāgram, śraddha atikramu mārapathasya darśika uttama mokṣapathasya. bījamapūtiku hetu guṇānāṃ śraddha virohaṇi bodhidrumasya, vardhani jñānaviśeṣasukhānāṃ śraddha nidarśika sarvajinānām (quoted in Śs, B2-3).

79. BCA, p. 19.

80. BCA, p. 18.

81. SED, p. 718.

82. La Vallée Poussin (1898), p. 102.

83. Id., p. 103.

84. chandaṭṭho abhiññeyyo, chandassa mūlaṭṭho abhiññeyyo, chandassa pādaṭṭho abhiññeyyo, chandassa padhānaṭṭho abhiññeyyo, chandassa ijjhanaṭṭho abhiññeyyo, chandassa adhimokkhaṭṭho abhiññeyyo, chandassa paggahaṭṭho abhiññeyyo,

chandassa upaṭṭhānaṭṭho abhiññeyyo, chandassa avikkhepaṭṭho abhiññeyyo, chandassa dassanaṭṭho abhiññeyyo (Paṭis, I-19; II-123, based on trsl. by Gethin [1992], p. 102).

85. Gethin (1992), p. 85.

86. mahārāja, evam eva saṃbodhau chandam śraddhām prāthanām praṇidhim gacchan api, tiṣṭhan api niṣannaḥ api śayanaḥ api jāgrad api bhuñjānaḥ api piban api satatasamitam anusmara manasikuru bhāvaya (BCA, p. 18 This passage is also quoted in Kamalaśīla's *Bhāvanākrama* and, according to this text, it comes from the *Āryarājāvavādakasūtra*).

Chapter 5

1. Godman (1985), p. 1.

2. meroḥ api yadāsaṃgāt na bhasmāpi upalabhyate, kṣaṇāt kṣipanti māṃ tatra balinaḥ kleśaśatravaḥ. na hi sarvāni aśatrūṇāṃ dīrgham āyuḥ api īdṛśam, anādyantaṃ mahādīrghaṃ yat mama kleśaśatravaḥ. sarve hitāya kalpante ānukūlyena sevitaḥ, sevyamānāḥ tu amī kleśāḥ sutarāṃ duḥkhakārakāḥ (BCA, IV-31-33).

3. BCA, IV-28.

4. etad hi baḍiśaṃ ghoraṃ kleśabāḍiśikārpitam, yataḥ narakapālāḥ tvāṃ krītvā pakṣyanti kumbhiṣu (BCA, VI-89).

5. atra grahī bhaviṣyāmi baddhavairaḥ ca vigrahī, anyatra tadvidhāt kleśāt kleśaghātānubandhinaḥ (BCA, IV-43).

6. kvāsau yāyānmanmanaḥstho nirastaḥ sthitvā yasmin madvadhārthaṃ yateta, na udyogo me kevalaṃ mandabuddheḥ kleśāḥ prajñādṛṣṭisādhyā varākāḥ. (BCA, IV-46).

7. na kleśā viṣayeṣu na indriyagaṇe na api antarāle sthitāḥ, na ataḥ anyatra kuha sthitāḥ punar amī mathnanti kṛtsnaṃ jagat māyā eva iyam ataḥ vimuñca hṛdaye trāsaṃ bhajasva udyamam, prajñārthaṃ kim akāṇḍa eva narakeṣu ātmānam ābādhase (BCA, IV-47).

8. amī varākāḥ paramārthataḥ vicāryamāṇāḥ (BCA, p. 71).

9. BHS, p. 343.

10. Dayal (1932), pp. 165–66.

11. cittasyākopanatā (BCA, p. 77).

12. krodhādinivṛttacittam (BCA, p. 77).

13. kauśika, jātyandhānāṃ śataṃ vā sahasraṃ vā apariṇāyakānām abhavyaṃ mārgāvataraṇāya, kutaḥ punar nagarānupraveśāya; evam eva, kauśika, acakṣuṣkāḥ

pañca pāramitā jātyandhabhūtā bhavanti vinā prajñāpāramitayā apariṇāyakāḥ, vinā prajñāpāramitayā abhavyā bodhimargāvataraṇāya, kutaḥ eva sarvākārajñatānagarānupraveśāya! (quoted in BCA, pp. 264–65).

14. prajñāpāramitāparigṛhītāḥ etāḥ pañca pāramitāḥ pāramitānāmadheyaṃ labhante (BCA, p. 265).

15. SED, p. 623.

16. Id., p. 622.

17. BCA, VI-1.

18. SED, p. 772.

19. BCA, p. 161.

20. evaṃ dveṣadoṣān vibhāvyam sarvopāyena tadvipakṣabhūtāṃ kṣāntim utpādayet (BCA, p. 123).

21. Dayal (1932), p. 209.

22. BCA, p. 123.

23. na kiñcit asti tadvastu yadabhyāsasya duṣkaram, tasmāt mṛduvyathā abhyāsāt soḍhavyā api mahāvyathā. śītoṣṇavṛṣṭivātādhvavyādhibandhanatāḍanaiḥ, saukumāryaṃ na kartavyam anyathā vardhate vyathā (BCA, VI-14 and 16).

24. bodhisattvaḥ sarvārambaṇavastuṣu sukhām eva vedanāṃ vedayate na duḥkhām, na aduḥkhasukhām (BCA, p. 126).

25. tathā sarvasattveṣu na maitracittam mayā nikṣeptavyam. antaśaḥ na dagdhasthūṇāyām api pratighacittam utpādayitavyam (BCA, p. 141).

26. SED, p. 716.

27. D, I-14.

28. na udyogo me kevalaṃ mandabuddheḥ (BCA, IV-46).

29. yadi prītisukhaṃ prāptam anyaiḥ stutvā guṇārjitam, manaḥ tvaṃ api taṃ stutvā kasmāt evaṃ na hṛsyati? (BCA, IV-76).

30. he manaḥ tvam api kimiti harṣasukham na anubhavasi? (BCA, p. 151).

31. aniṣṭakaraṇāt jātam iṣṭasya ca vighātanāt, daurmanasya āśanaṃ prāpya dveṣaḥ dṛptaḥ nihanti mām. tasmāt vighātayiṣyāmi tasya āśamam ahaṃ ripoḥ, yasmāt na madvadhādanyat kṛtyam asya asti vairiṇaḥ (BCA, VI-7, 8).

32. seyyathâpi bhikkhave ayaṃ kāyo āhāraṭṭhitiko āhāraṃ paṭicca tiṭṭhati anāhāro no tiṭṭhati, evaṃ eva kho bhikkhave pañca nīvaraṇā āhāraṭṭhitikā āhāraṃ paṭicca tiṭṭhanti anāhārā no tiṭṭhanti (S, V-64–65).

33. na tu paramārthataḥ kiñcit iṣṭam aniṣṭaṃ vā saṃbhavati (BCA, p. 123).

34. avicārayataḥ daurmanasya utpadyate (and) vicārya daurmanasya nivartanam eva varam (BCA, p. 124).

35. Gethin (1994), p. 177.

36. kaḥ kasmai druhyati paramārthataḥ yena aparādhini kvacit kasyacit aparādhe tasya dveṣaḥ yuktaḥ (BCA, p. 133).

37. BCA, VI-31.

38. sadā kalyāṇamitraṃ ca jīvitārthe api na tyajet, bodhisattvavratadharaṃ mahāyānārthakovidam. (BCA, V-102).

39. kalyāṇamitram vande aham satprasādāt ca vardhate (BCA, X-58).

40. tasmāt stutyādighātāya mama ye pratyupasthitāḥ, apāyapātarakṣārthaṃ pravṛttāḥ nanu te mama (BCA, VI-99).

41. ataḥ kalyāṇamitrāni te na apakāriṇaḥ (BCA, p. 160).

42. dveṣaḥ teṣu kathaṃ mama (BCA, VI-100).

43. bhūmiṃ chādayituṃ sarvāṃ kutaḥ carma bhaviṣyati, upānaccarmamātreṇa channā bhavati medinī (BCA, V-13).

Chapter 6

1. buddhaṃ gacchāmi śaraṇaṃ yāvadā bodhimaṇḍataḥ, dharmaṃ gacchāmi śaraṇaṃ bodhisattvagaṇaṃ tathā (BCA, II-26).

2. Subhuti (1994), p. 128.

3. BCA, p. 125.

4. santi asmin kāye aśītikṛmikulasahasrāṇi, tāni anena eva ojasā sukhaṃ viharantu (BCA, p. 104).

5. samyaksaṃbodhau buddhatve yaccittaṃ sarvasattvasamuddharaṇābhiprāyeṇa tatprāptyartham adhyāśayena manasikāraḥ (BCA, p. 9).

6. SED, p. 1233.

7. BHS, p. 418.

8. asaṃprajanyacaureṇa smṛtimoṣānusāriṇā, upacitya api punyāni muṣitāḥ yānti durgatim. kleśataskarasaṃgho 'yam avatāragaveṣakaḥ, prāpya avatāraṃ muṣṇāti hanti sadgatijīvitam (BCA, V-27, 28).

9. ye kecit samādhihetavaḥ prayogāḥ, te śīle 'nugatāḥ iti. tasmāt samādhyārthinā smṛtisamprajanyaśīlena bhavitavyam (BCA, p. 88).

10. tasmāt smṛtiḥ manodvārāt na apaneyā kadācana, gatāpi pratyupasthāpyā saṃsmṛtyāpāyikīṃ vyathām (BCA, V-29).

11. asaṃprajanyacittasya śrutacintitabhāvitam, sacchidrakumbhajalavat na smṛtāvavatiṣṭhate (BCA, V-25).

12. etad eva samāsena saṃprajanyasya lakṣaṇam, yatkāyacittāvekṣāyāḥ pratyavekṣā muhuḥ muhuḥ (BCA, V-108).

13. cirāt prāptaṃ kṣaṇavaraṃ smṛtvā smṛtvā muhurmuhuḥ, dhārayāmi īdṛśaṃ cittam aprakampyaṃ sumeruvat (BCA, V-58).

14. SED, p. 1488.

15. BHS, p. 506.

16. kiṃ vīryaṃ kuśalotsāhaḥ tadvipakṣaḥ kaḥ ucyate? ālasyaṃ kutsitāsaktiḥ viṣādātmāvamanyanā. avyāpārasukhāsvādanidrāpāśrayatṛṣṇayā, saṃsāraduḥkhānudvegāt ālasyam upajāyate (BCA, VII-2, 3).

17. kleśavāgurikāghrātaḥ praviṣṭo janmavāgurām, kim adya api na jānāsi mṛtyorvadanam āgataḥ. svayūthyānmāryamāṇāṃstvaṃ krameṇa eva na paśyati, tathāpi nidrāṃ yāsyeva caṇḍālamahiṣo yathā. bhayenodvīkṣyamāṇasya baddhamārgasya sarvataḥ, kathaṃ te rocate bhoktuṃ kathaṃ nidrā kathaṃ ratiḥ (BCA, VII-4-6).

18. yāvatsaṃbhṛtasaṃbhāraṃ maraṇaṃ śīghram iṣyati, santyajyāpi tadālasyam akāle kiṃ kariṣyasi? idaṃ na prāptam ārabdham idam ardhakṛtaṃ sthitam, akasmāt mṛtyuḥ āyātaḥ hā hataḥ asmi iti cintayan (BCA, VII-7, 8).

19. jīvamatsya iva asmi iti yuktaṃ bhayam iha eva te, kiṃ punaḥ kṛtapāpasya tīvrāt narakaduḥkhataḥ (BCA, VII-11).

20. Polanyi (1975), p. 155.

21. aviṣādabalavyūhatātparyātmavidheyatā, parātmasamatā ca eva parātmaparivartanam (BCA, VII-16).

22. athāpi hastapādādi dātavyam iti me bhayam, gurulāghavamūḍhatvaṃ tanme syāt avicārataḥ (BCA, VII-20).

23. triṣu māno vidhātavyaḥ karmopakleśaśaktiṣu, mayaiva ekena kartavyam iti eṣā karmamānitā (BCA, VII-49).

24. sthāma ārabdha-dṛḍhatā (BCA, p. 187).

25. See Crosby and Skilton's translation of the *Bodhicaryāvatāra* for an interesting discussion regarding the negative and the positive connotations of the term māna.

26. SED, p. 1261.

27. nīcaṃ karma karoti anyaḥ kathaṃ mayyapi tiṣṭhati. mānāt cet na karomi etat māno naśyatu me varam. mānena durgatiṃ nītā mānuṣye 'pi hatosavāḥ, paripiṇḍāśino dāsā mūrkhā durdaśanāḥ kṛśāḥ (BCA, VII-51, 57).

28. Matics (1970), pp. 63-4.

29. ye sattvāḥ mānavijitāḥ varākāḥ te na māninaḥ, mānī śatravaśaṃ na eti mānaśatruvaśāḥ ca (BCA, VII-56).

30. Matics (1970), p. 30.

31. Id., p. 64.

32. Id., p. 65.

33. Gethin (1994), p. 352.

34. ekâyano ayaṃ bhikkhave maggo sattānaṃ visuddhiyā sokapariddavānaṃ samatikamāya dukkhadomanassānaṃ atthāgamāya ñāyassa adhigamāya nibbānassa sacchikiriyāya yadidaṃ cattāro satipaṭṭhānā (D, II-290).

35. Gethin (1994), p. 64.

36. Id., p. 66.

37. prajñāpradhānāḥ dānādayaḥ guṇāḥ ucyante (BCA, p. 263).

38. dātṛdeyapratigrāhakāditritayānupalaṃbhayogena (BCA, p. 263).

39. iyaṃ kauśika prajñāpāramitā bodhisattvānāṃ mahāsattvānāṃ dānapāramitām abhibhavati, śīlapāramitām abhibhavati, kṣāntipāramitām abhibhavati, vīryapāramitām abhibhavati, dhyānapāramitām abhibhavati (quoted in BCA, p. 264).

40. dānapāramitāsu dharmapravicayasvabhāvāyāḥ prajñāyāḥ pradhānatvāt (BCA, p. 263).

41. tathā hi dānam saṃbodhiprāptaye prathamaṃ kāraṇam, puṇyasaṃbhārāntarbhūtatvāt. tacca śilālaṃkṛtam eva sugatiparamparāṃ sukhabhogopakaraṇasaṃpannābhāvahadanuttarajñānapratilaṃbhahetuḥ. kṣāntiḥ api tadvipakṣabhūtapratighatapratikṣatayā dānaśīlasukṛtamayaṃ saṃbhāram anupālayantī sugatatvādhigataye saṃpravartate. etat ca śubhaṃ dānāditritayasaṃbhūtaṃ puṇyasaṃbhārākhyaṃ vīryam antareṇa na bhavati iti tad api ubhayasaṃbhārakāraṇatayā sarvāvaraṇaprahāṇāya samupajāyate. samāhitacittasya ca yathābhūtaparijñānam utpadyate iti dhyānapāramitāpi (BCA, p. 263).

42. evaṃ kṣamo bhajet vīryam vīrye bodhiḥ yataḥ sthitā, na hi vīryaṃ vinā puṇyaṃ yathā vāyuṃ vinā gatiḥ (BCA, VII-1).

43. vardhayitvaivam utsāhaṃ samādhau sthāpayet manaḥ, vikṣiptacittaḥ tu naraḥ kleśadaṃṣṭrāntare sthitaḥ (BCA, VIII-1).

44. bhayotsavādisaṃbandhe yadi aśaktaḥ yathāsukham, dānakāle tu śīlasya yasmāt uktam upekṣaṇam (BCA, V-42).

Chapter 7

1. Guenther and Kawamura (1975), p. 35.

2. Id., p. 36.

3. Gethin (1994), pp. 344-5.

4. sattvalokam atha bhājanalokaṃ cittam eva racayati aticitram, karmajaṃ hi jagat uktam aśeṣaṃ karma cittam avadhūya ca na asti (MA, 6-89, quoted in BCA, p. 75).

5. sarvasattvahitasukhavidhānaikamanasaḥ (BCA, p. 32).

6. atha pratyapakārī syāṃ tathāpi ete na rakṣitāḥ,
hīyate ca api me caryā tasmāt naṣṭhāḥ tapasvinaḥ (BCA, VI-51).

7. BHS, p. 226.

8. SED, p. 317.

9. uttarottarataḥ śreṣṭhā dānapāramitādayaḥ, na itarārthaṃ tyajet śreṣṭham anyatra ācārasetutaḥ (BCA, V-83).

10. bodhisattvānāṃ yaḥ ācāraḥ śikṣāsaṃvaralakṣaṇaḥ saḥ eva kuśalajalarakṣaṇāya setubandhaḥ vihitaḥ (BCA, p. 103).

11. śikṣāsaṃvararakṣaṇena bodhicittasevanādinā ca kuśalapakṣasya ca vṛddhim kuryām (BCA, p. 144).

12. bodhicittagrahaṇapūrvakaṃ bodhisattvaśikṣāsamādānam (BCA, p. 5). bodhicittotpādaṃ pratipādya śikṣāsaṃvaragrahaṇam pratipādayan (BCA, p. 61). bodhisattvaśikṣā yadupāditabodhicittena bodhisattvena sadā karaṇīyam (BCA, p. 61).

13. yathā gṛhītaṃ sugataiḥ bodhicittaṃ purātanaiḥ, te bodhisattvaśikṣāyām ānupūrvyāḥ yathā sthitāḥ. tadvad utpādayāmi eṣaḥ bodhicittaṃ jagaddhite, tadvadeva ca tāḥ śikṣāḥ śikṣaṣyāmi yathākramam (BCA, III-22, 23).

14. atha khalu punaḥ tvam mahārāja, samyaksaṃbodhicittakuśalamūlavipakena anekakṛtyaḥ deveṣu upapannaḥ abhūḥ (BCA, p. 18).

15. asmāt tvam, mahārāja, bahukṛtyaḥ bahukaraṇīyaḥ asahaḥ sarveṇa sarvam sarvatha dānapāramitāyām śikṣitum yāvat prajñāpāramitāyām śikṣitum (BCA, p. 18).

16. bodhipraṇidhicittasya saṃsāre ‘pi phalaṃ mahat, na tu vicchinnapuṇyatvaṃ yathā prasthānacetasaḥ (BCA, I-17).

17. aśucipratimām imāṃ gṛhītvā jinaratnapratimāṃ karoti anarghām, rasajātam atīva vedhanīyaṃ sudṛḍhaṃ gṛhṇata bodhicittasaṃjñam. yugāntakālānalavat mahānti

pāpāni yat nirdahati kṣaṇena, yasyānuśaṃsān amitān uvāca maitreyanāthaḥ sudhanāya dhīmān (BCA, I-10, 14).

18. kṛtva api pāpāni sudāruṇāni yadā āśrayāt uttarati kṣaṇena, śūrāśrayeṇa iva mahābhayāni na aśrīyate tat katham ajñasattvaiḥ (BCA, I-13).

19. sarvabuddhabodhisattvāryaśrāvakapratyekabuddhapṛthakjanānām ātmanaḥ ca atītānāgatapratyutpannāni kuśalamūlāni piṇḍayitvā, tulayitvā, anumodayasva. agrayā anumodanayā anumodya ca sarvabuddhabodhisattvapratyekabuddhāryaśrāvakāṇam pūjākarmāni niryātaya. niryātya ca sarvasattvasādhāraṇāni kuru tataḥ sarvasattvānām yāvat sarvajñatāpratilambhāya sarvabuddhadharmaparipūraṇāya dine dine traikālyam anuttarāyām samyaksaṃbodhau pariṇāmaya (BCA, p. 18).

20. jagat adya nimantritaṃ mayā sugatatvena sukhena cāntarā, purataḥ khalu sarvatāyinām abhinandantu surāsurādayaḥ (BCA, III-33).

21. vipulasugandhiśītalasaroruhagarbhagatāḥ, madhurajinasvarāśanakṛtopacitad-yutayaḥ, munikarabodhitāmbujavinirgatasadvapuṣaḥ, sugatasutāḥ bhavanti sugatasya puraḥ kuśalaiḥ (BCA, VII-44).

22. BHS, p. 323.

23. Id.

24. Sangharakshita (1966), p. 454.

25. Id.

26. esā, bhikkhave, yaṃ passaddhakāyo sukhaṃ vediyati. sukhino, bhikkhave, ne cetanāya karaṇīyaṃ cittaṃ me samādhiyatū ti (A, X-1, ii).

27. evam abdhātoḥ api na evam bhavati—ahaṃ bījam snehayāmi iti. tejodhātoḥ api na evam bhavati—ahaṃ bījam paripācayāmi iti. vāyudhātoḥ api na evam bhavati—ahaṃ bījam abhinirharāmi iti. ākāśadhātoḥ api na evam bhavati—ahaṃ bījasya anāvaraṇakṛtyam karomi iti. ṛtoḥ api na evam bhavati—ahaṃ bījasya pariṇāmanākṛtyam karomi iti (Śāl).

Conclusion

1. BCA, p. 18.

Bibliography

A. Original works

Anaṅgavajra.

1987ed *Prajñopāyaviniścayasiddhi*, in *Guhyādi-aṣṭasiddhi-saṅgraha*, ed. Samdhong Rinpoche. Rare Buddhist Text Project. Varanasi, India: Central Institute of Higher Tibetan Studies.

Aṅguttara-nikāya,

1960ed ed. Bhikkhu J. Kashyap. Nālandā-Devanāgarī-Pāli-Series, Vol. 4. Bihar, India: Pāli Publication Board.

Candrakīrti.

1960ed *Prasannapadā*, ed. Dr. P. L. Vaidya. Buddhist Sanskrit Texts, No. 10. Darbhanga, India: Mithila Sanskrit Institute.

Daśabhūmikasūtra,

1967ed ed. Dr. P. L. Vaidya. Buddhist Sanskrit Texts, No. 7. Darbhanga, India: Mithila Sanskrit Institute.

Dīgha-nikāya,

1903ed eds. T. W. Rhys Davids and J. Estlin Carpenter, Vols. 1–3. London: Pali Text Society. [Reprint 1982]

Gaṇḍavyūhasūtra,

ed. Dr. P. L. Vaidya. Buddhist Sanskrit Texts, No. 5. Darbhanga, India: Mithila Sanskrit Institute.

Kamalaśīla.

1980ed *Bhāvanākrama*, in *Minor Buddhists texts*, ed. G. Tucci, Part 2. Rome: Instituto Italiano per il Medio ed Estremo Oriente.

Majjhima-nikāya,
1979ed ed. V. Trenckner. Text Series No. 60. Vol. 1. London: Pali Text Society.

Nāgārjuna.
1978ed *Vigrahavyāvartanī*, eds. E. H. Johnston and Arnold Kunst. Delhi, India: Motilal Banarsidass Publishers. [Reprint 1990]
1986ed *Mūlamadhyamakakārikā*, ed. David J. Kalupahana. Albany: State University of New York Press.

Paṭisaṃbhidāmagga,
1905–7ed Vols. 1–2, ed. A. C. Taylor. London: Pali Text Society.

Śālistambasūtra,
1950ed ed. N. Aiyaswami Sastri. Adyar Library. Adyar LS. No. 76.

Saṃyutta-nikāya,
1884–98ed Vols. 1–5, ed. L. Feer. London: Pali Text Society.

Śāntideva.
1961ed *Śikṣāsamuccaya*, ed. Dr. P. L. Vaidya. Buddhist Sanskrit Texts, No. 11. Darbhanga, India: Mithila Sanskrit Institute.
1988ed *Bodhicaryāvatāraḥ*, Commentary by Shri Prajñākaramati. Varanasi, India: Bauddha Bharati.

Sutta-nipāta,
1924ed P. V. Bapat. Bibliotheca Indo-Buddhica, No. 75. Delhi, India: Sri Satgura Publications. [Reprint 1990]

Vibhaṅgaṭṭhakathā,
1923ed in *Sammohavinodanī*, ed. A. P. Buddhadatta. London: Pali Text Society.

Visuddhimagga,
1950ed ed. H. C. Warren, revised D. Kosambi. Harvard.

B. Translations and commentary of original works

Bareau, André.
1950 *Asaṃskṛta*. Thèse de Doctorat. Paris le 31 Mai 1950. Université de Paris.

Barnett, Lionel D.
1909 *The Path of Light*. London: John Murray. 1959 [Reprint]. (BCA Trsl)

Batchelor, Stephen.
1979 *A Guide to the Bodhisattva's Way of Life*. Dharamsala, India: Library of Tibetan Works and Archives. 2nd edition published in 1981. (BCA Trsl)

Bendall, Cecil and William Henry Denham Rouse.
1971 *Śikṣāsamuccaya*. Delhi, India: Motilal Banarsidass [Reprint]. (Śs Trsl)

Bhattacharya, Kamalaswar.
1978 *The Dialectical Method of Nāgārjuna*. Delhi, India: Motilal Banarsidass [Reprint 1990]. (Vv Trsl)

Crosby, Kate and Andrew Skilton.
1996 *Śāntideva. The Bodhicaryāvatāra*. Oxford: Oxford University Press. (BCA Trsl)

Dalai Lama, H. H (14th).
1988 *Transcendent Wisdom: A Commentary on the Ninth Chapter of Śāntideva's Guide to the Bodhisattva Way of Life*. Ithaca, New York: Snow Lion Publications.

Driessens, Georges.
1993 *Vivre en héros pour l'éveil*. Trad. du tibétain. Paris: éditions du Seuil. (BCA Trsl)

Ensink, J.
1955 *De grote weg naar het licht: Een keuze uit de literatuur van het Mahāyāna Buddhisme*. Uit het Sanskrit vertaald en toegelicht. Amsterdam: De Arbeiderspers. Second edition published in 1973, Amsterdam: Wetenschappelijke Uitgereij. (Chapter 2).

Finot, Louis.
1920 *La marche à la lumière*. (Les Classiques de l'Orient, 2.) Paris: éditions Bossard. (BCA Trsl)

Horner, I. B.
1957 *The Collection of the Middle Length Sayings*. Vol. 1. London: Pali Text Society. (M Trsl)

Kanakura, T.
1958 *Satori e no Michi*. Kyoto: Heirakuji Shoten.

Kia-Hway, Liou and Benedykt Grynpas.
1980 *Philosophes taoïstes: Lao-tseu, Tchouang-Tseu, Lie-Tseu*. Paris: Gallimard et Unesco.

La Vallée Poussin, Louis de.
1892 *Bodhicaryāvatāra: Introduction à la pratique de la sainteté bouddhique*. Muséon 11: 87–115 Reprinted in 1896. (Chapters 1–4, 10)
1896 *Śāntideva: Bodhicaryāvatāra. Exposition à la pratique des bodhisattvas*. Muséon 15: 306–18. (Chapter 5) (BCA Trsl)
1898 *Bouddhisme: études et matériaux*. London: Luzac.
1907 *Introductions à la pratique des futurs Bouddhas, poème de Śāntideva*. Paris: Librarie Blond. (BCA Trsl)

1923–31 *L'Abhidharmakośa de Vasubandhu.* 6 Vols., Paris. (Abhidh-k Trsl)

Matics, Marion L.
1970 *Entering the Path of Enlightenment.* London: Macmillan. (BCA Trsl)

Pezzali, Amalia.
1975 *Il Bodhicaryāvatāra di Śāntideva.* Bologna: Egidi.

Saddhatissa, H.
1985 *The Sutta-Nipāta.* London: Curzon Press. (Sn Trsl)

Schmidt, Richard.
1923 *Der Eintritt in den Wandel in Erleuchtung (Bodhicaryāvatāra).* Ein buddhistisches Lehrgedicht des VII. Jahrhunderts n. Chr. Aus dem Sanskrit übersetzt. Dokumente der Religion, vol. 5. Paderborn: Ferdinand Schöning.

Sharma, Parmananda.
1990 *Śāntideva's Bodhicaryāvatāra.* Vols. 1–2. New Delhi, India: Aditya Prakashan. (BCA Trsl)

Steinkellner, Ernst.
1981 *Śāntideva: Eintritt in das Leben zur Erleuchtung (Bodhicaryāvatāra).* Lehrgedicht des Mahāyāna aus dem Sanskrit übersetzt von Ernst Steinkellner. Diederichs Gelbe Reihe, vol. 34. Düsseldorf: Eugen Diederichs.

Wallace, Vesna A. and Wallace B. Alan.
1997 *A Guide to the Bodhisattva Way of Life.* Ithaca, New York: Snow Lion Publications. (BCA Trsl)

Walshe, Maurice.
1987 *Thus Have I Heard: The Long Discourses of the Buddha.* London: Wisdom Publications. (D Trsl)

Woodward, F. L. and Hare, E. M.
1936 *The Book of Gradual Sayings.* Vol. 5. London: Pali Text Society. (A Trsl)

C. Secondary literature

Adams, Charles J.
1984 "Islam and Christianity: The Opposition of Similarities," in *Mediaeval Studies*: 6. 287-306.

Blofeld, John
1970 *The Way of Power: A Practical Guide to the Tantric Mysticism of Tibet.* London: George Allen and Unwin Ltd.

Borne, Etienne
1984 "Teilhard de Chardin," in *Dictionnaire des religions.* ed. Paul Poupard. Paris: Presses Universitaires de France. pp. 1673–74.

Brecht, Bertholt.
1967 *Gesammelte Werke.* ed. Elisabeth Hauptmann. 20 v. Frankfurt am Main, Germany: Suhrkamp.

Dargyay, L.
1981 "The View of Bodhicitta in Tibetan Buddhism," in *The Bodhisattva Doctrine in Buddhism.* ed. Kawamura. Canadian Corporation for Studies in Religion. Waterloo, Canada: Wilfrid Laurier University Press. pp. 95–109.

Dayal, Har.
1932 *The Bodhisattva Doctrine in Buddhist Sanskrit Literature.* London: Kegan Paul.

Desjardins, Arnaud.
1969 *The Message of the Tibetans.* London: Stuart & Watkins.

Embree, Ainslie T. ed.
1988 *Sources of Indian Tradition.* Vol. 1. New York: Columbia University Press.

Gethin, R. M. L.
1992 *The Buddhist Path to Awakening: A Study of the Bodhi-Pakkhiyā Dhammā.* Leiden, Netherlands: Brill.

Godman, David. ed.
1985 *Be As You Are: The Teachings of Sri Ramana Maharshi.* London: Arkana.

Govinda, Anagarika Brahmacari.
1961 *The Psychological Attitude of Early Buddhist Philosophy.* London: Rider.

Gregory, Peter N.
1987 *Sudden and Gradual: Approaches to Enlightenment in Chinese Thought.* Honolulu: University of Hawaii Press.

Griffiths, Paul J.
1986 *On Being Mindless: Buddhist Meditation and the Mind-Body Problem.* La Salle, Ill.: Open Court.

Guenther, Herbert V. and Leslie S. Kawamura.
1975 *Mind in Buddhist Psychology.* Translation of the Tshe-mchog-gling Ye-shes-rgyal-mtshan's *Sems dang sems byung gi tshul rnam pa bshad pa'i sdom tshig rin po che'i phren ba.* Emeryville, Calif.: Dharma Pub. [1975].

Gyatso, Geshe Kelsang.

1988 *Universal Compassion: A Commentary to Bodhisattva Chekhawa's Training the Mind in Seven Points*. London: Tharpa Publications.

1989 *Meaningful to Behold: A Commentary to Shantideva's Guide to the Bodhisattva's Way of Life*. London: Tharpa Publications.

Gyatso, Lobsang.

1997 *Bodhicitta: Cultivating the Compassionate Mind of Enlightenment*. Ithaca, New York: Snow Lion Publications.

Hayes, Richard.

1988 *Dignaga on the Interpretation of Signs*. Dordrecht, Netherlands: Kluwer Academic Publishers.

1994 "Nāgārjuna's Appeal," in *Journal of Indian Philosophy*, Vol. 22, No. 4. Kluwer Academic Publishers, pp. 299–378.

Hori, G., Victor Sōgen.

1994 "Teaching and Learning in the Rinzai Zen Monastery," in *Journal of Japanese Studies*. 20:1. pp. 5–35.

Hopkins, Jeffrey.

1984 *The Tantric Distinction: An Introduction to Tibetan Buddhism*. London: Wisdom Publications.

Jayatilleke, K. N.

1963 *Early Buddhist Theory of Knowledge*. Delhi, India: Motilal Banarsidass.

de Jong, J. W.

1975 "La légende de Śāntideva," in *Indo-Iranian Journal*. Vol. 16, No. 3, pp. 161–82.

Joshi, L. M.

1971 "A Survey of the Conception of Bodhicitta," in *The Journal of Religious Studies*. Dept. of Religious Studies, Punjabi University, Patiala, Vol. 3, No. 1. pp. 70–79.

Kalupahana, David J.

1986 *Nāgārjuna: The Philosophy of the Middle Way*. Albany: State University of New York Press.

Katz, Nathan.

1982 *Buddhist Images of Human Perfection*. Delhi, India: Motilal Banarsidass.

Kiyota, M., ed.

1978 *Mahāyāna Buddhist Meditation: Theory and Practice*. Honolulu: University Press of Hawaii.

1982 *Tantric Concept of Bodhicitta: a Buddhist Experimential Philosophy*. Madison, Wis.: South Asian Area Center, University of Wisconsin-Madison.

Kōgen, Mizuno.
1982 *Buddhist sutras, Origin, Development, Transmission.* Tokyo: Kōsei Publishing.

Kulkarni, N. G.
1989 "The Yoga of Patañjali," in *Some Non-Vedānta Systems of Indian Philosophy.* Pune, India: Datta Lakshmi Trust. pp. 63–76

Lama Zopa Rinpoche.
1993 *Transforming Problems into Happiness.* Boston: Wisdom Publications.

Lamotte, Etienne.
1958 *Histoire du Bouddhisme indien.* Louvain: Université de Louvain.

Mai, Tong Ba.
1994 "The Role of Reason in the Search for Nirvāṇa." M. A. thesis. McGill University, Montreal, Canada.

Masefield, P.
1986 *Divine Revelation in Pali Buddhism.* Colombo/London: Sri Lanka Institute of Traditional Studies/George Allen & Unwin.

Nakamura, Hajime.
1989 *Indian Buddhism.* 2d ed. Delhi, India: Motilal Banarsidass.

Nanayakkara, S. K.
1961 "Bodhicitta," in *Encyclopedia of Buddhism.* ed. G. P. Malalasekera, O. B. E. II, pp. 184–188.

Nyanaponika, Thera.
1969 *The Heart of Buddhist Meditation.* York Beach, 1984 [Reprint].

Pezzali, Amalia.
1968 *Śāntideva, Mystique Bouddhiste des VIIe et VIIIe siècles.* Firenze, Italy: Vallecchi Editore.

Polanyi, Michael.
1962 *Personal Knowledge: Towards a Post-Critical Philosophy.* Chicago and London: University of Chicago Press.

Polanyi, Michael and Harry Prosch.
1975 *Meaning.* Chicago and London: University of Chicago Press.

Potter, Karl H.
1963 *Presuppositions of India's Philosophies.* Wesport, Conn.: Greenwood Press Publishers, 1976. (paperback edition of 1972 reprint).

Pye, Michael.
1978 *Skilful Means, A Concept in Mahāyāna Buddhism.* London: Duckworth.
1990 "Skillful Means and the Interpretation of Christianity," in *Buddhist-Christian Studies,* 10, pp. 37-41.

Radhakrishnan, S. and Moore, C. A. eds.
1957 *A Source Book in Indian Philosophy.* Princeton: Princeton University Press. [Reprint 1973].

Reat, Ross N.
1990 *Origins of Indian Psychology.* Berkeley: Asian Humanities Press.

Reps, Paul.
1957 *Zen Flesh, Zen Bones.* Harmondsworth, England: Penguin.

Ruegg, David Seyford.
1981 *The Literature of the Madhyamaka School of Philosophy in India.* Wiesbaden, Germany: Otto Harrassowitz.

Saddhatissa, H.
1971 *The Buddha's Way.* London: George Allen and Unwin, 1985 [Revised].

Sangharakshita.
1966 *A Survey of Buddhism.* 3rd ed. Bangalore, India: Indian Institute of World Culture.
1970 *The Three Jewels.* New York: Doubleday.

Schmithausen, Lambert.
1987 *Ālayavijñāna: On the Origin and the Early Development of a Central Concept of Yogācāra Philosophy.* Studia Philologica Buddhica. Tokyo: International Institute for Buddhist Studies.

Sendler, Egon. S. J.
1981 *L'icône: Image de l'invisible, éléments de théologie, esthétique et technique.* Collection Christus No. 54. Desclée de Brouwer.

Shah, S. M.
1987 *The Dialectic of Knowledge and Reality in Indian Philosophy.* Delhi, India: Eastern Book Linkers.

Sopa, Geshe Lhundup and Jeffrey Hopkins.
1976 *Practice and Theory of Tibetan Buddhism.* London: Rider.

Sprung, G. Mervyn, ed.
1973 *Two Truths in Buddhism and Vedānta.* Dordrecht, Netherlands: Reidel.

Streng, J. F.
1971 "The Buddhist Doctrine of Two Truths as Religious Philosophy," in *Journal of Indian Philosophy.* 1 Kluwer Academic Publishers, pp. 262–71.

Subhuti.
1994 *Sangharakshita: A New Voice in the Buddhist Tradition.* Birmingham: Windhorse Publications.

Suzuki, D. T.
1950 *Essays in Zen Buddhism* (2d and 3rd series). London: Rider.
1970 *Outlines of Mahayana Buddhism*. New York: Schocken Books. [Reprint of 1907 by Luzec, London.]

Vetter, Tilmann.
1988 *The Ideas and Meditative Practices of Early Buddhism*. Leiden and New York: E. J. Brill.

Williams, Paul.
1989 *Mahāyāna Buddhism*. London: Routledge.

Yu, David.
1974 "Skill-in-Means and the Buddhism of Tao-sheng," in *Philosophy East and West*. 24. pp. 413–27.

D. Dictionaries and glossaries

Apte, Vaman Shivaran.
1986 *The Practical Sanskrit-English Dictionary*. Kyoto, Japan: Rinsen Book. [Reprint].

Conze, Edward.
1967 *Materials for a Dictionary of the Prajñāpāramitā Literature*. Tokyo: Suzuki Research Foundations.

Edgerton, Franklin.
1953 *Buddhist Hybrid Sanskrit Grammar and Dictionary*. Delhi, India: Motilal Banarsidass. [Reprint 1985].

Hodge, Stephen
1990 *Introduction to Classical Tibetan*. Warminster, England: Aris & Phillips.

Kale, M. R.
1972 *A Higher Sanskrit Grammar*. Delhi, India: Motilal Banarsidass. [Reprint 1988].

Jäschke, Heinrich, August.
1990 *A Tibetan-English Dictionary*. Kyoto, Japan: Rinsen Book. [Reprint].

Rhys Davids, T. W. and William Stede.
1989 *Pali-English Dictionary*. Delhi, India: Munshiram Manoharlal Publishers Pvt. Ltd. [Reprint].

Webster's New Collegiate Dictionary.
1977 Springfield, Massachusetts: G. & C. Merriam.

Index